Teaching Atwood's
The Handmaid's Tale
and Other Works

Approaches to Teaching
World Literature
Joseph Gibaldi, series editor

For a complete listing of titles,
see the last pages of this book.

Approaches to Teaching Atwood's *The Handmaid's Tale* and Other Works

Edited by

Sharon R. Wilson,
Thomas B. Friedman,
and
Shannon Hengen

The Modern Language Association of America
New York   1996

© 1996 by The Modern Language Association of America
All rights reserved. Printed in the United States of America
For information about obtaining permission to reprint material from
MLA book publications, send your request by mail (see address below),
e-mail (permissions@mla.org), or fax (212 533-0680).

Library of Congress Cataloging-in-Publication Data

Approaches to teaching Atwood's The handmaid's tale and other works /
edited by Sharon R. Wilson.
    p.   cm.—(Approaches to teaching world literature : 56)
    Includes bibliographical references (p.   ) and index.
    ISBN 0-87352-735-6. — ISBN 0-87352-736-4   (pbk.)
    1. Atwood, Margaret Eleanor, 1939– —Study and teaching. 2. Atwood,
Margaret Eleanor, 1939– —Criticism and interpretation.
3. Atwood, Margaret Eleanor, 1939– Handmaid's tale. 4. Feminism and
literature—Canada—History—20th century. 5. Women and literature—
Canada—History—20th century. I. Wilson, Sharon Rose.
II. Series.
PR9199.3.A8Z53   1996
813'.54—dc20   96-6231
ISSN 1079-2652

"A Feminist and Psychoanalytic Approach in a Women's College" is reprinted
from *Brutal Choreographies: Oppositional Strategies and Narrative Design in the
Novels of Margaret Atwood,* by J. Brooks Bouson (Amherst: U of Massachusetts
P, 1993). © 1993 by The University of Massachusetts Press

Cover illustration of the paperback edition: drawing by Margaret Atwood,
reproduced in the Talese-Doubleday edition of Atwood's *Good Bones and Simple
Murders* (1994). Used with permission of the artist

Printed on recycled paper

Published by The Modern Language Association of America
10 Astor Place, New York, New York 10003-6981

CONTENTS

PREFACE TO THE SERIES

In *The Art of Teaching* Gilbert Highet wrote, "Bad teaching wastes a great deal of effort, and spoils many lives which might have been full of energy and happiness." All too many teachers have failed in their work, Highet argued, simply "because they have not thought about it." We hope that the Approaches to Teaching World Literature series, sponsored by the Modern Language Association's Publications Committee, will not only improve the craft—as well as the art—of teaching but also encourage serious and continuing discussion of the aims and methods of teaching literature.

The principal objective of the series is to collect within each volume different points of view on teaching a specific literary work, a literary tradition, or a writer widely taught at the undergraduate level. The preparation of each volume begins with a wide-ranging survey of instructors, thus enabling us to include in the volume the philosophies and approaches, thoughts and methods of scores of experienced teachers. The result is a sourcebook of material, information, and ideas on teaching the subject of the volume to undergraduates.

The series is intended to serve nonspecialists as well as specialists, inexperienced as well as experienced teachers, graduate students who wish to learn effective ways of teaching as well as senior professors who wish to compare their own approaches with the approaches of colleagues in other schools. Of course, no volume in the series can ever substitute for erudition, intelligence, creativity, and sensitivity in teaching. We hope merely that each book will point readers in useful directions; at most each will offer only a first step in the long journey to successful teaching.

Joseph Gibaldi
Series Editor

PREFACE TO THE VOLUME

The Canadian writer Margaret Atwood has established an international reputation as a novelist, poet, and critic, receiving numerous literary prizes. The international Margaret Atwood Society was founded in 1984 and in 1992 became an allied organization that meets in conjunction with the Modern Language Association.

Margaret Atwood's works are widely taught in world literature, comparative literature, humanities, women's studies, Canadian studies, emerging English literatures (formerly Commonwealth literature), American literature, English literature, science-fiction, and communications courses in universities, colleges, junior colleges, and secondary schools not only in the United States and Canada but throughout the world. In addition, *The Handmaid's Tale*, currently the most widely taught Atwood text in the United States, is used in economics, political science, sociology, film, business, and other disciplines outside the humanities, and it has been adopted by several universities (e.g., George Mason, Miami University) as a required text for all undergraduates.

Because of Atwood's popularity, individual works, especially *The Handmaid's Tale*, are often taught outside the context of the Atwood canon, Canadian literature, or even the field of literature. Despite Atwood's initial success as a poet—beginning with the Canadian Governor General's Award for *The Circle Game* (1966)—and the notoriety of *Survival: A Thematic Guide to Canadian Literature* (1972), teachers and students in the United States are sometimes unaware of her poetry and literary criticism. Often, too, such readers are not trained to approach works with specifically Canadian content (*Survival*; *The Journals of Susanna Moodie*, 1970; *Surfacing*, 1972). At the same time, some Canadian teachers, failing to recognize or appreciate the extra-Canadian contexts of Atwood's work (e.g., feminism, mythology), undervaluing Canadian literature and culture, or resenting her role as national "icon," see her as only a parochial Canadian nationalist or a one-note self-publicist. Too frequently, cross-disciplinary scholars interested in content are unprepared to examine style and prefer a single, unambiguous message to multifaceted themes, whereas poststructuralists suspicious of authorial intentionality and single meaning may ignore issues students find most significant. Many readers are still unaware of Atwood's published visual art, including book covers for *True Stories* (1981), cover and illustrations for *The Journals of Susanna Moodie*, and political comics for *This Magazine*, or have never heard of the Margaret Atwood Papers at the University of Toronto.

Nonetheless, Atwood has, as noted, enjoyed both critical and popular success. Much sought after for readings and often interviewed, Atwood frequently appears on television and has been in several films, including *Not a Love Story*. Critics have addressed such themes as identity, Canadian nationalism, struggle for survival, sexual politics, and shamanism and concentrated on animal, mirror, camera, and other images in Atwood's work. As indicated by the contributors to this volume, scholars have taken a multiplicity of approaches to Atwood's work, including formalist, autobiographical and biographical, thematic, Marxist, historical, phenomenological, existentialist, structuralist, generic, feminist, psychological and psychoanalytic, archetypal and Jungian, mythic, linguistic, hermeneutic, reader-response, cross-disciplinary, comparative, manuscript, ecological, and deconstructive approaches.

Paradoxically discussed as realist or modernist, feminist or antifeminist, often in terms of readers' traditional expectations, Atwood's work poses a number of challenges to scholars, teachers, and students. Atwood's departures from realism into surrealism and magical realism (Irvine, *Sub/version* 44–45; S. Wilson, *Sexual Politics* 295–97) and her denial of expected fiction structures and closures—the sense in which she "writes beyond the ending" (DuPlessis 6)—pose difficulties. As early *Surfacing* critics illustrate, Atwood's experimentation with a wide range of narrative possibilities (framed and self-reflexive narrative; interior monologue; represented speech; and unreliable, developing, self-conscious, and multiple narrators) and her use of comedy, parody, satire, and irony—especially a subversive, doubled discourse (Hutcheon, "Circling" 170) and a characteristically Canadian self-deprecation—invite careful reading. Some readers undervalue the shifts from third to first person in *The Edible Woman* and *Life before Man* and from present to future tense near the end of *Bodily Harm*.

In addition, scholars and teachers of Atwood texts are challenged by her biblical, mythical, literary, folktale, cinematic, historical, and other kinds of intertexts and allusions; her varied genres and generic parodies (e.g., comedy of manners, the fantastic, fabulation, Gothic, romance, thriller, antinovel, dystopian, bildungsroman, kunstlerroman, life writing); her sensitivity to the nuances and complexities of language and visual image; and her commitment to such issues as feminism, human rights, and Canadian nationalism. Atwood's powerful themes, the focus of much criticism, cannot be fully understood outside genres and techniques (metafiction, antifiction, self-conscious narration, intertextuality, magical realism, parody, irony, deconstruction of national and cultural myths) frequently identified with the discourse of postmodernism (S. Wilson, "Deconstructing" 54–55; Hutcheon, *Canadian Postmodern* 1–25, 138–57 and "Circling," 168–69). Atwood deconstructs phallocentric narratives and synthesizes the often similar techniques identified with feminist, postmodernist, and postcolonialist theory into a revisionist form (S. Wilson, *Sexual Politics* 28; see also the essays by Brydon, Manley, Merivale, and Wilson in this volume).

Thus teachers and students of Atwood's work need contexts for understanding and appreciating it, including discussion of Atwood's complex style. This volume, intended primarily for United States and Canadian audiences, not only provides literary, biographical, Canadian, feminist, generic, and interdisciplinary contexts: it offers varied theoretical, critical, scholarly, and pedagogical approaches to Atwood's work, including a case study of *The Handmaid's Tale*.

The structure of the volume, based on survey responses and essay proposals, reflects a progression from pedagogical backgrounds to practical teaching approaches in frequently offered courses to, finally, more innovative teaching approaches and courses. The selection of essays reflects the editors' desire to provide practical guidance and challenges to the kinds of teachers most likely to use this volume. Because of the large number of Atwood texts— among them, poetry volumes that are out of print and thus not available for study in most classes—we have not included essays on *For the Birds* (1990), *Princess Prunella*, *Strange Things*, every short story, many major poems, uncollected work, most of the rare poetry volumes published with Charles Pachter's visual art (see the "Materials" section in this volume), or Atwood's introductions, including those to the volumes she has edited: *The Oxford Book of Canadian Short Stories in English* (1986) and *The New Oxford Book of Canadian Verse in English* (1982). In the case of the poetry volumes, we do not discuss *Morning in the Burned House* (1995), published while this volume was in press, but we do offer short references to, or discussions of, one or two poems in *Double Persephone* (1961), *The Circle Game* (1966), *The Animals in That Country* (1968), *Procedures for Underground* (1970), *Two-Headed Poems* (1978), and *True Stories* (1981). Similarly, we make only brief allusions to Atwood's visual art, *Second Words* (1982), *The CanLit Foodbook* (1987), *Good Bones* (1992), *Good Bones and Simple Murders* (1994), and *The Robber Bride* (1993). Since the survey indicates which texts are taught most frequently, and in what settings, the essays were, to some extent, selected with this information in mind. For comparative purposes, some texts, such as the widely taught "This Is a Photograph of Me" (*Selected Poems*; *The Circle Game*), are, like *The Handmaid's Tale*, discussed from several perspectives. In addition, some essays inform teachers of possibilities they may have overlooked.

Part 1, "Materials," has five sections: Background, Survey Issues, Primary Works, Atwood Criticism, and Teaching Aids. Part 2, "Approaches," consists of an introduction and these sections: Backgrounds; Classrooms; A Case Study: *The Handmaid's Tale*, with its own overview; and Pedagogical Challenges and Opportunities. We thank all our colleagues who completed questionnaires and submitted essays (a list of respondents appears at the end of the volume) and, most of all, congratulate the writers included here for essays both perceptive and practical. The editors acknowledge with thanks the help of former Laurentian University students Patricia Ames and Susan Vanstone in preparing the volume's works-cited list.

Part One

MATERIALS

Background

Historical Forces and Political Issues

Atwood's first book, *The Circle Game*, was published in 1966, when Canadian cultural and political nationalism was on the rise. Pierre Trudeau would become prime minister in 1968, immediately following the centennial year of Canadian Confederation and its attendant festivities, especially Expo '67 in Montreal, ushering in an unprecedented surge of pride in and optimism about Canada. In the present age, with its designations of "postmodern" and "postnational," and with a strong, persistent pull away from federal authority by the province of Quebec, Canadian nationalism may seem a useless sentiment from the past. Yet because it has been a topic of recurring interest to Atwood, it can still help illuminate the historical and political contexts of her oeuvre.

The future of Canada (and so of Canadian nationalism) seems tied to the issues of Quebec separatism and free trade, among others. The richest sources of information about Atwood's position on these issues are the following: the interviews collected in Earl Ingersoll's *Margaret Atwood: Conversations* (see especially G. Gibson; M. E. Gibson; Oates, "Dancing"; Davidson; Hammond, "Articulating"; and FitzGerald and Crabbe); Atwood's *Survival*, in which she delineates the notorious victim positions Canadians have adopted to survive in the face of domination by imperial powers; and her *Second Words*. More or less neutral on the matter of separatism, but clearly opposed to free trade, Atwood advocates a Canada worth preserving, a Canada never explicitly defined but based on historical differences between her country's economic and foreign policies and those of the United States (see Hengen). Her witty and brief piece "The Only Position," in *If You Love This Country: Facts and Feelings on Free Trade*, edited by Laurier LaPierre, serves as introduction to her stance on that issue.

As background to Atwood's approach to Canadian culture, her critics agree that Northrop Frye's *The Bush Garden* is invaluable, particularly his notion of the "garrison mentality" that pervaded early Canadian writing. Her philosophical attitude toward the United States is likely to be clearer to those who have read the Canadian philosopher George Grant's *Technology and Empire* or *Technology and Justice*, in which he warns against worship of progress as the highest human good, at the expense of nature.

More general background sources include a pocket-size book by Kenneth McNaught, *The Pelican History of Canada*; and, Stephen Graubard, editor, *In Search of Canada*. The annual Canada Report in the December issue of *Maclean's* magazine would also put readers in touch with major Canadian events and Canadians' attitudes to them. Since the country has not yet conceded that it has entered a postnational age, the most appropriate context for studying Atwood's work remains that of Canadian culture.

Feminist Background and Issues

An appropriate background for understanding the feminist contexts of Atwood's writing is the work of other Canadian feminist critics, particularly
Linda Hutcheon, Shirley Neuman and Smaro Kamboureli, and Barbara Godard, for the movement in Canadian and United States feminist criticism
since the early 1970s has been toward valuing difference and acknowledging
diversity of race, class, nationality, and sexual identity. But Canadian feminist criticism is of course indebted to that of the United States, Britain,
France, and developing countries. For an overview of the feminist critical
agenda in the United States since the 1970s, an agenda that has helped to
shape its Anglo-Canadian counterpart, see Naomi Schor's "Feminist and
Gender Studies" and the earlier work by Elaine Showalter.

Germinal discussions of the feminist critical perspective in the United
States, from a poet-critic's point of view, appear in the work of Adrienne
Rich, whose poetry and prose are still excellent starting points for novices
in the field. Rich discusses *Surfacing* in her *Of Woman Born*; Atwood
reviews *Of Woman Born* in her *Second Words*. Four United States feminist
critics whose more or less recent monographs include particular, sustained
mention of Atwood's writing are Rachel Blau DuPlessis, Lorna Irvine, Roberta Rubenstein, and Gayle Greene, among a host of other critics who
refer at least in passing to Atwood's oeuvre. And Judith McCombs, in her
"Country, Politics, and Gender in Canadian Studies," has examined twenty
years of Atwood's reception in Canada and the United States, concluding
that the most frequently recurring issue her critics cite is a lack of warmth.

An initiating voice in the recent movement toward specificity in analyses
of sexual politics might be Gayatri Chakravorty Spivak, whose *The Postcolonial Critic* broaches such issues of relevance to Atwood's work as identity,
postmodernism, and power (see also Spivak's *In Other Worlds: Essays in
Cultural Politics*). The Canadian critic best known for analyses of the Canadian postmodern is Hutcheon, whose discussions of Atwood's work (among
others) in her *Canadian Postmodern* and *Splitting Images: Contemporary
Canadian Ironies* are especially valuable for situating Atwood's work in a
Canadian cultural milieu.

In the same vein is *Language in Her Eye: Views on Writing and Gender
by Canadian Women Writing in English*, edited by Libby Scheier et al.,
whose opening piece is by Atwood. Finally, two widely referred-to works
of Canadian feminist criticism that serve as historical and bibliographical
introductions to the field are Godard's *Gynocritics/Gynocritiques* and Neuman and Kamboureli's *A Mazing Space*.

Survey Issues

Responses to the questionnaire show that the pedagogy developing in Atwood studies is thriving and varied. Her work is taught in general education
humanities and liberal arts programs, as well as in Canadian studies, women's
studies, even business, and, of course, English programs, in formats ranging
from lecture to student-led seminars, using traditional, interdisciplinary,
and team teaching, with 10 to 150 and more students, in secondary schools,
colleges, and universities across North America and in Europe and Asia (see
the names and affiliations of questionnaire respondents). The most frequently
taught novel after *The Handmaid's Tale* is *Surfacing*, while all the novels
have been used, as have the short stories, poems, and literary criticism,
especially *Survival*; perhaps the most popular single volume of poetry is *The
Journals of Susanna Moodie*, followed by any of the editions of selected
poems; and *Bluebeard's Egg* is the preferred short story collection.

Respondents provided many suggestions for background reading to prepare the beginning teacher of Atwood's work, the most often noted of which
are these: Atwood's *Survival* and *Second Words*, Frye's *The Bush Garden*
(as noted above), Grimm's fairy tales, the Bible, New's *Literary History of
Canada*, and the *Oxford Companion to Canadian Literature*, as well as
works by the following, each listed at least twice: Barr, Bartkowski, Chodorow, Gilligan, Hutcheon, Ingersoll, Kauffman, Lauter, Rich. (See the
works-cited list for recommended works by these authors and by the following authors, whose works were listed once: C. Allen, Belenky et al., Brady,
Brans, Brownmiller, Buss, Cluett, DeShazer, Dooley, Forché, Fox-Genovese,
Friedan, Hancock, Jung, Kaler, Ketterer, King, Klinck, Korte, Mandel and
Taras, McCarthy, Northey, Ostriker, Petrone, Plaskow, Schreiber, Snitow,
St. Andrews, Stewart, Stimpson, and Yalom; also mentioned once were
Atwood's afterword to *The Mare's Egg*, by Carole Spray, and the Atwood
entry in *Contemporary Authors*.) The most commonly suggested sources
of literary criticism for teachers are book reviews and, particularly, inter-
views, in addition to works by the following: Christ, Cixous, Davey,
C. Davidson, Davidson and Davidson, Fetterley, Grace, Grace and Weir,
Howells, Malak, Mallinson, McCombs, Mendez-Egle, Moi, Rigney, Rosenberg, and VanSpanckeren and Castro.

The major background and critical works recommended to students in-
clude some of those already mentioned, as well as works by de Lauretis,
Dembo, Felski, Godard, Irvine, Jones, Keith, P. Miller, Montefiore, Mul-
vey, Neuman and Kamboureli, New, Ortner, Rubenstein, Scheier et al.,
Waugh, and Woolf. More general literary theorists such as Bakhtin, Bal,
Barthes and Sontag, Beauvoir, Cixous, Foucault, Irigaray, Kristeva, and
Turner were also cited, and so were general references to histories of the
Gothic romance and of folklore. Most frequently mentioned, however, were
Atwood's own works as background to one another.

By far the most often mentioned audiovisual material cited was the film version of *The Handmaid's Tale*, with some respondents using it as an example of comparatively bad art. The National Film Board of Canada documentary *Margaret Atwood: Once in August*, an interview with the writer, is highly recommended, as are any of her taped readings. Some teachers show slides of the Group of Seven Canadian artists or of native art, or indeed of Atwood's own watercolors; some classes examine contemporary media images of women. Bringing in related disciplines, some teachers discuss recent feminist debates on pornography (Dworkin) or current film theory (Bordwell; Bordwell and Thompson).

The aspects of Atwood's work that are most likely to be treated in the classroom parallel those addressed in Atwood criticism, discussed below: gender politics and women's roles, women's attitudes to the body, narrative voice and design, language, subversion of traditional literary forms (e.g., dystopian/utopian, Gothic), revisionist mythmaking, history, satire, irony, Canadian nationalism, spirituality, and the environment. Particularly successful assignments are also wide-ranging, from the more familiar techniques of reading journals and holding small-group discussions, to the more exotic: conducting choric readings; copying Atwood's style; writing alternative endings or movie scripts; creating a male dystopia; taking on, in creative writing or skits, the persona of the Commander or other Atwoodian figures; scrambling lines of poetry to consider resolution. Favorite essay topics are Atwood's men, humor, mothers, mother-daughter relationships, and the quest motif.

Respondents note that the elements of Atwood's life and writing that seem most troublesome may actually be most interesting: her feminist anger, her bashing of males and the United States (the latter especially concerning readers in the United States), her public persona and international fame, the coldness and unreliability of her narrators, and her pessimism. Approaches to her work that appear effective are, of course, the feminist (listed by almost every respondent) and the following rich array of methods: psychoanalytic, deconstructionist, archetypal, Canadian nationalist, comparative, historical, formalist, reader-response, generic, New Critical, dialogic, ecological, postmodernist and poststructuralist, narratological, thematic, religious, and Marxist. Discourse theory has also proven useful. In the light of this list, perhaps the respondents who described their approach as eclectic offered the best advice.

Happily, most of the material that respondents wished to see in this volume is in fact included. The bibliography of primary and secondary sources addresses an almost unanimous request, as do Rosenberg's biographical essay, Wilson's introduction, and our sections on background and teaching aids. The volume also includes, as asked for, commentary on Atwood's use of language, genre, gender, and humor. The issue of Atwood's Canada seems to continue to vex her teachers in the United States, and for them the Backgrounds section is especially recommended (see also Bennett and Cooke, and Brydon, in this volume).

Primary Works

The most immediate concern for teachers must be the availability of a literary text for classroom use, but the accuracy and consistency of the editions of an author's primary texts should be of similar importance. Fortunately, most of Margaret Atwood's primary texts are readily available and textually accurate, but teachers must be aware that the very availability and accuracy of the editions present some problems. Discrepancies between the original Canadian editions and United States and British reprints of Atwood's poetry and fiction range from differences in size, format, and pagination to more serious alterations in the selections of poems and in the texts of her novels.

Of Atwood's ten individual collections of poetry published since 1966, seven remain in print in Canada, but only two in the United States (*Morning in the Burned House* was published in a United States edition in September 1995). A number of editions of Atwood's selected poems, which have appeared since 1976, have attempted to compensate for the unavailability of the earlier poetry volumes. However, in only a few cases have these editions reprinted a volume of poetry in its entirety. For example, *Selected Poems* (Oxford UP, 1976; Houghton, 1976; Simon, 1978) includes all the poems from *The Journals of Susanna Moodie* (1970) but provides only a selected number from each of the other five volumes Atwood had published by 1974 (*The Circle Game*, 1966; *The Animals in That Country*, 1968; *Procedures for Underground*, 1970; *Power Politics*, 1971; and *You Are Happy*, 1974). The texts of individual poems are accurate, but, without access to the original volume as a whole, the teacher (and the student) will find it impossible to reconstruct the placement of a single poem and, perhaps, will miss contextual meanings.

Since *Selected Poems*, five further editions of selected poems have been published; teachers of Atwood's poetry must be aware of the differences among these editions. *Selected Poems II: Poems Selected and New 1976–1986* (Oxford UP, 1986) is substantially different from the 1987 Houghton Mifflin edition with the same title. The Oxford edition of *Selected Poems II* (176 pages) includes a selection of poems from *Two-Headed Poems* (1978), *True Stories* (1981), *Murder in the Dark* (1983), and *Interlunar* (1984) and a concluding section entitled "New Poems (1985–86)." The Houghton Mifflin edition of *Selected Poems II* (147 pages) omits the selections from *Murder in the Dark*, a volume that has not appeared in its entirety in the United States. *Selected Poems, 1965–1975* (Houghton, 1987; Virago, 1991) was published, it appears, to make up for the fact that Simon and Schuster allowed the first United States edition of the selected poems to go out of print; both the United States and the British editions reproduce the 1976 Oxford edition of *Selected Poems*, but the Virago edition, titled *Poems 1965–1975*, includes a new introduction by Atwood. Finally, *Selected Poems: 1966–1984* (Oxford UP, 1990) provides a convenient, one-volume overview of Atwood's poetic accomplishment. Atwood's poems frequently appear in a wide variety of literary, Canadian studies, and women's studies anthologies.

The editions of Atwood's eight novels and five collections of short fiction present fewer problems of availability but pose more difficulties in terms of consistency and textual accuracy. The most serious pedagogical and scholarly problem in the editions of Atwood's fiction occurs in the 1976 Popular Library and 1987 Fawcett Crest editions of *Surfacing* (1972). Both of these United States editions exhibit numerous typographical errors. As Sandra Donaldson demonstrates in the Notes & Queries column in the *Newsletter of the Margaret Atwood Society* (1992), the errors in the 1987 edition, particularly those involving verb tenses, interfere with students' ability to understand the work fully. Teachers in the United States can order the 1994 New Canadian Library (McClelland) edition of *Surfacing* for a more accurate classroom text.

As W. J. Keith points out, a textual problem in *The Edible Woman* results from inconsistencies in the spelling of Marian McAlpin's surname (*Introducing* 28–29). Her name is variously spelled "MacAlpin" and "McAlpin" in the original editions of the text published in 1969 (Toronto: McClelland; Boston: Little; London: Deutsch). The New Canadian Library (McClelland, 1973) compounds the error by spelling the protagonist's name "McAlpine." Since Keith pointed this fact out, the New Canadian Library has issued a revised edition of the novel (1989) that corrects the earlier errors. This text appears in a New Canadian Library series that, under the general editorship of David Staines, has had the mandate for the past decade of providing accurate editions of works of Canadian literature. In addition, the New Canadian Library has reissued a number of previously out-of-print Canadian works of fiction. The only two Atwood novels for which the New Canadian Library currently has the rights are *The Edible Woman* and *Surfacing*. Teachers should note as well that the 1980 Virago edition of *The Edible Woman* includes an introduction by Atwood herself, which is reproduced in *Second Words*.

The novels published between *Lady Oracle* (1976) and *The Robber Bride* (1993) present far fewer textual problems, since fewer differences occur between Canadian, United States, and British editions and between hardcover and paperback editions. Often the only differences are those of cover illustration, typeface, and pagination; the latter, admittedly, is a problem for students who use an edition different from their instructor's. Although there is always a discrepancy in pagination between Canadian and United States hardcover editions (up to and including *The Robber Bride*), Atwood's publishers seemed to have made a conscious effort, starting with *Bodily Harm* (1981), to print identical paperback editions. With the exception of *The Handmaid's Tale* (1985), whose United States paperback rights are held by Ballantine, the recent novels have been published in simultaneous, identical paperback editions by McClelland and Stewart–Bantam (Seal Books) in Canada and Bantam in the United States. The advantage to scholars of this arrangement is obvious, since citations to Canadian and United States editions will no longer require laborious conversion of page number from one edition to the other. The editors of this volume, in fact, have provided chapter numbers along with the publisher's name and the page number for references to Atwood's novels; we hope that this practice will facilitate the conversion from Canadian to United States editions and vice versa.

Atwood's collections of short fiction present a different textual challenge: the Canadian, United States, and British editions of *Dancing Girls* and of *Bluebeard's Egg* contain different stories. Correspondence, collected in the Margaret Atwood Papers, between Atwood and the United States publisher Simon and Schuster, indicates that the United States edition of *Dancing Girls and Other Stories* would differ from the Canadian edition in its selection of stories. When the United States edition appeared in 1982 (five years after the Canadian text), it replaced "The War in the Bathroom" and "Rape Fantasies" with two stories Atwood had published in the interim: "Betty" and "The Sin Eater." When *Bluebeard's Egg* was published in Canada in 1983, it contained both "Betty" and "The Sin Eater." When the United States edition of this second fiction collection appeared in 1986 (with the subtitle *and Other Stories*), it included two new stories, "The Whirlpool Rapids" and "Walking on Water," separated from the rest of the text under the title "Two Stories about Emma." These two stories, of course, replaced the two that had previously appeared in the United States edition of *Dancing Girls*. In the case of both collections, the British editions (Virago) are identical to the United States editions. Atwood's 1992 collection of prose pieces and short fictions, *Good Bones*, has been published in Britain by Bloomsbury in an edition identical to the Canadian. Until 1994, neither *Good Bones* nor *Murder in the Dark* was available in the United States. A 1994 compilation of the two works, entitled *Good Bones and Simple Murders* (Doubleday), contains twenty-three stories from *Good Bones*, eleven from *Murder in the Dark*, and a new story.

All of Atwood's novels (up to and including *Cat's Eye*) and a number of volumes of her poetry, especially *The Journals of Susanna Moodie*, have been translated into various western European and Scandinavian languages and Japanese.

Aside from poetry and fiction, Margaret Atwood has written literary criticism, book reviews, speeches, children's books, and a nonfiction work, and she has produced a number of works of visual art. Her major work of literary criticism, *Survival*, and her collection of speeches, reviews, and articles,

Second Words, are both still in print. *Second Words* is available in a United States edition (Beacon, 1984), but *Survival* must be ordered in the Anansi edition. In 1995 Oxford University Press published Atwood's 1991 Clarendon lectures in the volume *Strange Things: The Malevolent North in Canadian Literature*. Atwood's first three books for children—*Up in the Tree* (1978), *Anna's Pet* (1980), and *For the Birds* (1990)—demonstrate her attitudes toward children, family, and, particularly in the latter, the environment. In late 1995, Atwood published another children's story, *Princess Prunella and the Purple Peanut*; Atwood set this whimsical homage to language in eighteenth-century France, a time period she has been researching in connection with her own family history. Another work meant for a young audience, *Days of the Rebels: 1815–1840*, is Atwood's historical narrative of the events leading up to (and the aftermath of) the failed rebellions of Louis Joseph Papineau in Lower Canada and William Lyon Mackenzie in Upper Canada, both of whose actions played a vital role in the nation's subsequent development.

A number of Atwood's uncollected prefaces, forewords, afterwords, and introductions to the work of others can be valuable aids to teaching her oeuvre. Foremost among these is her 1986 introduction to the Virago edition of Susanna Moodie's *Roughing It in the Bush* (reprinted in the 1987 Beacon edition); this introduction serves as an effective companion text to Atwood's poetry volume *The Journals of Susanna Moodie*. The introductions to three literary anthologies Atwood edited during the 1980s provide important insights into her views on literature: *The New Oxford Book of Canadian Verse in English* (1982); *The Oxford Book of Canadian Short Stories in English* (coed. with Robert Weaver, 1986); and *The Best American Short Stories, 1989* (coed. with Shannon Ravenel, 1989). In all three cases, Atwood not only justifies her selections but also reveals much about her literary standards. In a similar vein, her foreword to the *Cambridge Guide to Literature in English* (1988) reveals something of Atwood's outlook on the formation and continuity of literary canons. Also of note is her short foreword to a collection of essays on Canadian literature by scholars in India, *Ambivalence: Studies in Canadian Literature* (Juneja and Mohan v–vi). Other uncollected Atwood pieces of possible aid to the teaching of her own works include her afterword to Margaret Laurence's *A Jest of God* (1988), which tells us a great deal of why Atwood sees Laurence as a vital precursor; her critique of another Canadian writer in "A Double-Bladed Knife: Subversive Laughter in Two Stories by Thomas King" (in *Native Writers and Canadian Writing*, 1990), which reflects on her use of disruptive ironic humor; and her foreword to the volume *Charles Pachter* (1992), which describes her collaboration and friendship with a Canadian visual artist and the visual dimension that informs her own imaginative response to the world.

Margaret Atwood has also produced thirteen limited-number, privately printed editions of her poetry in the form of *livres d'artiste* or *livres de peintre*, with illustrations by Atwood herself or other artists, primarily Pachter. Many of the poems in these editions have subsequently appeared in commercially published collections of her work, but some have never been reprinted. The Metropolitan Toronto Reference Library, the Thomas Fisher Rare Book Library at the University of Toronto, and the Art Gallery of Ontario, also in Toronto, own a number of these limited-edition works, but most are held in private collections. Atwood's other visual art includes a drawing for the cover of *Good Bones*, collages in *The Journals of Susanna Moodie*, and comic strips. Rarely studied or used by teachers, Atwood's comic-strip art appeared under the pseudonym B.G. (Bart Gerrard) in the influential Toronto magazine devoted to education issues, *This Magazine Is about Schools* (now titled *This Magazine*). Atwood's regular strip, "Kanadian Kultchur Komics," ran from the January–February 1975 to the July–August 1978 issue of the magazine; the satiric targets of the twenty-two strips were Canadian nationalism, sexual politics, and other social issues. In the July–August 1975 issue, Atwood introduced her self-deprecating persona "Survival Woman." For more information on Atwood's visual art in conjunction with her poetry and these limited editions, see Sharon R. Wilson's article "Sexual Politics in Margaret Atwood's Visual Art" in Kathryn VanSpanckeren and Jan Garden Castro's *Margaret Atwood: Vision and Forms* (1988), and Wilson's chapter on Atwood's visual art in her study *Margaret Atwood's Fairy-Tale Sexual Politics* (1993).

In other areas of artistic endeavor, Atwood has written a number of unpublished teleplays, among them *Heaven on Earth*, produced jointly by BBC Wales and CBC and telecast in 1987, and *Grace Marks*, produced on CBC television in January 1974 as *The Servant Girl*; a stage play, *Forbidden Christmas*, which was also scripted for television; a libretto for the work of Canadian composer John Beckwith, *Trumpets of Summer: Choral Suite for Mixed Chorus, Four Soloists and Male Speaker*; and several as-yet-unproduced screenplays, including ones for her own novels *The Edible Woman*, *Surfacing*, *Lady Oracle*, and *Cat's Eye* and, with Graeme Gibson, one for Margaret Laurence's novel *The Diviners*. Atwood's visual art, her unpublished play and screenplays, and manuscripts and correspondence relating to her published works can be found in the Margaret Atwood Papers at the Fisher Rare Book Library. Teachers and scholars contemplating a visit to Toronto to examine the collection can now order the fifty-page *Guide to the Margaret Atwood Papers* from the library (Martyn). The guide provides an overview of the collection, with detailed information on the contents of each of the nearly one hundred boxes of materials currently comprising the papers.

Atwood Criticism

Several clear indications of Atwood's stature in the contemporary literary milieu are the books, articles, and doctoral dissertations on her writing, and the panels given at MLA and other conferences. As of this writing, twenty-nine books have appeared treating only Atwood's work, while many other recent books contain chapters on Atwood; innumerable scholarly and popular articles and reviews emerge regularly. Thirty-seven dissertations have had Atwood's work as their exclusive subject, while sixty-two more have referred to her writing along with that of other writers. Scholarly discussions devoted exclusively to her oeuvre have taken place in panels at the MLA convention each year since 1984 (and one in both 1977 and 1978), with two panels being offered annually since 1992. The Atwood Society has members from around the world.

The year 1988 marked publication of *Critical Essays on Margaret Atwood*, edited by Judith McCombs, whose introduction surveys critical response to Atwood's writing through *The Handmaid's Tale*, including monographs by Sherrill Grace, Frank Davey, and Jerome Rosenberg, and *The Art of Margaret Atwood*, edited by Arnold E. Davidson and Cathy N. Davidson. Particular attention should be given to McCombs's bibliographic review of the controversy surrounding Atwood's *Survival* (7–8)—a debate familiar to Canadianists but virtually unknown to others. In the review, McCombs essentially weighs the relevance of *Survival* to other critics' understanding of Canada and Canadian literary culture. The debate is significant because of the emphasis placed on *Survival* by non-Canadianist respondents to our questionnaire (see also Friedman in this volume).

In 1991 McCombs and Carole L. Palmer published *Margaret Atwood: A Reference Guide*, which contains an update of Atwood criticism to that year; the guide includes discussion of Barbara Hill Rigney's monograph *Margaret Atwood* and of studies edited by Beatrice Mendez-Egle and by Kathryn VanSpanckeren and Jan Garden Castro. Especially helpful in the guide is mention of Atwood criticism abroad—in Australia, India, Italy, France, German-speaking Europe, Scandinavia, and other Commonwealth and European countries (xi).

In the 1988 volume, McCombs classifies approaches to Atwood's work as follows:

> [They are] focused on themes and patterns of social criticism; feminism and women's literature; Canadian literature; Gothic and popular genres; re-enacted or transformed myth and, lately, folklore. The linguistic, formal, structuralist, postmodern, and manuscript approaches have been fewer, but will no doubt increase. (2)

To this list might be added psychoanalytic and postcolonial methodologies. Four books on Atwood, all published in 1993, explore her feminism. Among other aspects of Atwood's oppositional strategies, J. Brooks Bouson discusses what she calls the protofeminism of *The Edible Woman*, the cultural feminism of *Surfacing*, and the antifeminist backlash terrors of *Bodily Harm* and *The Handmaid's Tale*. Sharon Rose Wilson examines the sexual politics of Atwood's fiction, poetry, and visual art; Eleonora Rao connects feminism in Atwood's novels with genre and narrative theory; and Shannon Hengen discusses a peculiar kind of Canadian feminism as related to nationalism during and since the mirror stage of Atwood's writing, in the late 1970s to early 1980s. Hilde Staels's 1995 study analyzes Atwood's novels through *The Robber Bride* from a narratological and semiotic perspective and includes an interview with the author. A collection of essays published in 1994, edited by Colin Nicholson, is the first of its kind from the United Kingdom; it addresses Atwood as Canadian and feminist from a range of critical perspectives. A 1995 collection, edited by Lorraine M. York, studies the variousness not only of Atwood's later work but also of approaches to it. Work in progress in the category of manuscript scholarship is McCombs's *First Surfacings: The Creative Metamorphoses in Margaret Atwood's Manuscripts*, an extensive study of the writer's papers at the Fisher Rare Book library. Forthcoming is Sonia Mycak's psychoanalytic and phenomenological reading of the fiction, entitled *In Search of the Split Self*.

Teachers of Atwood should be aware of the Canadian Fiction Studies Series, published and forthcoming by ECW Press in Toronto. Five titles have appeared to date: W. J. Keith's *Introducing Margaret Atwood's The Edible Woman*; George Woodcock's *Introducing Margaret Atwood's Surfacing*; Margery Fee's *The Fat Lady Dances: Margaret Atwood's Lady Oracle*; Carol Beran's *Living over the Abyss: Margaret Atwood's Life before Man*; and Lorna Irvine's *Collecting Clues: Margaret Atwood's Bodily Harm*. Lee Briscoe Thompson's study of *The Handmaid's Tale* is forthcoming.

Reviews of Atwood's work in and since 1991 have appeared in the major print media in the United States and Canada, as well as in British and European newspapers and magazines, and have been largely favorable. For discussion of *Wilderness Tips*, see Davidson in this volume; for reference to *Good Bones* and *The Robber Bride*, see Sharon Wilson (in this volume and *Sexual Politics*).

Exhaustive discussion of the wealth of Atwood criticism is simply not possible here. Readers are encouraged to consult the annual bibliography published in the *Newsletter of the Margaret Atwood Society* for a complete survey of each year's primary and secondary works.

Teaching Aids

Teachers of Atwood's poetry and fiction have access to a variety of sources for background information on the author and her work. We have divided these pedagogical aids into the following categories: bibliographies; interviews, including a filmed documentary; sound recordings; films based on Atwood's works; and teaching guides.

Until fairly recently, the most complete Atwood bibliography was the two-part entry in *The Annotated Bibliography of Canada's Major Authors*, compiled by Alan J. Horne (1979). This work has been superseded by McCombs and Palmer's *Reference Guide*; see the preceding section, on Atwood criticism. To supplement and update these reference guides, we recommend that teachers consult the annual "Atwood Checklist" included in the *Newsletter of the Margaret Atwood Society*. This checklist, compiled by Palmer from 1987 to 1992 and continued by Loretta P. Koch in 1993, includes primary texts, reviews, interviews, critical articles, dissertations, and chapters of books on Atwood's works. Back issues of the *Newsletter* from 1987 to 1993, as well as earlier annual issues from 1984 to 1986, are available from the society.

The society itself is an important forum for gathering and sharing information about the teaching of Atwood's works and may well be regarded as a teaching aid. The society, founded in 1984 by Jan Garden Castro, is an international association of scholars, teachers, and students who share an interest in the work of Atwood. Its main goal is to promote scholarly study of her works by providing opportunities for members to exchange information and ideas. In addition to the society's *Newsletter*, which now appears semiannually, the society organizes at least two sessions devoted to papers on Atwood's works at the annual MLA convention. The present volume, in fact, grew out of discussions among society members, who expressed the desire to see a collection of essays detailing pedagogical approaches to her works. Teachers interested in joining the society should write Mary Kirtz, University of Akron, Akron, OH 44325.

Interviews with Margaret Atwood give teachers important insights into her life, her writing methods, her political and social views, and her own analysis of her poetic and fictional achievements. Atwood is an articulate, humorous, and shrewd, though often deceptive, interviewee; like her poems and fiction, interviews with Atwood can be exercises in narrative misdirection and should be approached with a certain wariness. As with other authors, her answers provide important background material but do not represent definitive readings or evaluations. Ingersoll's *Margaret Atwood: Conversations* (1990), the first published collection of Atwood interviews, offers a valuable compilation up to 1989. These conversations, conducted at different times in her career and reprinted from a variety of publications, give teachers a chance to examine her evolving views. One important interview with

Atwood was conducted by Mary Morris in 1986 and published as "The Art of Fiction CXXI" in *Paris Review* in 1990. It also appears in the 1992 Virago edition of Ingersoll's volume. Two widely available recorded interviews provide useful information for introducing Atwood in the classroom. In the one-hour audio interview with Jan Garden Castro, taped in April 1983 in Saint Louis, Atwood speaks about source material that inspired her work, her views on women and the women's movement, her attitudes toward imperialism, and her love of the Canadian wilderness. Hermione Lee's video interview with Atwood, part of the British *Writers in Conversation–Writers Talk. Ideas of Our Time* series, was originally released in a two-cassette, 92-minute version, and was reissued for the United States market in a 52-minute cassette as part of the *Writers on Writing* series. More recent interviews with Atwood are included in the annual checklist in the Atwood Society's *Newsletter.*

A National Film Board of Canada documentary, Michael Rubbo's *Margaret Atwood: Once in August* (1984), provides a useful perspective on Atwood, showing her interacting with her family at their cabin in Ontario's Algonquin Park, the putative landscape (if not the actual setting) of *Surfacing.* Rubbo, an Australian, attempts to demonstrate an autobiographical parallel between Atwood's own life and that of her novels' central female characters, particularly the protagonist of *Surfacing;* the attempt fails, and Atwood cleverly, and humorously, turns the tables on the director. A shorter version of this documentary, *Atwood and Family*, was released in 1985. The main benefit of this documentary in the classroom is its portrayal of a relaxed Atwood in a natural setting and the demonstration of her sardonic humor (see Rosenberg in this volume).

Aside from interviews and the documentary, several audio recordings may be effective teaching aids. A number of commercial recordings with Atwood or others reading her poetry and fiction have been released, although not all are currently available. Audio recordings of Mia Anderson reading from *The Journals of Susanna Moodie* (CBC, 1969) and of Atwood herself reading from *The Circle Game, The Animals in That Country*, and *Power Politics* (*Margaret Atwood Reading*, High Barnet, 1973), from *The Animals in That Country* and *Power Politics* (*Poetry and Voice*, Caedmon, 1992), and from *Power Politics* (*Twist of Feeling*, CBC, 1980), as well as recordings of her prose readings—"Unearthing Suite" (*Margaret Atwood Reads*, American Audio Prose, 1983) and selections from *Bodily Harm* (*Margaret Atwood Reads*, American Audio Prose, n.d.) and *The Handmaid's Tale* (*Margaret Atwood Reads*, American Audio Prose, 1986)—allow students to hear the distinctive, rather deadpan voice she uses for public readings. Since 1987 and the growth in popularity of books on tape, usually abridged audio versions of popular literary works, many of Atwood's books have appeared in this format, including the following: *Bluebeard's Egg and Other Stories*, read by Patricia Vandenberg Blom (Brilliance, 1987); *The Handmaid's Tale*, read by Julie

Christie (Durkin Hayes, 1987, 1992); *Murder in the Dark,* read by Clare Coulter (Coach, 1989); *Cat's Eye,* read by Kate Nelligan (Bantam, 1989); *Stories from* Wilderness Tips, read by Helen Shaver (Bantam, 1991); and *The Robber Bride,* read by Blythe Danner (Bantam, 1993).

Two short films based on Atwood's poetry may be useful teaching aids, but neither is widely available: *Reflections: Progressive Insanities of a Pioneer* (Cinematics Canada, 1972; Universal, 1974) and *The Journals of Susanna Moodie* (Tranby, 1972). Both enact the mood and ideas of the poems through rather heavy-handed visual imagery. Two of Atwood's novels have been adapted for the screen and released as feature films. The Québecois filmmaker Claude Jutra directed an adaptation of *Surfacing* (Pan-Canadian, 1979), starring American actors Joseph Bottoms and Kathleen Beller and Canadian actor R. H. Thomson. The German director Volker Schlondorff's *The Handmaid's Tale* (Cinecom, 1989) enjoyed far wider distribution (and a larger publicity budget) than the previous film and is available on HBO video (1990). This film also starred better-known actors, including Natasha Richardson, Robert Duvall, and Faye Dunaway. See Kirtz's and Hewitt's articles in this volume for discussions of film adaptations of Atwood's works and their usefulness for teaching.

In addition to the ECW readers' guides to Atwood's individual works mentioned in the section on Atwood criticism in this volume, some guides meant for teachers of Atwood's works should be noted. Lars Thompson's volume *A Teacher's Guide for* The Handmaid's Tale (1990), published as part of the series Companions to Literature, targets predominantly high school literature teachers. The guide contains important information, interpretations, sample discussion questions, and suggestions for teaching approaches that can be used profitably by college instructors. *York Notes on* The Handmaid's Tale, by Coral Ann Howells, is a study guide for secondary and first-year university students in England. Finally, a brief word about a series perhaps regarded as somehow antithetical to the pedagogical enterprise—Coles Notes. Two volumes in this series are devoted to individual works by Atwood: the first deals with *Surfacing* (1982); the second, with *The Edible Woman* (1983). Each provides a fundamental analysis of the novel, complete with a summary of each chapter, a discussion of themes, literary techniques, and characterization, and gives sample questions for discussion and further analysis. The second volume was written by the noted Canadian scholar Elspeth Cameron and is particularly valuable as a teaching preparation resource.

Part Two

APPROACHES

Introduction

The essays that follow are divided into four sections. The first section, on backgrounds, offers biographical, feminist, literary-historical, Canadian, intertextual, sociocultural, and postcolonial perspectives from experienced scholar-teachers.

In tracing the "mystery" of Atwood's identity, Jerome Rosenberg discusses Atwood's early background in the Canadian bush, her college publications, career, friends, marriage and divorce, various jobs, and life with writer Graeme Gibson and their daughter. In an essay based on their dramatic presentation at the 1991 MLA Convention, Donna Bennett and Nathalie Cooke place Atwood in Canadian literary history by using a collage of quotations from the writer, including the voice of her literary foremother, Susanna Moodie, to locate the shaping forces of Atwood's work. In addition, they show that Atwood has been instrumental in creating a new Canadian canon since the mid-1970s. Lorraine M. York focuses on satire and gender politics in *Murder in the Dark, Power Politics, The Edible Woman,* and *Lady Oracle.* York also discusses her use of a reader questionnaire on Atwood's feminism in both undergraduate and graduate courses to demonstrate how the writer's opposition of socialized behavior and accepted modes of discourse evokes hostility and reverence among students and critics.

Using definitions of postcolonial theory and practice developed by Bill Ashcroft, Gareth Griffiths, and Helen Tiffin and by Robert Young, Diana Brydon outlines what a postcolonial focus on Atwood's work can help readers see that other perspectives might obscure or ignore. Progressing beyond the "violent duality" of the first book on Atwood, by Sherrill Grace, Brydon confronts the question "How can we know *and* respect the other?" in examining readings from *The Circle Game, The Journals of Susanna Moodie, Surfacing, Bodily Harm, The Handmaid's Tale, Cat's Eye,* and "Death by Landscape" (*Wilderness Tips*). Sharon R. Wilson's essay examines the Atwood canon from an intertextual background and provides guidelines for teaching intertexts, such as *The Wizard of Oz* in *Life before Man* and snake myth in *Interlunar*, in a variety of courses, including an introduction to literature and a course focused entirely on Atwood. Drawing on feminist theory, Wilson discusses how Atwood's fiction, poetry, and essays are illuminated by knowledge of her intertexts: stories within a larger story.

The "Classrooms" section offers practical advice on teaching Atwood's works in a variety of courses and institutions and to varied students. In his essay on *Survival*, Thomas B. Friedman discusses Atwood's prime work of literary criticism, particularly her major organizing principles with reference to Canadian literature. He demonstrates ways in which the text can serve as a guide to certain assumptions about national identity, minorities, art, and literature in a cross-disciplinary class on the history of Canadian ideas.

Sally A. Jacobsen presents thematic and structural approaches to Atwood's poems and "Rape Fantasies," a story from the Canadian edition of *Dancing Girls*, in one of the most widely used anthologies, particularly in women's studies programs or women's literature classes. As Jacobsen points out, this approach could work in a general studies literature class as well. Calling on a variety of Atwood poems, short fiction, and novels, Kathryn VanSpanckeren explores how, as a postmodern fabulist "summoning up an interactive simulacrum of reality at once compelling and patently false," Atwood fools the reader with trickster narrators and text. Through the use of specific assignments and guided discussion, according to VanSpanckeren, Atwood's works can provide powerful models for creative writing students.

Teaching Atwood in the department of communication, Carol L. Benton shows that Atwood's poetry demands the active participation of the reader in opening up the text's potential for comic interpretation. Using phenomenological theory to underscore her view, Benton describes the pedagogical and theoretical implications of this reader-centered approach in communication classes. Garry Leonard demonstrates how *Surfacing* and *Bodily Harm* and other novels draw on Atwood's keen understanding of advertising principles and consumerism, both of which encode gender roles and sexual orientation. He provides practical guides for student presentations and teacher exercises. In the final essay in this section, Patricia Merivale explores the relation of gender and genre codes in *Murder in the Dark*'s three postmodern genres: the prose poem, the detective story, and the artist parable. Drawing on her experience teaching this text in several graduate seminars, and quoting Atwood's regendered appropriation of a famous Baudelaire line, Merivale examines why so few female writers choose to work in two of these genres.

The "Case Study" section discusses tactics that have been used to teach *The Handmaid's Tale* to diverse audiences in a variety of settings, including sociology or women's studies classes, a team-taught utopia class in the Netherlands, a class of traditional-age and returning adult students in a women's college, a folklore and literature course, freshman composition or introduction to literature, and courses at both a private Catholic college and an open admissions university. In addition, this section addresses tactics appropriate to the religious, business, and political science settings mentioned in the survey. *The Handmaid's Tale* was chosen as a case study because, as the questionnaire confirms, it is the most frequently taught of Atwood's works, offered to a wider variety of students in a wider variety of departments and programs than any of her other texts. This section begins with a detailed overview of the case study essays.

Continuing the pedagogical focus of part 2 with greater attention to speculative issues, the fourth section, "Pedagogical Challenges and Opportunities," invites instructors to explore new possibilities. Written by experienced teachers of Atwood's texts, these essays suggest innovative ideas for courses or present new or creative approaches, in some cases one the teacher is currently preparing. These essays offer valuable approaches to teaching Atwood and challenge teachers to develop their own creative strategies.

Marlene Kadar's essay deals with a course that is gaining considerable interest: life writing. She examines the generic boundaries and internal contradictions of autobiography and biography as evidenced in *The Journals of Susanna Moodie* and shows how analysis of personal-expression forms, such as the journal or the memoir, helps in teaching Atwood's work in undergraduate humanities, graduate comparative literature, and life-writing classrooms. Positing a new genre for Atwood's texts, this essay also demonstrates how Atwood's works provide students with writing models in innovative classrooms. Helane Levine-Keating proposes that *You Are Happy* can be used for teaching imagery, irony, and allusion in an introduction to poetry class; for exploring the female poetic landscape and voice in a women in literature class; for examining the thematic and imagistic integrity of the poetic sequence in a contemporary poetry class; and for probing the nature of gender and power politics in a women's studies class. Moving from the tragic vision of the female quest to the positive, comic vision of the woman hero, she also suggests that this series of poems can best be approached from the notion of mythic transformation. Shuli Barzilai uses a feminist, psychoanalytic approach to teaching *Surfacing* in a voyages of discovery class, focusing on the English novel, at Hebrew University. Using Freud's castration theory in reference to the mother's role, Barzilai investigates whether this novel's "patrilineal orientation" diverges from the male quest-romance.

Theodore F. Sheckels, Jr., shows how various critical approaches can be taught in an undergraduate theory course, using Atwood's works as exemplars. For example, *Life before Man* can teach rhetorical criticism; *Surfacing* and *Bodily Harm*, reader-response; and *The Handmaid's Tale*, structuralism. Examining the challenges *Cat's Eye* poses for classroom discussion, Judith McCombs analyzes Atwood's novel as a departure from the classic Joycean model. According to McCombs, Atwood plays with concepts of the artist and self, of creativity and aesthetics, of feminism, ethics, and art. McCombs draws on such material as right-brain, visual thinking and the work of contemporary painters to demonstrate her approach. McCombs proposes that the novel can be taught in a course titled A Portrait of the Artist as Various Persons, to include texts by James Joyce, Alice Munro, Harriette Arnow, Virginia Woolf, Doris Lessing, Sinclair Ross, Margaret Laurence, Michael Ondaatje, and Paul Hiebert. Finally, Arnold E. Davidson, who has taught the *Wilderness Tips* collection of stories in both undergraduate and graduate Atwood courses in English and Canadian studies, suggests that the conjunction of "wilderness" and "tips" (as in "household tips") situates the stories between, in Peter Dale Scott's terminology, "the raw and the Fryed." Focusing on "Wilderness Tips," "Death by Landscape," and particularly "Hairball," Davidson explores how Atwood collapses the distinctions (inner-outer, fixed-free, wild-settled, dead-alive) on which her stories turn and how the works themselves undermine the distinction between stories and novel—more unnatural categories that the wilderness of the text teaches us not to impose.

Atwood's works can be, and are, taught in as many ways as those of any other writer. In addition, however, because *The Handmaid's Tale* compels students' direct involvement in the text, some instructors have developed unique classroom approaches, including teaching a science-fiction class in a Handmaid's costume in order to blur distinctions between reality and fiction. The essays in part 2 all offer teachers guidance to understanding the contexts, themes, styles, and genres of Atwood's texts.

For example, after reading introductory material on Atwood's feminism and background (York, Wilson), case-study, and challenge essays, teachers may design their own approaches to Atwood's feminism. They could investigate her criticism of North American social and cultural institutions evident in interviews, essays, and literary work (see Hewitt in reference to *The Handmaid's Tale*); relate her work to the female-prominent Canadian canon (Bennett and Cooke), to other English-language works by women writers (Jacobsen's use of *The Norton Anthology of Literature by Women*), or to world women writers. They could contrast Atwood's deconstruction of genre, myth, fairy tales, and other intertexts with the way such writers as Homer, the Grimms, and Joyce treat this material (see Merivale, Bouson, Barzilai, Wilson, Levine-Keating, Manley, McCombs). By pairing such nineteenth-century texts as Moodie's *Roughing It in the Bush*, Brontë's *Jane Eyre*, or Gilman's "The Yellow Wallpaper" and *Herland* with twentieth-century texts, including Atwood's, teachers might also use Atwood's works to teach feminist literary tradition. Further, Atwood's texts have been important in the development of feminist criticism and theory (see Kolodny 79–80, 82–84; Greene, *Changing the Story* 166–90), and they continue to provide concrete exempla of issues raised by Julia Kristeva, Hélène Cixous, and Luce Irigaray in feminist criticism and women's studies courses (see Wilson, Barzilai in this volume; Hengen, *Margaret Atwood's Power*).

Similarly, Atwood's works might introduce or illustrate Gothic, romance, or dystopian traditions; the study of literature and film or literature and art; critical theory and various critical approaches; the technique of parody; intertextuality; the prose poem; life writing; postmodernism; or postcolonialism (see Barzilai, Kirtz, McCombs, Sheckels, Kadar, Brydon).

Many essays included here model innovative approaches to active learning. For example, Jacobsen stimulates students to discuss their own experiences related to literature (including gender and identity issues) in exams, papers, and class discussions. As noted earlier, York uses a student questionnaire as a stimulus to discussion of student and critics' attitudes toward Atwood. Leonard asks half of his students to bring to class advertisements for products used by men and the other half, advertisements for products used by women. After students write responses about gender encoding,

Leonard puts some of these responses on the chalkboard, to guide students to more specific readings of cultural encoding in Atwood's novels. For other creative techniques, see also VanSpanckeren and Benton.

Disproving some teachers' assumptions about the incompatibility of specialized research and teaching, professors can make innovative use of archival and manuscript material and rare texts, not only in graduate and advanced courses including or focusing on Atwood but also in undergraduate general education courses. Slides of Atwood's visual art, housed in the Thomas Fisher Rare Book Library at the University of Toronto (reproduced in S. Wilson, *Sexual Politics*) effectively introduce students to typical and recurring images and themes and invariably elicit students' own interpretations. When presented as brief background and indication of no-longer-banished authorial intention, discussions of Atwood's manuscript revisions can humanize a famous author and hearten students engaged in their own attempts to write and refine language. See, for example, these archival studies: Beran, "George, Leda," on *Lady Oracle*; Godard, "Telling It Over Again," on *Double Persephone* and other early works; McCombs, "Politics, Structure" on poetry (another on fiction is in preparation); Patton, "Tourists and Terrorists," on *Bodily Harm*; and Sharon Wilson, *Sexual Politics*, on numerous works.

"Who Is This Woman?"

Jerome Rosenberg

"Who is this woman?" That's the question asked, mockingly, by novelist Graeme Gibson, as he, Margaret Atwood herself (sitting, with a paper bag over her head), and other members of the Atwood clan gather around a table for a scene in Michael Rubbo's film *Margaret Atwood: Once in August* (National Film Board of Canada, 1984). In the film, Rubbo acts as on-screen interviewer apparently doing battle with an only almost-compliant Atwood, whose life he is attempting to define. Rebuffed in his efforts to extract the supposed psychic wound that explains the dark vision of contemporary life haunting Atwood's fiction, he has given the tools of his craft over to the Atwood family to create, as it were, their own video biography.

If you believe Rubbo, this woman is a puzzle wrapped in an enigma, a personality whose cheerless stored secrets challenge her family's vision of a happy individual deeply committed to the well-being of her relatives and friends.

If you believe her family, Margaret Atwood is a woman whose compassion nearly (but not quite) exceeds her capacity to help all those who seek her aid—whether it be her work in helping to organize the Canadian Writers' Union in the early 1970s, her active support of the Penticton Indian Band Native Writing School in British Columbia in the early 1990s, or her more private acts of kindness to her friends.

If you believe her critics—certainly those who surfaced during the days of her emergence as a significant Canadian writer—this woman is an octopus, a Medusa, a shrill witch attempting—with her world-class fame—to take over the Canadian literary scene. Or trying—with her passionate political and social pronouncements—to delve into issues (the environment, AIDS, free trade) somehow beyond her competence as a woman writer.

Who is this woman? Who is this woman who has evoked in the minds of those who would define her so many contradictory images and emotions?

This much is known. Margaret Atwood—"Peggy" to her relatives and friends—was born on 18 November 1939, in Ottawa, Ontario. Her father, Carl Atwood, an entomologist then working for the government and studying (among other things) the damage done to the northern forests by the spruce budworm, packed up every spring with his family and headed out from Ottawa to the woods on the boundary between Ontario and Quebec—there to experience surroundings and events rather different from those they encountered in the city. Her mother, Margaret Killam Atwood, likes to tell the story, for example, of the bear that one day encroached on their camp, looking for food, and the way that she confronted the animal and frightened it away (fictionalized in the novel *Surfacing*, this event has been confirmed by Atwood as being part of the family's personal history and lore [*Surfacing*, McClelland, 79; ch. 9; qtd. in Cooper]).

The family, which included Peggy's older brother, Harold (born 1937), and later her younger sister, Ruth (1951), usually spent six or seven months of each year in this wilderness environment, returning to civilization during the winter. As Atwood describes it in a 1973 essay: "Highway 17 was my first highway, I traveled along it six months after I was born, from Ottawa to North Bay and then to Temiskaming, and from there over a one-track dirt road into the bush. After that, twice a year, north when the ice went out, south when the snow came, the time between in tents . . ." ("Travels Back" 28).

Civilization for the family was Ottawa until 1945, then a year in Sault Sainte Marie, after which Carl acquired a position on the faculty of the University of Toronto and the family—while still making spring and summer excursions to the northern Ontario and Quebec bush until 1961—settled in Toronto. Although this nomadic life was unconventional—Atwood has noted that she didn't spend a complete year in school until she was eleven years old—she remembers the experience as not being so very "unusual . . . children do not find anything that happens to them unusual." And it did provide a kind of education for the developing writer not available to her peers. The movement from bush to city, from city to bush, "meant . . . there were . . . two environments that I could feel comfortable in" (Rosenberg, unpublished conversation).

Although Atwood has half-seriously characterized her years from age eight to sixteen as a "sterile" or "dark period" in her writing career, it is also true that, from 1952 through 1957, while attending Leaside High School in Toronto, she contributed poems and essays to the school magazine *Clan Call* and engaged in other activities that showed her artistic bent (Miner

180; Draine 368). Her apprentice work continued once she entered the English honors program at the University of Toronto's Victoria College, where she received her baccalaureate degree in 1961. While studying at "Vic," Atwood had her work published in the college magazines *Acta Victoriana* and *The Strand*, and placed (for the first time) a poem in a major literary journal, *The Canadian Forum*. In 1961 she published *Double Persephone*, a collection of seven poems that serve as a point of departure for her later work. That same year she received the college's E. J. Pratt Medal for her poetry.

It was at Victoria College, also, that Atwood met Dennis Lee, a fellow student and writer who subsequently became a literary confidant for Atwood and served as editor on several of her major works. She also came into contact with Jay Macpherson, a poet and professor at Victoria, who became Atwood's friend. Reading through Macpherson's personal library collection of Canadian writers provided Atwood with her first inkling that a Canadian literary tradition actually existed. And she studied under the world-renowned literary critic Northrop Frye, who probably influenced the emerging writer's intellectual growth in various ways but who, Atwood has said, served the essential purpose of recommending to her "at some point that I not run away and become a waitress" (Struthers 22).

In 1961 Atwood journeyed to Cambridge, Massachusetts, to do graduate work (under a Woodrow Wilson Fellowship) at Radcliffe College. After completing her master's degree in 1962, Atwood spent an additional year beginning work on a doctorate at Harvard, where she met James Polk, an American writer also studying at the university. She spent the next two years away from Cambridge, first returning to Toronto, where she worked for a market research firm, and then moving on, in 1964–65, to Vancouver, where she taught literature and composition at the University of British Columbia. In 1965–67, Atwood was back at Harvard, continuing her doctoral work, with aid from a Canada Council grant. At the same time, significant events in her life and career accelerated: she published her first major book of poems, *The Circle Game* (1966), which won Canada's prestigious Governor General's Award (1967); she took first prize in the Centennial Commission Poetry Competition, for the manuscript of what was to be her second collection, *The Animals in That Country*; and she married James Polk.

These early years, from 1967 through 1973, were filled with an assortment of teaching positions—at Sir George Williams University in Montreal (1967–68), at the University of Alberta in Edmonton (1969–70), at York University in Toronto (1971–72), and at the University of Toronto (1972–73). Atwood was also writing during these years: *The Animals in That Country* was published in 1968; her first novel, *The Edible Woman*, in 1969; two books of poems, *The Journals of Susanna Moodie* and *Procedures for Underground*, in 1970; another poetry collection, *Power Politics*, in 1971; and, perhaps most important, the two volumes of 1972 that catapulted Atwood into the public eye—her critically acclaimed second novel, *Surfacing*, and her controversial book of Canadian literary history, *Survival*.

In 1973, Atwood divorced Polk and moved with the writer Graeme Gibson to a farm near Alliston, Ontario. Gibson and Atwood had met in 1970 at a party for the poet Milton Acorn. Atwood, as she recalled later, was not especially impressed with Gibson at that point, though she congratulated him on the quality of his novel *Five Legs* (1969). The relationship developed. And, today, the domestic side of Atwood's life seems well settled. She and Gibson have lived together since 1973, in Alliston, and then Toronto—with excursions along the way to such places as Australia, Afghanistan, and the south of France. Their daughter, Jess, was born in 1976.

By 1973, Atwood had reached a coveted status among writers, at least among writers whose works were recognized as having critical merit: financial security on the basis of her writing alone. She was on the threshold of her recognition as an international literary figure; and, in the years that followed, the honors and awards piled up as swiftly as her books. She has been the recipient of various honorary degrees: from Trent University (1973); Queen's University (1974); Concordia University (1980); Smith College (1982); the University of Toronto (1983); Mount Holyoke, the University of Waterloo, and the University of Guelph (all in 1985); and the University of Montreal (1991). She has received (among a score of other honors) the City of Toronto Book Award and the Canadian Booksellers Association Award (for her third novel, *Lady Oracle*) and a second Governor General's Award (for *The Handmaid's Tale*); and she was one of six nominees for Britain's prestigious Booker Prize (for *Cat's Eye*). Her activities also speak to her renown: in 1991, for example, she gave four well-received lectures in the prestigious Clarendon Lecture Series in Oxford, England. And she has been suggested as a possible candidate for the Nobel Prize.

If there's a mystery in all this, as Michael Rubbo's film would suggest, it may only be the increasingly common one faced by any talented woman confronting the delicate balance between conventional life and extraordinary career. Atwood herself said it best, maybe, as she looked at her life in the late 1980s and attempted to characterize it as neither more nor less than ordinary:

> I now live a life that is pretty close to the leaves-in-the backyard model I [once] thought would have been out of bounds forever. . . . I bake (dare I admit it?) chocolate chip cookies, and I find that doing the laundry with the aid of my washer-dryer is one of the more relaxing

parts of my week. I worry about things like remembering Parents' Day
at my daughter's school and running out of cat food.

("Great Unexpectations" xvi)

Who is this woman? More, perhaps, than this image of domesticity; less,
probably, than the mystery sought by Michael Rubbo. "She had eluded us,"
insists Rubbo, as he ends his film, his boat skidding away from the Atwoods'
island refuge. Perhaps. But, again, if there is a mystery here, it may have
to reside—at least for now—in the eye of the beholder.

A Feminist by Another Name:
Atwood and the Canadian Canon

Donna Bennett and Nathalie Cooke

> I see feminism as part of a large issue: human dignity.
> That's what Canadian nationalism is about, what
> feminism is about, and what black power is about.
> They're all part of the same vision.
>   —*Margaret Atwood*, "Defying Distinctions"

Prologue: The Mask

When Margaret Atwood, in 1970, re-created the experience and reinvented the voice of the nineteenth-century Canadian settler Susanna Moodie in *The Journals of Susanna Moodie*, she provided herself and Canadians with a literary foremother that they needed just then. In the opening of that collection of poems, Atwood imagines Moodie cutting the eyes out of her own picture as a way of seeing her relationship to her new world. This image also suggests to the reader the masks that Atwood and her contemporaries created, ways of seeing the present through what they took to be the empty eyes of the Canadian past.

In what follows, we wish to hold up a series of verbal "masks"—that is, to present a collage of quotations from Atwood (especially from Atwood's Moodie poems) and from her Canadian contemporaries, as a way of locating some of the forces that initiated and have continued to shape Atwood's work. (Poems are from *The Journals of Susanna Moodie* except as noted.)

To an international audience, much of Atwood's writing—both poetry and prose—appears primarily feminist in its emphasis; but to a Canadian audience it is distinctly Canadian, even nationalist. One of the reasons that the same elements of the text signal one thing for feminists and another for Canadians is that Canadians, like feminists, have had to construct themselves out of a larger culture in which they felt invisible. In the late 1960s each group began a journey into an unknown region that lacked maps and even names for what the groups would discover.

In 1832, Susanna Moodie departed from an England in which identities were all too clear and all too fixed and subsequently discovered a landscape unfamiliar and without definition that she now had to call home. Like Moodie, feminists and Canadians of Atwood's generation left behind the safety of belonging, however marginally, to an established society and set forth to found their own country. Being at home, they realized, was a question not so much of place as of vision.

Arriving, with the Wrong Baggage

Atwood has Susanna Moodie notice that things are different in a new land:

> Is it my clothes, my way of walking,
> the things I carry in my hand
> —a book, a bag with knitting—
> the incongruous pink of my shawl
>
> this space cannot hear
> . . . .
> The moving water will not show me
> my reflection.
>
> The rocks ignore.
>
> I am a word
> in a foreign language.   ("Disembarking at Quebec" 11)

This disorientation is characteristic of the experience of being in an unknown landscape. In this kind of space, Atwood tells us:

> A compass is useless; also
> trying to take directions
> from the movements of the sun,
> which are erratic;
> and words here are as pointless
> as calling in a vacant
> wilderness.
>   Whatever I do I must
> keep my head. I know
> it is easier for me to lose my way
> forever here, than in other landscapes
>   ("Journey to the Interior," *Circle Game*, Anans, 58)

For Canadians, this alien landscape is not an imaginary one. The poet Dennis Lee, who was Atwood's fellow student at Victoria College, University of Toronto, talks of this discovery:

> My sense when I began writing, about 1960—and this lasted five or six years—was that I had access to a great many words: those of the British, the American, and (so far as anyone took it seriously) the Canadian traditions. . . . All around me—in England, America, even in Canada—writers opened their mouths and words spilled out like crazy. But increasingly when I opened mine I simply gagged; finally,

the words no longer came. . . . To discover that you are mute in the
midst of all the riches of a language is a weird experience. . . . Those
of us who stumbled into this kind of problem in the nineteen-sixties
. . . were suffering the recoil from something Canadians had learned
very profoundly in the fifties. To want to see one's life, we had been
taught, to see one's own most banal impulses and deeper currents
made articulate on paper, in a film, on records—that was ridiculous,
uppity.   ("Cadence, Country, Silence" 155–56)

Awakening in an alien landscape of their own, Canadians and women had
to learn how to distinguish their voices from that of the dominant culture:
they had to learn to use their voicelessness. The silences Lee speaks of that
may make one feel bereft of identity were a necessary step in Canadian
writing, because Canadians had to fall mute, had to absent themselves. As
Lee says in *Civil Elegies* (1968):

> I learned to dwell among absence in jubilee,
> declaring that all things which release us, all things
>   which speed us into
> calamity, as Canada, are blessed.   ("Seventh Elegy")

These absences are common in Canadian literature of this period. The hero
of Leonard Cohen's novel *Beautiful Losers* is, as the poet Eli Mandel comments, "most present at the point where he is most absent from himself"
("City" 122). Maggie Vardoe of Ethel Wilson's novel *Swamp Angel* and Lou,
the protagonist of Marian Engel's *Bear*, must vanish from civilization—as
must many of Atwood's characters—before they can look through their own
eyes. By disappearing and falling silent, Canadians, like Atwood, began to define and speak out of their invisibility. What seems simple anti-Americanism
in *Surfacing* and elsewhere is more the voicing of what Canadians are not.
    For example, Atwood, in a passage that has been taken as about the
relationship between men and women, speaks as the Canadian backdrop to
the American cowboy:

> Then what about me
>
> what about the I
> confronting you on that border
> . . . .
> you ride towards, the thing you can never lasso
>
> I am also what surrounds you:
> my brain
> scattered with your

tincans, bones, empty shells,
the litter of your invasions.

I am the space you desecrate
as you pass through.
("Backdrop Addresses Cowboy," *Animals in That Country* 51)

Departure: Arriving Home, at Last

Discovering one's invisibility is but the first step in the journey toward self-discovery. Canadians had to ask themselves, How do you learn *how* to speak yourself into existence?

The poet and novelist Robert Kroetsch explains:

> At one time I considered it the task of the Canadian writer to give names to his experience, to be the namer. I now suspect that on the contrary, it is his task to un-name. . . . The Canadian writer's particular predicament is that he works with a language, within a literature, that appears to be authentically his own, and not a borrowing. But just as there was in the Latin word a concealed Greek experience, so there is in the Canadian word a concealed other experience, sometimes British, sometimes American. . . . In recent Canadian fiction the major writers resolve the paradox—the painful tension between appearance and authenticity—by the radical process of demythologizing the systems that threaten to define them. Or, more comprehensively, they uninvent the world. . . .
>
> The most conspicuous example is the novel *Surfacing* by Margaret Atwood.   ("Unhiding" 58)

Two methods of unnaming characterized this generation. Some writers—such as bp Nichol, Daphne Marlatt, Robert Kroetsch, and George Bowering—took apart language and story, finding in the consequent disorder some real sense of themselves and their work. We can see in Atwood's *The Circle Game* how she, like others, found voice only among the fragments of silence:

> Talking was difficult. Instead
> we gathered coloured pebbles
> from the places on the beach
> where they occurred.

> They were sea-smoothed, sea-completed.
> They enclosed what they intended
> to mean in shapes

as random and necessary
as the shapes of words

and when finally
we spoke
the sounds of our voices fell
into the air   single and
solid and rounded and really
there   ("Some Objects of Wood and Stone" 61)

The other kind of unnaming is similar to the feminist efforts to reclaim the underlying powers of womanhood. This unnaming is found in the work of Canadian writers who sought to break through surfaces to a deeper, mythic level, connecting the land to its people.

Atwood's contemporary the poet Gwendolyn MacEwen tells us:

This land like a mirror turns you inward
And you become a forest in a furtive lake;
The dark pines of your mind reach downward,
You dream in the green of your time,
. . . .
Explorer, you tell yourself this is not what you came for
. . . .
You had meant to move with a kind of largeness,
You had planned a heavy grace, an anguished dream.

But the dark pines of your mind dip deeper
. . . .
In an elementary world;
There is something down there and you want it told.
                    ("Dark Pines under Water")

Mythic unnaming penetrates most of Atwood's work. For example, throughout her life in the new country, Atwood's Moodie senses that the land and its creatures erase her identity; she tells us that she "was crept in / upon by green" and that "the animals / arrived to inhabit" her ("Departure from the Bush" 26), but it is not until she is dead and buried in a land she had fought against that she truly learns what it has to teach her:

I see now I see
now I cannot see

earth is a blizzard in my eyes

I hear now
        the rustle of the snow

      the angels listening above me
         thistles bright with sleet
         gathering

    waiting for the time
    to reach me
    up to the pillared
    sun, the final city
. . . .
      (but the land shifts with frost
      and those who have become the stone
      voices of the land
      shift also and say

    god is not
    the voice in the whirlwind

    god is the whirlwind

    at the last
    judgement we will all be trees   ("Resurrection" 58–59)

Atwood's work and that of many writers of her generation break down the lines of demarcation between the landscape and its people. This identification with place is not entirely benign. Not only do we see characters dive deep under the surface to find lost meaning; we also see that this identification changes them, enables them to gain powers that both strengthen and endanger. Atwood explains in "Procedures for Underground," from the volume of the same name:

    For this gift, as for all gifts, you must
    suffer: those from the underland

    will be always with you, whispering their
    complaints, beckoning you
    back down; while among us here
    you will walk wrapped in an invisible
    cloak. Few will seek your help
    with love, none without fear.   (25)

Putting in the Bush Garden

This discovery of a numinous world connected with the land is accompanied by a longing for a past. As Earle Birney puts it, "it's only by our lack of ghosts / we're haunted" ("Can. Lit."). This longing for history is an aspect of unnaming Canadian literature into existence. Not only is the need for ancestors a theme in the work of Robertson Davies and Margaret Laurence (who ends her Manawaka series of novels with an emphasis on "inheritors"), but ancestors themselves, both real and symbolic, begin to be incorporated into Canadian writing of this period. Leonard Cohen sends his characters out to find Catherine Tekakwitha (*Beautiful Losers*). Rudy Wiebe brings into focus such western Canadians as Louis Riel (*The Scorched Wood People*), Big Bear (*The Temptations of Big Bear*), and Albert Johnson (*The Mad Trapper*). Margaret Laurence treats Moodie's sister Catherine Parr Traill as a secular saint (*The Diviners*). The poet John Newlove vividly re-creates a crucial event from the narrative of the Canadian explorer Samuel Hearne. And, of course, Atwood shows us a Susanna Moodie whose experience spoke not only of the historical person but also of Canadians in general. The Canadian reclamation of a lost past is similar to feminist efforts to discover foremothers. Because this generation of Canadians lacked an indigenous tradition against which to rebel, the introduction of a past into fiction and poetry creates a doubled identity—older and newer voices are found to speak in dialogue. And even a single character, such as Atwood's Moodie, can speak with both an old voice and a new one.

> Two voices
> took turns using my eyes:
>
> One had manners,
> painted in watercolours,
> used hushed tones when speaking
> of mountains or Niagara Falls,
> composed uplifting verse
> and expended sentiment upon the poor.
>
> The other voice
> had other knowledge:
> that men sweat
> always and drink often,
> that pigs are pigs
> but must be eaten
> anyway, that unborn babies
> fester like wounds in the body,
> that there is nothing to be done
> about mosquitoes;
>
> One saw through my
> bleared and gradually
> bleaching eyes, red leaves,
> the rituals of seasons and rivers

> The other found a dead dog
> jubilant with maggots
> half-buried among the sweet peas.   ("The Double Voice" 42)

Not only did this generation of Canadian writers create a tradition within its own texts; it also helped form the Canadian canon as we know it. The writing of Atwood's generation takes up more of the canon than one would expect for works from a recent period in a national literature. The influence of Atwood and her literary contemporaries goes beyond their own creative work. These writers have themselves created surveys, anthologies, and many of the important critical statements about the nature of Canadian literature. They accomplished what women and minorities sometimes seek to achieve; building the canon after their own aesthetics, they have relocated the center and placed themselves there.

But this not a conventional center. As Atwood and her generation became the elders of Canadian literature, they resisted a picture of Canadian writing as entirely established or fixed. Robert Kroetsch tells us:

> Canadian writing takes place between the vastness of (closed) cosmologies and the fragments found in the (open) field of the archaeological site. It is a literature of dangerous middles. It is a literature that, compulsively seeking its own story . . . comes compulsively to a genealogy that refuses origin, to a genealogy that speaks instead, and anxiously, and with a generous reticence, the nightmare and the welcome dream of Babel.   ("Beyond Nationalism" 71)

In fact, what is important to Canadian writers of Atwood's generation is, finally, not so much that they have created a fixed tradition. It is that the fluid tradition they have created frees them from a stultifying past and a marginality to a center that was *never* there.

When Atwood was asked, in 1976, about the Canadian tradition in fiction "over the last few years," she reacted to the assumptions in the question:

> Four or five years ago you wouldn't have been asking me that. Instead, you would have been asking me, "Is there a Canadian tradition?" or saying, "I don't think there is a Canadian tradition." But now your question simply assumes that there is one and we go on from that. And that's a big change. It means that people don't have to scramble around trying to make a Canadian tradition. There already is one and you can work out of it. You don't have to be so self-conscious all the time. You can take off in different directions. It allows you more free-

dom. Instead of being at that stage that we were at for so long of having to *name* everything and *justify* everything . . . and *describe* everything . . . You can just take it for granted that it's perfectly O.K.

("Playing Around" 60–61)

It is tempting to say that Atwood and her generation created themselves as they helped bring Canadian literature into existence.

Are There Weeds in the Garden?

But in Canadian literature a tradition, even a recently created one, is not to be trusted. The generation that has followed Atwood's has learned from hers a deep-set resistance. In *The Journals of Susanna Moodie*, Atwood has us discover that the process of becoming part of the land does not stop with one generation.

Ironically, today Atwood in particular, and the writers of her generation in general, are seen as embodying the authority that they saw as external and inauthentic to their experience. The historian Michael Bliss expresses the degree of this authority when he describes this generation as "literary nationalists, personified most clearly by Margaret Atwood, [who] emerged as national sages and seers" (8). Today, as a new generation seeks its own space, Atwood becomes a central figure from which new departures will be measured, not only in literary but also in popular circles. She has become a kind of icon. Brian Fawcett, in the course of a defense against what he calls "the outbreak of 'let's-bash-Atwood,'" points out that even the Vancouver vocal group Sarcastic Mannequins has a recording suggesting that "Atwood has a Canadian flag tattooed on her posterior" (8).

The rejection of Atwood (which tends to appear in the book chat of critics and the parodies and lampoons of writers) comes at a time when Canada's national identity, won painfully and well in the late 1960s and 1970s, is endangered. The nationalism of Atwood's generation seems to speak neither to the multiethnic reality of Canada's cities nor to the current split between Canada's traditional English-French solitudes. It seems, in fact, an ideal lost in a receding past. However, as Atwood warns us at the end of *The Journals of Susanna Moodie*, once a past becomes integrated into the land, subsequent generations can never entirely free themselves. They have the ancestors that once seemed absent and unreachable.

In Atwood's version of things, one of those ancestors becomes Moodie, riding on a bus in modern Toronto:

It would take more than [death] to
  banish
me: this is my kingdom still.
. . . .

Though they buried me in monuments
of concrete slabs, of cables
though they mounded a pyramid
of cold light over my head
though they said, We will build
silver paradise with a bulldozer
. . . .

                    I have
my ways of getting through.
. . . .

I am the old woman
sitting across from you on the bus,
her shoulders drawn up like a shawl;
out of her eyes come secret
hatpins, destroying
the walls, the ceiling

Turn, look down:
there is no city;
this is the centre of a forest

your place is empty
                    ("A Bus along St. Clair: December" 60–61)

Satire: The No-Woman's Land of Literary Modes

Lorraine M. York

When I began to teach Canadian literature in 1985, one of my most surprising classroom discoveries was the violently polarized responses toward Canada's most widely recognized writer, Margaret Atwood. No writer on the Canadian curriculum, in my experience, excites as much reverence—and its reverse emotion, hostility—as Atwood. As seasoned teachers of Atwood will testify, her parodic litany of the catcalls lobbed in her direction by professional reviewers is echoed by a significant portion of classroom readers: "Witch, man-hater, man-freezing Medusa, man-devouring monster. The Ice Goddess, the Snow Queen" ("If You Can't" 20). As Atwood's own list suggests, her feminist concern makes her a prime target for this sort of verbal abuse. But this explanation has always left me unsatisfied; celebrated feminist writers such as Alice Walker and Charlotte Perkins Gilman, to name two American examples, do not inspire such vicious *personal* demonizations. And so, in my search for a pedagogical explanation, I hit on the twin variables of gender and literary mode; Atwood is demonic because much of her feminist writing participates in a literary mode that is inevitably gendered male: satire.

In her contribution to the volume *Language in Her Eye*, edited by Libby Scheier, Sarah Sheard, and Eleanor Wachtel (1990), Atwood recalls that "any woman who began writing when I did, and managed to continue, did so by ignoring, as a writer, all her socialization about pleasing other people by being nice"("If You Can't" 18). Though Atwood did not specifically locate her subversive nonniceness in terms of literary mode, the connection is not far-fetched. The business of the satirist is precisely to say nonnice things, and the pantheon of canonized satirists convened in one place would make for a nightmarish house party: Swift, Juvenal, Pope, Dryden, Smollett, Addison . . .

As this list suggests, the satiric pantheon is marked by its gender as well as by its capacity for venom—or, to be more precise, the two qualities are theoretically associated in the mode of satire itself. Satire is gendered male, though most of the students who react in hostile ways to Atwood aren't consciously aware of that; any woman who writes satire runs afoul of one of the most sacred of female stereotypes: woman as noncritical, private individual. Such was my hypothesis. I then needed a methodology that would test its validity, and I decided on a twofold approach. The first step was to survey the critical literature on satire, to determine the degree to which the gendering of the satiric mode was embedded in the very discourse that seeks to describe and analyze it. Step two was the direct canvassing, by questionnaire, of McMaster University literature students' responses to Atwood's work.

Step one produced results beyond my expectations. I *did* expect that a survey of the major critical works on satire would reinforce the idea of the satiric canon as a male one, and in this respect I was not surprised; references to women writers of satire usually amounted to one citation, in each of the works of criticism, to Jane Austen, Mary McCarthy, or Dorothy Parker. The indexes did, of course, include several references to female victims of satire. Several of these indexes included a passive item such as "women satirized" or "women, attitudes toward." Not one indexed "women satirists." What was more revealing, however, was the rhetoric of those critical works (written mostly by men), a rhetoric that often brought the critic into implicit or even explicit collaboration with the male satirist–female object of satire opposition. Here are some examples:

> The satirists do not confine themselves to the sexual behavior of woman; others of her foibles attract their attention.   (Pollard 18)

> Dean Swift's pathological horror of the human body . . . would have made it difficult for him to love even a healthy, well-exercised, well-bathed, scentless Greek beauty; but, surrounded by the lazy, unwashed, flea-bitten women of the eighteenth century, who covered their smells with perfumes and their pimples with "beauty patches," he was nearly driven insane with disgust . . . The eighteenth century. That was the era when a lady of the French court would have an enema administered to her while she was chatting with her guests. That was the era when Lady Mary Wortley Montagu, on being told that her hands were rather dirty, replied, "You should see my feet!"
>   (Highet 227–28)

These critics equate satire with documentary representation; Arthur Pollard's comment apropos of Swift's "On a Beautiful Young Nymph Going to Bed" sums up this elision: "the realism almost makes us forget the satire" (19). Us?—the male critics of satire, that is, collaborators with its male gaze.

Any rhetoric of satire criticism and theory must also take into account the well-worn military metaphor. Satire is invariably figured as a military ambush; to cite Northrop Frye's aphoristic definition, "satire is militant irony" (*Anatomy* 223). The related metaphors of weaponry are prevalent throughout the standard critical studies (Pollard 1; Highet 23; Elliott 195; Kernan 94). A more recent study, George A. Test's *Satire: Spirit and Art* (1991), is so conscious of satire's masculinist-military legacy that an entire section is devoted to satire's association with aggression. Test concludes, "So the aggression of satire comes with the territory" (18), unconsciously spawning yet another military metaphor himself.

What does a woman writer—or, more to the point, a feminist writer—make of such a legacy? Clearly, one route is to adopt the mode and turn its masculinist weapons against the very concept of masculinist weaponry. From her earliest fiction, this has been Margaret Atwood's project, and it appears most prominently in two of her novels, *The Edible Woman* (1969) and *Lady Oracle* (1976), one of her poetry collections, *Power Politics* (1971), and one collection of prose poems and short fictions, *Murder in the Dark* (1983).

One of the most celebrated moments in the first of these works, *The Edible Woman*, shows a weapon being trained on the main character, Marian—but, of course, it is a metaphorical one:

> Marian came slowly from the corner. She was breathing quickly. She reached out one hand, forcing herself to touch it.
> "What's the matter with me?" she said to herself. "It's only a camera."
> (McClelland, 1981; 242; ch. 26)

As Perry Nodelman and Sheila Page, among others, have observed, the camera takes its place in *The Edible Woman* alongside the gun as a piece of stultifying patriarchal technology. Still, Marian echoes her own words near the end of the novel, when, mouth full of her woman-cake, she replies to Ainsley's accusation, "You're rejecting your femininity!": " 'Nonsense,' she said. 'It's only a cake' " (286; ch. 30). The verbal analogy drawn between Marian's liberating sponge-woman and Peter's imprisoning camera might seem troubling, unless one sees that cake as a counterweapon. To be more precise, I see the cake-woman as satire itself: a mode that has traditionally objectified and consumed woman. Now Marian, like Atwood, is baking the satire herself; the features of the cake-woman refer metonymically to the various conditions of life as a mid-twentieth-century woman, conditions that the novel has satirized and counterconsumed (the commodification of beauty, the repression of the intellect). Viewed in this light, the title of *The Edible Woman* refers, self-consciously, to the satirical text itself, which Atwood's readers are invited to take and eat.

Lady Oracle marks a return to the satirical text as consuming body—most self-consciously in the figure of that rather rotund consuming body, the young Joan Foster. Indeed, the opening metaphor, of Joan's life having "a tendency to scroll and festoon like the frame of a baroque mirror" (Seal-Bantam, 3; ch. 1) also functions as a metaphor for the satiric text. As Atwood wrote to Jerome Rosenberg, the author of the Twayne study of her work, "In *Lady Oracle* I set out to write a book that was all tangents" (Rosenberg, *Margaret Atwood* 112)—all scrolls and festoons. Such is the nature of satire: to consume by directing streams of scathing ridicule in all directions. A short list of *Lady Oracle*'s targets might include the Canadian literary establishment, avant-garde visual arts, bourgeois proprieties of the 1950s Torontonian variety, spiritualism, and part-time revolutionaries.

In her 1974 article on Canadian humor "What's So Funny?" Atwood observed that "much Canadian political satire has been in verse form. . . . Its targets are usually abuses within the body politic" (*Second Words* 183). A few years earlier, Atwood had made her own contribution to Canadian satirical poetry about the body politic—but in *Power Politics* the political body is that of woman, and it is firing the satirical salvos rather than receiving them. Again, the baroque festoons are in evidence; the lovers wander through the poem cycle from snowbanks, to movies, to restaurants, to guest bedrooms, to "A different room, this month" (11), shifting "from east to west" (26)—in short, through various dimensions. In one poem, untitled, they self-consciously inhabit a baroque interior:

> We are standing facing each other
> in an eighteenth century room
> with fragile tables and mirrors
> in carved frames. . . .   (44)

This satire, too, though it focuses on one male-female couple, spills over its frame in baroque fashion; as Rosenberg (*Margaret Atwood*) and Judith McCombs ("*Power Politics*: The Book and Its Cover") have pointed out, *Power Politics* details the multifarious masks and strategies of sexual power struggles in a dizzying textual game of repetition and variations.

But Atwood is most clearly revising the (male) satiric tradition in her more recent work *Murder in the Dark*. One of the best examples is "Simmering," which takes Atwood's wry dissection of "power politics" in that earlier poetry collection one step further. Now Atwood uses the stylistic and rhetorical trappings of traditional satire for purposes that are utterly subversive of satire's gendered nature. "Simmering" is a *conte*, a short, witty Voltairean tale, which opens with a sarcastic commentary on the male-female division of cooking labor: barbecuing as male, baking as female. But from there the satire festoons into the raucously absurd—and timely: women nervously sipping port (!) in the living room while their husbands take over the kitchen, sending gales of "somehow derisive laughter from behind the closed kitchen doors" (33). This is Margaret in Lilliput, but the gendered reversal of the satiric mode would no doubt irritate the author of *Gulliver's Travels*.

I then turned from my own investigations of satire's gender and Atwood's playful reversals to the responses of some of her readers. Would I find some connection between readers' general feelings about Atwood's writing and the gendering of satire I had discerned? To guard against forced results, I deliberately set up my student questionnaire so as to elicit those general opinions about Atwood's work before asking respondents to consider the specific variable of satire:

1. What works by Margaret Atwood have you read? Don't worry if you can't recall specific titles; describe what you've read as clearly as you can.
2. Have you studied her work? (Or are you going to, in this course?) How often?
3. What is your basic response to Atwood's work? Like? Dislike? Why?
4. Satire has been described as "a mode of writing that exposes the failings of individuals, institutions, or societies to ridicule and scorn" (Baldick 198). Is Atwood a satirist, in your view?
5. If you believe that Atwood *is* a satirist, how does that aspect of her work affect your opinion of her?

The questionnaire also included the advice "Do not worry if you have studied or read very little of Margaret Atwood's work, or if your memory of that study or reading is very dim. I would like to hear from *all* readers." I did not want those students whose impressions of Atwood have derived more from media myth than from study or reading to count themselves out of the survey.

First, the raw results: Out of the approximately 200 McMaster undergraduates who completed the questionnaire, 14% had never read anything by Atwood, 25% had read one novel only, 6% had read her poetry only, and 55% had read more than one item. (Of those, 17% listed more than 3 items.) About 67% had studied Atwood before, and a further 12% indicated that, although they hadn't studied Atwood to date, they would be studying her in the present course. The response to question 3 substantiated my opening observation that classroom opinions of Atwood tend to be polarized; the term *polarization*, indeed, turns out to be mathematically indicative, since students were divided, 55%–45%, with Atwood's admirers taking the rather slim lead. Reasons for the dislike were many, but they sorted themselves into three categories: putative "man-hating," lack of sense of humor (?), and destructive criticism. The third reason, in particular—variations of which were cited in 34% of dislikers' comments—was of interest to me, since students tended to amplify it in their responses to question 5. Most of the students, in fact, merely repeated their earlier assertion.

An overwhelming majority—87%—of the students agreed that Atwood was a satirist, with 6% falling in the "I don't know" contingent and 7% disputing the appropriateness of particular terms of the definition as applied to Atwood (i.e., she exposes the failings of individuals but not of institutions or societies). Of the students who acknowledged Atwood as a satirist, virtually all of those who disliked her works found reasons also to dislike Atwood because she is a satirist. Particularly pungent comments include these: "She never has anything positive or constructive to say"; "She only satirizes men, not women"; and, most rich in gender associations, "Atwood is shrill!" As a result, I was left with the impression that the final question had touched a nerve in Atwood-resistant readers. Satire does seem, in the minds of many readers, to be associated with unacceptable forms of female deportment: noncompliance, critique of sexual relations, barbed invective.

Lest I give the impression that only the Atwood haters are worth study, I close with a discovery about the classroom admirers of Atwood. Like their colleagues, they tended to read Atwood's satire in terms of their personal feelings about Atwood's work as a whole: "I really like Atwood because she knows her targets and she hits them every time!" "She's said a lot of things about male-female relationships that women have been afraid to say before. Afraid of not being too popular?" "She's got this wonderfully nasty voice!" Obviously, to enjoy Atwood the satirist is to challenge gender associations, to hold that saying the unsayable is a positive rather than a negative act for women, that the military metaphor can be wielded by women, that the female satirist decides to sacrifice popularity, and that a nasty voice can be a wonderful one too.

Whatever these students found in the works—or myths—of Margaret Atwood—the nasty or the wonderful—their responses helped me to understand that satire is the no-woman's land of literary modes and that any woman who steps into that heavily bombarded landscape is bound to attract both medals and shell fire.[1]

NOTE

[1] I would like to think my colleagues Carl Ballstadt and Roger Hyman for taking the time and trouble to distribute questionnaires to their students, and the students themselves for their generosity and frankness.

Beyond Violent Dualities:
Atwood in Postcolonial Contexts

Diana Brydon

Postcolonial is a relatively new theoretical term that is currently being used in a bewildering variety of ways by different critics. At its most basic level, the term refers to a criticism dedicated to understanding and combating colonialism, particularly as it manifests itself through discourse, the linguistic system that structures writing and speech. Postcolonial criticism revalues indigenous cultures that were invaded, conquered, and denigrated under imperialism. It analyzes their literatures. And it seeks to understand the structure of thought that made imperialism possible, by examining "Eurocentrism," the belief that European cultures were superior to cultures that had developed in other parts of the world. In *The Empire Writes Back*, Bill Ashcroft, Gareth Griffiths, and Helen Tiffin use the term *postcolonial* "to cover all the culture affected by the imperial process from the moment of colonization to the present day," locating the postcolonial in a shared experience of colonization and in a shared resistance to the "assumptions of the imperial centre" (2). Gayatri Spivak suggests that *postcolonial* is becoming the name for "a new object of investigation—'the third world,' 'the marginal' " ("Poststructuralism" 222). Although the term is becoming institutionalized within the academy, she prefers to reserve its use for questioning rather than consolidating knowledge, for what the African writer Ngũgĩ wa Thiong'o has called "decolonising the mind."

As these definitions imply, the postcolonial, like the feminist, is an engaged criticism. It addresses unequal power relations, theorizes agency for the oppressed (agency being the creation of an active role beyond victimhood), recuperates lost or occluded histories, and questions traditional boundaries drawn between public and private lives. But where feminism primarily addresses gender oppression, postcolonialism focuses on cultural, economic, and political oppressions based on ethnicity, nation, and race. Atwood invites a combined feminist and postcolonial approach, both explicitly in her criticism and implicitly in her fiction and poetry.

The challenge for the teacher is to develop a postcolonial pedagogy aligned to the goals of postcolonial criticism, one that encourages class interaction, values personal experience, and questions the foundations of knowledge within an imperialist system. Strategies will vary according to the composition and location of the class. For Canadian students, Atwood presents an image of Canada more comfortably received in Ontario than in British Columbia, but it is an image Canadians can claim and contest simultaneously. Students in the United States, who may assume that she is an American writer, may be tempted to read Atwood against the Canadian grain of her work. A postcolonial approach, accentuating the differences between Canadian and United States perspectives, would stress her Canadian qualities and explain why Canadians value them. Even when Atwood sets a text outside Canada, she writes from a Canadian perspective.

Although Atwood's *Survival* (1972) has generally been read as a nationalist text, its nationalism has seldom been interrogated from a postcolonial perspective, which recognizes that *nationalism* means differently in different contexts. Canadian nationalism of the 1960s was inspired in part by the struggles for autonomy launched by anti-imperialist movements throughout the Third World, yet its homogenizing tendencies within Canada made it seem as totalizing as imperialism to those disenfranchised by its mandate. Nationalism in the settler-invader colony has no original, pre-Conquest past to legitimate its existence; it must make a strength of its obviously constructed character, relying on consensus building for the future rather than appeals to a shared past. As a self-proclaimed "political manifesto" (13), *Survival* identifies Atwood as a politically committed writer in the tradition of African writers such as Ngũgĩ wa Thiong'o and Chinua Achebe, seeking to build her nation and arguing that the literature of her place requires understanding within its own terms and not as judged against the false universalism of a dominant English or American imperialism. *Survival* marks an early recognition in Canadian literary criticism of Canada's status as a colony and what that status might mean for Canadian writers and readers. But the book does not take that analysis far enough.

After partially defining a colony as "a place from which a profit is made, but *not by the people who live there*: the major profit from a colony is made in the centre of the empire," Atwood concludes that Canada's status as a colony makes the country a "collective victim" (35–36). Both of these concepts, of collective identity and of victimization, are important for understanding Atwood's postcolonial vision. As outlined in *Survival*, her four "victim positions" (which move from denial through acceptance and questioning to creative refusal of victimhood) anticipate and correspond to current attempts to theorize subaltern agency (Spivak, "Can the Subaltern Speak?").

Subaltern is Spivak's term for an oppressed and silenced subject position. Since the subaltern is someone who by definition has been denied the power of independent action or speech, theorists question how such a person may achieve agency and change that status. For Atwood, Canada exists in such a subaltern state. Yet Atwood's focus on the necessity of theorizing a Canadian subaltern agency disappeared in *Survival*'s reception. Victims claimed all the critical attention. Atwood's political insight was translated into a static formalist paradigm. Such a recuperation of her postcolonial critique into a thematic aesthetic itself invites criticism from a postcolonial position. Whose interests might such a reading serve? A book designed to arouse Canadians to seek greater control over the direction of their country is read in a way that encourages apathy and defeatism. A potential challenge to the status

quo is deflected. Instead of changing how we see the world, Canadian literature can be added to the curriculum through this kind of formalist reading
without changing anything.

Similarly, in her fourth "victim position," in which "Victor/Victim games
are obsolete" (39), Atwood predicts the possibility of moving beyond this
"violent duality" (*Journals* 62), or "Manichean aesthetic" (JanMohamed), to
create instead nonrepressive alternatives to such colonialist models. Yet
again the reception of the book stressed the crippling binary bind rather
than the active quest to move beyond dualities. With postcolonial theory,
Atwood shares her desire for a world beyond the victor/victim games of
imperialism, but the reception of *Survival*, which blunted the theory's critical edge, suggests that more is needed than Atwood's prescribed effort of
will.

Robert Young outlines the philosophical dimensions of the challenge in
White Mythologies: "the real difficulty has always been to find an alternative
to the Hegelian dialectic" (6). The first book on Atwood, Sherrill Grace's
Violent Duality (1980), shows this Hegelian pattern structuring Atwood's
work. Grace concentrates on the tension between art and life as "the central
dialectic" (130). Grace later revises her focus to argue that "from the beginning of her career, Atwood has tried to find a third way, a non-Cartesian
way, to think of and structure images of personal and social life" (Grace and
Weir 3). To develop that third way, we need to ask the questions made
urgent by contemporary postcolonial insistence, questions such as: "How
can we know *and* respect the other?" (Young 14).

For Atwood, this question marks the point where art and life converge.
She concludes *Second Words* with this observation:

> If writing novels—and reading—have any redeeming social value, it's
> probably that they force you to imagine what it's like to be somebody
> else.
> Which, increasingly, is something we all need to know.
>   ("Writing the Male Character" 430)

As the "somebody else" of the dominant imperial gaze, Atwood the Canadian writer is always conscious of understanding both the view from the
center, whether that be New York or London, and the view from home, a
Canadian place that seems marginal to the rest of the world. At the same
time, however, she is acutely aware of the fractured nature of being Canadian, part of a settler-invader colony, officially both bilingual and multicultural, with a colonized native population contesting its claim to the land, a
population the colonizers would prefer to absorb and forget. To be Canadian,
as she argues in the afterword to *The Journals of Susanna Moodie*, is to be
violently torn between alternative interpellations, like a schizophrenic, and
hence to exist only in process.

Canadians' complicity in colonization, in the genocide and marginalization of the country's indigenous inhabitants as well as in their own domination by foreign economic and cultural interests, emerges as an important theme in Atwood's work when it is read from a postcolonial perspective. The famous diving scene of recognition in *Surfacing* shifts its meaning when read in this light. The canonical interpretation sees the nameless protagonist finding her repressed memory of her aborted child in this incident. Without denying this interpretation, a postcolonial reading would identify a more deeply repressed, implied recognition here of the fact that the narrator's Canada is founded on the genocide of First Nations peoples. Earlier critics see the Indian pictographs as serving a thematic function, unproblematically marking the heroine's decontextualized appropriation of a shamanic quest. A postcolonial critic might note the ambivalence and guilt that mark this moment as a sign of Canadians' inability to come to terms with the history of violent invasion that contradicts their chosen image as the world's peacemakers, the "sweet Canadians" Dr. Minnow so ironically refers to in *Bodily Harm*. As native writers are now pointing out, white Canadians cannot so easily incorporate native mythologies into their own attempts to manufacture a sense of belonging in this place. *Surfacing*'s uneasy references to actual native people suggest that the narrator knows this, though she wishes to deny it:

> I was remembering the others who used to come. There weren't many of them on the lake even then, the government had put them somewhere else, corralled them, but there was one family left . . . Every year they would appear on the lake in blueberry season . . . condensing as though from the air . . . and then disappearing around a point or into a bay as though they had never been there. . . . It never occurred to me till now that they must have hated us.
>
> (McClelland, 85–86; ch. 10)

Even as the protagonist acknowledges the basis for their hatred, she employs the colonialist rhetoric used to depersonalize and contain their threat, the language that characterizes them as a disappearing race, closer to the landscape, mysterious, inscrutable—above all, other. Whereas the family romance seems resolved by the end of the novel—father and mother have been dealt with, and Joe is about to be faced—this other dilemma remains, unsurfaced and unresolved, as the ghost less easily exorcised.

"Death by Landscape," a story in *Wilderness Tips*, in returning to an obsession first articulated in "This Is a Photograph of Me," the first poem in Atwood's *Selected Poems* (Oxford UP), makes the point more self-consciously. Lois feels "a wordless unease" when she looks at the Group of Seven landscape paintings she owns, paintings that reinforce the *terra nullius*, or empty lands, theory used to justify European colonization of the "New" World. Lois intuitively understands that the apparently empty landscape is inhabited: "it's as if there is something, or someone, looking back out" (Seal-Bantam, 102). The story invents a plausible reason for this unease: Lois's friend Lucy has disappeared in this landscape. But Lucy's mysterious disappearance, like that of the schoolgirls in the Australian novel *Picnic at Hanging Rock*, by Joan Lindsay, replaces settler-invader anxiety about "disappearing" the original inhabitants of the land with the fearful desire that the newcomers too may achieve such a disappearance and merging with the territory they have stolen, thus displacing the original inhabitants with their own presence.

Knowing now that the native peoples view the ritual imitation of Indians that was part of life at Camp Manitou as yet another, more insidious form of theft, Lois protests that such behavior was not "making fun. She wanted to be an Indian. She wanted to be adventurous and pure, and aboriginal" (110). Lois feels that Indians should be flattered that she envies their authenticity, rather than angry that she wishes to take over their identity. She refuses to see that by wishing to *be* the other, she contributes to the other's annihilation. As Atwood's story suggests, Canadians are far from resolving their unease with a history that casts them in such a bad light. Canadians prefer pretending that their only history lies in landscape. Atwood shows Canadians this aspect of themselves, as an amnesia they can no longer afford.

The denial or suppression of history is a classic imperialist technique of control, as Atwood demonstrates in *The Handmaid's Tale*, a book that turns away from colonial negotiations of identity toward an analysis of life at the center of an empire. Rewriting history from the point of view of the conqueror is bad enough. Mistaking the postcolonial recognition that all judgments are culture-specific as an authorization for refusing moral judgment entirely is much worse. Professor Pieixoto's statement that the reader's job "is not to censure but to understand" (McClelland, 315; "Historical Notes") is revealed contextually as a serious abdication of responsibility, similar to that of "the gentleman from the Canadian government" who tells Rennie that "of course we don't make value judgements. . . . we just allocate aid for peaceful development" (*Bodily Harm*, McClelland, 293, 296; ch. 6).

The Handmaid's Tale calls for resistance on a double front: both to those who would devise Gileadean empires and to those who would merely study them. Postcolonial criticism calls for more than understanding; it insists on action for social change. As Atwood's "Bread," in *Murder in the Dark*, demonstrates graphically, bread's meaning is entirely context-specific, yet it always points to an inescapable material reality for which we are ultimately responsible. The choices we make have material consequences. Our privileged lives are intertwined with those who suffer elsewhere. "Freedom that exists as a result of the servitude of others is not true freedom," Atwood writes.

She adds: "Oppression involves a failure of the imagination: the failure to imagine the full humanity of other human beings" ("Disneyland" 131–32).

After the Handmaid's tale of ritual abuse, brainwashing, incarceration, and constant policing, Pieixoto's posturing sounds beside the point. He sees Offred as data to be processed; her full humanity eludes him. But *The Handmaid's Tale* creates that humanity for readers willing to disengage themselves from Pieixoto's sterile rationalism. By framing Offred's story with his response, the text demands that we go beyond the only readings that he can offer. By ending in the conference classroom, as the professor yields the floor to his audience, inviting questions and dialogue, Atwood yields her narrative to her readers, inviting response to the dilemmas she has set us.

As Offred claims: "I tell, therefore you are" (279; ch. 41). This revision of the Cartesian formula "I think, therefore I am" stresses the interdependence of all of us in the contemporary world. The violent duality of the victim/victor model is surpassed. Offred offers readers of *The Handmaid's Tale* their own agency, calling us into existence as witnesses. We become students who can learn our own humanity through vicariously suffering its denial to others. That experience may prepare us to defend the human community wherever it is threatened.

Atwood shares with postcolonial writers elsewhere a belief in the power of the word: to communicate, to share, to transform, to convert, to separate, to shake and topple tyrannies, to save lives, and to end them. Respecting the power of the word, Gilead forbids its handmaids reading. Scenes of reading, and of classroom learning, recur in Atwood's texts as important moments of choice, moments in which characters can accept or resist the options offered them by an official world. The old imperialist rhetoric of the British Empire is mocked in *Cat's Eye* through a caricature that exposes its insidious indoctrination as ludicrous yet powerful (McClelland, 79; ch. 15). Other texts, such as "The Boys' Own Annual, 1911" (in *Murder in the Dark*), show that power more nakedly.

Whether her target is the old British Empire, the new United States one, or a composite picture of horrific totalitarian states drawn from around the world, Atwood's writing seeks to create in her readers an ability to imagine themselves into the lives of others in a way that creates respect for their differences. Some readers dislike the way that her first person narrators refuse to let us subsume ourselves in total identification with them; yet this refusal of identification is essential to her desire to help us to know and respect the other. Unlike Lois, we cannot afford the wish to *be* the other; unlike Pieixoto, we cannot afford the luxury of disengagement. Reading Atwood's texts is a postcolonial education in learning to balance distance and involvement, and in learning to see the ways in which we both are and are not the world.

Atwood's Intertextual and Sexual Politics

Sharon R. Wilson

Margaret Atwood's narrators and personae, nearly all failed or commercial "artists," suffer more than the female artist's usual double or triple "bind" (Juhasz 1; Trinh 6). Although the pain Atwood characters experience is most evident in the Caribbean of *Bodily Harm* and the Gilead of *The Handmaid's Tale*, nearly all Atwood artists suffer "bodily harm." Symbolically dismembered and cannibalized in a phallocentric civilization worshiping what Riane Eisler calls the dominator blade rather than the life-generating chalice (xvii), Atwood's artists, and through them her readers, typically face "massive involvement" (*Bodily Harm*, Bantam, 296) within their own bodies as well as in the body politic. Symbolically denied hands (*You Are Happy, Life before Man, Bodily Harm*, visual art), feet (*Lady Oracle*), head ("Women's Novels" in *Murder in the Dark* and *Good Bones and Simple Murders*, visual art), eyes (all the novels), ears, nose (*The Handmaid's Tale*), mouth (*The Edible Woman*, visual art), and breast (*Bodily Harm*), and even reduced to womb (*Surfacing, The Handmaid's Tale*), the amputated and crucified bodies of Atwood's females resemble those described by Julia Kristeva, Monique Wittig, and Lola Lemire Tostevin. Similarly, Atwood's males, victims as well as oppressors in the sexual war, most notably in her 1993 novel, *The Robber Bride*, symbolically lack hands, hearts, penises, and any apparent means of changing their stopped lives. Nevertheless, protagonists of both Atwood's poetry and fiction learn to speak the forbidden unspeakable (Kristeva 197) and recover amputated parts.[1]

Although students hoping to identify with characters like themselves may initially find this Atwood universe uninhabitable and may consider feminism, including Atwood's, "extreme," they can grow to appreciate and enjoy her work, and through it feminist theory, when they understand Atwood's techniques of presenting sexual politics. In teaching undergraduate and graduate courses devoted entirely to Margaret Atwood, as well as courses (Introduction to Literature, The Female Body, Images of Women in Literature and the Arts, World Literature by and about Women, and Contemporary Canadian Women's Fiction) that include Atwood, I have found that students of all types respond well to study of Atwood's intertexts, especially when they first *see* some of them, in Atwood's visual art or the film of *The Handmaid's Tale* (S. Wilson, *Sexual Politics* 35–81). Stories embedded within larger stories, creating a "play of referentiality" (O'Donnell and Davis ix–x), Atwood's intertexts include mythic, biblical, folk and fairy-tale, Native American, historical, literary, film, radio, comic-strip, advertising, and other well-known texts. These intertexts constitute material essential to understanding her work, including her essays, as well as material, such as *The Wizard of*

Oz and "Little Red Riding Hood," that is familiar and interesting to students. Atwood's intertexts influence her themes, motifs, images, characterization, and structures. Sometimes "reversing" and revisioning her embedded stories through parody or deconstruction (e.g., "Little Red Cap" in *The Handmaid's Tale*), Atwood uses intertexts to dramatize her characters' movement from symbolic dismemberment to transformation.

Well aware that her work has been influenced by Grimm and Andersen fairy tales, Greek myth, and the Bible (Atwood, audiotape recording for Wilson; Sandler, "Interview" 14), Atwood has called attention to these intertexts through titles, such as *Bluebeard's Egg* (1983), *The Robber Bride* (1993), and *Double Persephone* (1961); through epigraphs; and even through direct allusions, such as to the Grimms' "Rapunzel" and "Little Red Cap"; to goddess and classical myth; and to biblical names and settings, such as Jacob and Gilead. Because of the feminist attention they focus on their embedded narratives, both Atwood's fiction and poetry texts are feminist metanarratives, often feminist "meta–fairy tales." Resembling Salman Rushdie's *Haroun and the Sea of Stories*, Rosario Ferré's *The Youngest Doll*, A. S. Byatt's *Possession*, Toni Morrison's *Beloved*, and Anne Sexton's *Transformations*, most call attention to themselves as art, and they comment on— even parody—fiction, poetry, film, fairy tales, and other popular art conventions. In Atwood's metanarratives, her self-conscious narrators and personae tell the "other side" of fairy-tale, mythic, biblical, literary, popular-culture, historical, and life stories. Often the version they and most of us know is only one version anyway.

Atwood's recently published visual art, often untitled before publication, serves as an overview and introduction not only to some of her most predominant intertexts but also to the theme of sexual politics evident in both texts and intertexts. Her watercolor *Fitcher's Bird* is perhaps Atwood's most vivid portrayal of the Bluebeardian sexual politics suggested by two of her paradigmatic intertexts from the Grimms' *Die Kinder- und Hausmärchen*: "Fitcher's Bird" and "The Robber Bridegroom" (ATs 311, 955).[2] Both of these fairy tales suggest that underneath the promises of marriage, on the other side of the forbidden door and the disguises we all assume and project, lie dismemberment and death, even cannibalism, initially for the woman but finally also for the man. Such watercolors as the two about Frankenstein, the two about Anne Boleyn or Mary, Queen of Scots, the "Hanged Man" that is the basis for the cover of *Power Politics*, the comic Dracula (the *Portrait of Graeme Gibson*), and the covers for *True Stories* and *Murder in the Dark* all draw on these intertexts. The drawings *Amanita Caesarea*, *Egg*, *Cross-Section on Cloud*, and *Tarte as Salesman Kilodney*, *Garnie de Hornrims* and the watercolors *Undersea* and *Microscope Image* suggest related motifs. The Great Goddess of matriarchal mythology, including moon, snake, harpy, sphinx, bird goddess, and Hecate incarnations, is evident in such visual art as *Moon*, the covers of *Double Persephone* and *Good Bones*

(Canadian edition only), *Moodie Underground* in *The Journals of Susanna Moodie*, and these watercolors: *The Termite Queen, Mother Harpy and Chicks,* and *Sphinx* (reproduced in S. Wilson, *Sexual Politics*; see also Atwood, Papers). The drawings in *Good Bones and Simple Murders,* including the cover based on *The Termite Queen,* the female bird on the cover of this Approaches volume, a stump with toothed roots, and another female snake (n.pag., 34, 58), continue some of the same motifs.

The Grimms' fairy tales "Fitcher's Bird" and "The Robber Bridegroom" (Hunt and Stern 216–20, 200–04) underlie sexual political themes in every Atwood novel and most of the fiction collections. See especially "Bluebeard's Egg"; "Him," in *Murder in the Dark*; and "Alien Territory," in *Good Bones* and *Good Bones and Simple Murders.* These intertexts also shape motifs, images, structure, and such themes as the artist's marriage to death throughout her poetry, most explicitly in *Power Politics, You Are Happy, True Stories,* and *Interlunar.* The women in these fairy tales by the Grimms are much more than the passive victims of Perrault's "Blue Beard" (Zipes, *Beauties* 31–35): in "The Robber Bridegroom" the unnamed bride subversively tells her story, bringing death to those who cannibalize females; in "Fitcher's Bird," the woman uses goddess power, trickery, and disguise to bring her dismembered sisters back to life and, again, to punish the Bluebeard. Thus these embedded tales symbolize the "magic" of language, transformation, and wholeness throughout Atwood's work (see also S. Wilson, *Sexual Politics* 257–70; Manley, in this volume).

As a case in point, *Interlunar* (1984), featuring a poem entitled "The Robber Bridegroom," portrays "hollow" wasteland artists figuratively, sometimes literally, married to death. Like *Surfacing*'s narrator-illustrator, these *solde* females and males are divided from others and parts of themselves but are seeking transformation. As in *Bodily Harm* and *Murder in the Dark,* connected themes include sacrilege or debasement of art and of the sacred, natural, and human; humanity's simultaneous attraction to destruction and to creation; sexual/textual/cultural politics and the colonization of the alien "other"; the artist's heroic/ironic/parodic journey out of the wasteland/hell; and transformation toward individual and global wholeness or healing and wisdom, sometimes through special eating. Among shared motifs are magic, dismemberment, vision, eating, silence versus speech or singing (poetry), hands, and the folk motif—also used in *Double Persephone* and *Procedures for Underground*—of descent to the underworld of the dead (Stith Thompson, motif F81). Because potential artists are married to death, the "robber" is not simply a male or even patriarchy per se but a death-worshiping culture, a society in which art and the artist serve commercial, military, and colonial ends. By being part of this increasingly global culture, Atwood's artists thus become not just victims but "robbers" of life, colluding in their own and their world's cannibalism and dismemberment. Other intertexts include the Grimms' "The White Snake" (AT 673) and variants, "The Girl without Hands" (AT 706), and related European and native folktales (the search for the wife, AT 400), Great Goddess and classical myths (Eve/Lilith, Medusa, Lamia, Persephone, Orpheus and Eurydice, the Norse Mimir), native North American myths, legends, and folklore (Snake lore, Takánakapsáluk, Orpheo), other legends (the fisher king), biblical stories (Adam and Eve), literature (Dante, T. S. Eliot), and visual art (S. Wilson, *Sexual Politics* 229–57).

In addition to the Grimms' "Fitcher's Bird" and "The Robber Bridegroom," Atwood's novels use intertexts drawn from other fairy tales, myth, and other aspects of popular culture. In *The Edible Woman* (1969), Atwood's first published novel, "Hansel and Gretel," "Brier Rose," "Cinderella," and "Little Red Cap" (ATs 327A, 410, 510, 333; see Hunt and Stern) are important intertexts. In addition to "Fitcher's Bird" and "The Robber Bridegroom," Perrault's "Sleeping Beauty" ("The Sleeping Beauty in the Woods," Zipes, *Beauties* 44–51), Dodgson's *Alice in Wonderland*, Shakespeare's *Titus Andronicus*, *The Decameron*, "The Gingerbread Man," "Goldilocks and the Three Bears," and "Peter, Peter Pumpkin-Eater" illuminate the book's symbolic cannibalism. As Atwood points out (audiotape recording for Wilson), the Grimms' "The Juniper Tree" (AT 720; Hunt and Stern 220–29)—a fairy tale featuring a stepmother witch, decapitation, cannibalism, resurrection, and a real, dead mother associated with the Great Goddess's tree—is significant in *Surfacing* (1972), especially in the scene in which the narrator's mother appears to turn into a bird. Direct allusion to French Canadian *loup garou*, or werewolf, legends and to three French Canadian tales, "The Golden Phoenix," "The Fountain of Youth" (Barbeau and Hornyansky 7–25, 90–108), and a tale about hearing animal languages, similar to the Grimms' "The White Snake" (ATs 550, 551, 673), help show the narrator's symbolic and partly ironic shape change and rise from the ashes of past selves. In *Lady Oracle* (1976), Hans Christian Andersen's "The Red Shoes" (450–53) and the Powell and Pressburger film (1948) based on it, Andersen's "The Little Mermaid" (134–48), Triple Goddess myth, and popular Gothic romances reveal the double bind Joan Foster and all females face: they can "dance" *or* marry; they risk amputation of feet and tongue for attempting to do both. Although Joan cuts her feet, like the Robber Bride of the Grimms' tale and Rennie of *Bodily Harm* she tells her story and creates a future.

Atwood's more recent novels continue to depict Bluebeardian sexual politics. Despite Atwood's meticulous, paleontological attention to surface realism, down to the location of telephone booths and restaurants during the time period the book depicts (Atwood, Papers; *Life before Man* manuscripts), fantastic intertexts in *Life before Man* (1979) are especially numerous. They include L. Frank Baum's *The Wizard of Oz* (1899) and the Victor Fleming film (MGM 1939) based on it; the Grimms' "The Girl without Hands," "Rapunzel" (ATs 706, 310), and "Cinderella" ("Ashputtle") (ATs 510, 510A, 510B; Hunt and Stern 160–66, 73–77, 121–28); Perrault's "Cinderella" (Zipes, *Beauties* 25–30); Andersen's "The Snow Queen" (53–75); Washington Irving's "The Legend of Sleepy Hollow"; Mother Goose and other nursery rhymes; vampire and ghost legends; such films as *Jaws*; such radio programs as *Our Miss Brooks* (Beran, "Intertexts" 212); and visual art including Duchamp's *Nude Descending a Staircase* (S. Wilson, *Sexual Politics* 165–97). As in "Book of Ancestors" (*You Are Happy*) and "You Begin" (*Two-Headed Poems*), the characters of *Life before Man* must open themselves and reinhabit their bodies, including their hands (*Selected Poems*, Houghton and Oxford UP, 240; *Selected Poems II*, Houghton, 54; Oxford UP, 53).

Bodily Harm (1981), originally entitled "The Robber Bride" (Atwood, Papers; *Bodily Harm* manuscripts), also embeds the Grimms' "The Girl without Hands," *Oedipus Rex* and Oedipus legend, fisher king legend, Pandora myth, the biblical story of the Fall, current critical theories, and spy stories to explore marriage to death, within Rennie Wilford and within colonizing western culture. In *The Handmaid's Tale*, women's dismemberments are symbolized by societal color-coding of separate functions. Deprived not only of an individual name but of any control over her own body, Offred is the Grimms' Little Red Cap (see also Manley, in this volume), the biblical Bilhah, and both Persephone and Venus goddesses. Related intertexts include witch and she-wolf or female werewolf legends (Zipes, *Trials* 55, 64–90; Dworkin, *Woman Hating* 142–43; Walker 1068–70). Swift's "A Modest Proposal," Tennyson's "Sense and Conscience," Brontë's *Jane Eyre*, Austen's *Pride and Prejudice*, Dodgson's *Through the Looking Glass*, and Orwell's *1984* are also important.

Although the games of power politics in *Cat's Eye* (1988) are among women, the players still live in a patriarchal culture in which girls must take lessons in being feminine and compete for approval of daddy and fathergod. Intertexts in *Cat's Eye* include the Grimms' "Rapunzel," Andersen's "The Snow Queen," Triple Goddess myth, and Shakespeare's *King Lear* (S. Wilson, *Sexual Politics* 295–313). Finally, *The Robber Bride* (1993) again dramatizes the archetypal significance of the Grimms' "The Robber Bridegroom" and "Fitcher's Bird." It also draws on varied intertexts, ranging from Greek and Egyptian myth—including the snake goddess, Medusa, Mnemosyne (goddess of memory), the devouring mother, and Isis and Osiris myth—to mummy lore, mummy films, vampire legend, *Through the Looking Glass*, and "The Three Pigs." Sally Jacobsen suggests that the tales of E. T. A. Hoffmann, Offenbach's opera based on them, and "Pop Goes the Weasel" are intertexts (n. pag.). *The Wizard of Oz* may also be important (McCombs, "The Robber" n. pag.). Although some critics misread *The Robber Bride*'s female "cannibal" in the same way they did Cordelia in *Cat's Eye* (see Greene, Rev. 448–55, on the novel's misogyny), Zenia is not Atwood's first female Robber or Bluebeard. The novel again reminds us that although we play and project fairy-tale and mythic roles, we are human. Like Tony, the military historian who recognizes that history is a construct, we, too, spend our lives telling stories and wondering whether our characters resemble us or, from another angle, we resemble them.

Atwood's metanarratives usually consist of more than the two narrative strands, interwoven in dialectic with one another, that Anne Cranny-Francis finds characteristic of feminist fantasy (89). Atwood's frame narrative is always more than a revised version of one traditional fairy tale, and in deconstructing her fairy-tale and mythic intertexts, allowing the muted or silenced subtext to speak, Atwood usually heightens, exaggerates, or parodies the "embroidered" intertexts. In keeping with traditions of the romance forms (including literary fairy tales, fantasy, the fantastic, Gothic and ghost fiction, detective fiction, the thriller, and true romance) that Atwood knows and deconstructs so well, Atwood's intertextual narratives sometimes resemble what Eugène Vinaver describes as the interlace of medieval romance (*Form and Meaning* 22). See Atwood's unfinished doctoral dissertation, "Nature and Power in the English Metaphysical Romance of the Nineteenth and Twentieth-Centuries" (Atwood, Papers) and *Wilderness Tips* (McClelland, 9–37; Seal-Bantam, 3–39).

Atwood's metanarratives typically illustrate similar intertextual patterns and techniques. Although these techniques are interdependent and this listing is by no means exhaustive, it still constitutes an initial overview of Atwood's intertextual tactics. First, as in *Surfacing*, Atwood often builds a scene on a powerful fairy-tale image. Second, she frequently reverses the gender of the hero, "heroine," or other characters (third sons in "The Golden Phoenix," the Robber in "The Robber Bridegroom") to shift females from object to subject, sometimes doubling roles so that the same person may be both rescuer and rescuee and, in terms of divided archetypes or foils, princess and stepmother or witch. Sometimes men comically play roles assigned to women in the intertexts. Third, displacing the "truth" of canonical texts and inherited patterns and giving voice to the silenced, Atwood shifts the point of view from the fairy tale's usual privileged, reliable, third person narration (Jackson 26) to an unreliable third person center of consciousness or unreliable first person narration (see Booth 153; S. Wilson, *Sexual Politics* 31–32).

Fourth, Atwood uses tropes and symbols to enlarge the meaning of the ordinary (e.g., the fish bait and dead heron in *Surfacing*), especially to make the literal symbolic (e.g., the dismemberment in "Fitcher's Bird," the "treasure" the youth finds in "The Three Languages," the robbery in "The Robber Bridegroom," the prince's "rescue" and the princess's "awakening" in "Sleeping Beauty"). Fifth, retaining the magical transformations of fairy-tale plots, Atwood displaces the original plot line so that the silent or marginalized subtext of female experience is central (e.g., she makes the daughter and mother's feelings and motivations in "The Girl without Hands" the focus of *Life before Man*) (S. Wilson, *Sexual Politics* 31–32).

Sixth, keeping the fairy tale's binary opposition (VanSpanckeren, "Magic" 2) and its archetypal movement from "negative" to "positive," Atwood changes the intertext's resolution so that marriage or heterosexual relationship does not complete the woman's story (*The Edible Woman*); more commonly, she explodes and opens the resolution ("writes beyond the ending") (DuPlessis 6). Seventh, Atwood transforms, bends, or blends both tone and genre (e.g., making Fitcher and the Robber Bridegroom comic figures, simultaneously parodying and uncovering the tragic subtext in the costume gothic). Eighth, Atwood uses irony as a subversive doubled or split discourse (Hutcheon, "Circling" 170). Ninth, she uses language to defamiliarize (Shklovsky, "Art" 13–22, "Sterne's" 48–49), transgress (York, "Habits" 18), and often parody the traditional fairy-tale elements she employs to facilitate readers' unconscious recognition of intertexts: fairy-tale and mythic costumes (Offred's red clothing and basket in *The Handmaid's Tale*), settings (*Lady Oracle*'s labyrinth, *Cat's Eye*'s river of death / icy pool), props, events (the sibyl's trance in *Lady Oracle*), plots, themes, and motifs (animal languages in *Surfacing*, dancing in *Lady Oracle*). Choosing parodic antilanguage to create antinarratives resembling those of Beckett, Robbe-Grillet, and Sarraute, Atwood, in "There Was Once" (*Good Bones* 19–24; *Good Bones and Simple Murders* 20–24), deconstructs not only fairy-tale plots, readers, current critical approaches, and the genre but description, the sentence, and language (S. Wilson, *Sexual Politics* 30–33). Tenth, decolonializing in transition toward a postcolonial society, Atwood revises or reverses the norms or ideology of an intertext. For example, the danger in the Grimm fairy tale of Red Cap's going off the path becomes, in *The Handmaid's Tale*, the danger of staying on the Gileadean path. Finally, eleventh, by transgressing the conventions of language and culture (York 18) through puns, word play, figures of speech, and irony, by using delegitimation (creating an unexpected story), and by writing beyond the ending (DuPlessis 110, 6), Atwood engages readers in creating the text and remythifying patriarchally amputated intertexts (S. Wilson, *Sexual Politics* 33).

Atwood's intertexts therefore serve at least five purposes in her work: (1) to indicate the nature of her characters' cultural contexts (Beran, "Intertexts" 200); (2) to signify her characters'—and readers'—entrapment in preexisting patterns; (3) to comment self-consciously on these patterns—including the embedded fairy tales, myths, and related traditional stories—often by deconstructing constricting literary, folkloric, and cultural plots with "transgressive" language (York 6–7, 17) and filling in the gaps of female narrative; (4) to comment self-consciously on the frame story and other intertexts; and (5) to structure the characters' "magical" release from externally imposed patterns, offering the possibility of transformation for the novel's characters, for the country they partly represent, and for all human beings (S. Wilson, *Sexual Politics* 34).

Atwood's fairy-tale intertexts thus foreground sexual politics and other political issues, including those of the postcolonial condition. As Jack Zipes suggests, fairy tales present issues of power (*Fairy Tales* 67). Atwood links sexual politics, already a subtext in tales such as "Fitcher's Bird" and "The

Robber Bridegroom," to broader dominance and submission hierarchies, exposing issues of class, internal political fragmentation, and social, sexual, cultural, or religious orthodoxy. By doing so, her work raises many of the same questions as Eisler and other feminist theorists do about the possibility of human survival and evolution (S. Wilson, *Sexual Politics* 34). Contrary to most critical assessments, particularly of fairy tales, Atwood's previously unrecognized intertexts suggest possibilities beyond the amputations of body politics.

NOTES

[1] See Sharon Rose Wilson, *Sexual Politics* 16. Many of the ideas in this article are developed in greater detail in this book.

[2] Folklorists classify folktales with AT numbers based on the system cataloged in Antti Aarne and Stith Thompson's *The Types of the Folktale*. See this invaluable source for the geographical distribution and variations of these tale types; see Thompson's *Motif-Index of Folk-Literature* for classification of folk motifs.

Using Atwood's *Survival* in an Interdisciplinary Canadian Studies Course

Thomas B. Friedman

During the summer of 1989 the University of Toronto's University College asked me to teach an upper-level, interdisciplinary Canadian studies course titled Intellect and Imagination in English Canada for two years. I inherited a challenging calendar description from the instructor who had originally developed the course, a description that included the following: "an historical survey of critical thought and creative imagination in Canada . . . [that] will explore some of the traditions in the development of Canadian intellectual and artistic life." Along with this objective came a comprehensive bibliography of class readings in history, sociology, political theory, art history, imaginative literature, and two defining works of Canadian criticism: Northrop Frye's *The Bush Garden: Essays on the Canadian Imagination* (1971) and Margaret Atwood's *Survival: A Thematic Guide to Canadian Literature* (1972). Beyond their literary-critical objectives, Frye's and Atwood's works attempt a Canadian cultural critique by focusing on Canadian artistic expression as a source of "key patterns" of the Canadian imagination, a number of significant themes that Atwood states "constitute the shape of Canadian literature insofar as it is Canadian literature, and that shape is also a reflection of a national habit of mind" (*Survival* 13). *The Bush Garden* and *Survival* both announce and exemplify Canada's post-Centennial-era search for a usable concept of national identity through a systematic quest for national thematic patterns.

It was apparent to me that the inclusion of these two seminal works on the course reading list assumed an approach to Canadian intellectual history dominated by cultural nationalism and presupposed an organizational methodology that would stress an identifiable, distinctive Canadian imagination. Responding to these assumptions and deciding how to use *Survival*, in particular, to teach Canadian studies, I probed a number of related questions: Is *Survival* a prescriptively thematic text—that is, does Atwood hypothesize "a national habit of mind" and use it as a prescriptive organizing principle for her reading of literary texts, or does she use her readings of literary works to develop a theory of Canadian culture? In the face of two decades of postthematic—often trenchant—dismissals of Atwood's nonevaluative, selected search for themes in Canadian literature, can *Survival* be rehabilitated as a relevant and valuable text in the classroom? And, perhaps most far-reaching, is the search for themes itself, particularly for discovering and defining national motifs, a necessary exercise in a Canadian studies course?

In a 1985 speech at Princeton University entitled "After *Survival* . . . ," a deliberate echo of the final two words of the volume, Atwood admitted that part way through her writing of *Survival*, "the project grew more ambitious in scope" (37). A careful examination of the drafts of the book and Atwood's correspondence with her Anansi editor Dennis Lee (an endeavor currently being undertaken by Judith McCombs in *First Surfacings*) will, I am sure, reveal that the project not only grew more ambitious but also evolved in a radically different direction. As Atwood herself explains in *Survival*:

> This, then, is a description of what I intended to write: something that would make Canadian literature, as *Canadian* literature—not just literature that happened to be written in Canada—accessible to people other than scholars and specialists. . . . But I find that what I've written is something more, a cross between a personal statement, which most books are, and a political manifesto, which most books also are, if only by default.   (13)

As a result, as George Woodcock has noted, *Survival* is "a curious hybrid of a book" ("Bashful but Bold" 236); beyond its "utilitarian intent" and its "lists of recommended texts, 'useful books' and research resources which in themselves form a kind of survival course," *Survival* is, in Woodcock's estimation, "a polemical work" ("Poet as Novelist" 320), one "approaching a manifesto of nationalist cultural theory" ("Bashful but Bold" 232).

Reading *Survival* in preparation for teaching, I was struck not so much by Woodcock's sense of "one of those mildly exasperating books in which a brilliant intelligence has been unable to put the brakes on its activity and has run far ahead of a task it has undertaken" ("Poet as Novelist" 320) as by the difficulties posed by a critical work whose central tenets are articulated with such authorial self-effacement and so many cautionary warnings to its readers. The rhetorical tone of Atwood's prefatory chapter, "What, Why, and Where Is Here?," is particularly revealing. The chapter presents two intentions sometimes perceived as contradictory: the first, to write a "short, easy-to-use guide to Canadian literature"; the second, to search for "those patterns of theme, image and attitude which hold our literature together" (*Survival* 12). The first, modest aim relies on a rhetorical stance emphasizing Atwood's "amateur" status—"I'm a writer rather than an academic or an expert" (11)—and the repeated statements of "what this book is not"; Atwood claims it is nonacademic, nonevaluative, nonhistorical, nonbiographical, and "not particularly original" (12). The second purpose of the book is introduced with an unassuming tone—"it attempts one simple thing" (13). However, underneath the quiet language is an ambitious goal: to identify frequent, major thematic motifs in a country's literary works and, from them, postulate a single, definitive symbol of that nation's psyche.

Perhaps aware that her programmatic aim—especially in chapter 1 of the book, "Survival"—borders on critical audacity, Atwood carefully qualifies her language with such terms as "sweeping generalization," "possibly" and an overt warning: "(Please don't take any of my oversimplifications as articles of dogma which allow of no exceptions)" (31). As Paul Stuewe has pointed out, however, Atwood rapidly "progress[es] from equivocation to certainty" in the rhetoric of chapter 1 (17). In fact, Stuewe condemns what is perhaps the primary tenet of the book—"The central symbol for Canada . . . is undoubtedly (*Survival* 32)—apparently more for this rhetorical slippage than for the statement's actual validity or applicability, saying that "Atwood admits that her basic assumptions are dubious, but nonetheless uses them as the basis for further assertions which somehow acquire the status of obvious facts" (17). Another critic of Atwood's rhetorical techniques in *Survival*, Shuli Barzilai, has argued that what she calls the "rhetoric of ambivalence" and the "contradictory elements" of Atwood's arguments end up making the work an expression of a "cult(ure) of failure," a philosophy Barzilai—perhaps facetiously—describes as "I fail therefore I am." What these critics fail to discern is Atwood's ironic humor in these passages, humor that mocks her own qualified pretensions to authority.

However, neither the ambivalent rhetoric and the contradictions in its programmatic objectives nor its metamorphosis from literary guide to nationalistic cultural polemic directly addresses the issue of the suitability and effectiveness of *Survival* in the classroom. To me, classroom suitability rested less on the universality of Atwood's polemical statements than on the applicability of her literary-critical observations to the understanding of Canadian intellectual and imaginative history. In addition, Atwood's identification of specific themes in Canadian literature, not her implication that they are significant indicators of "a national habit of mind," seemed to me to be of primary importance for the teacher. If *Survival* was to be of pedagogical value, I felt, its literary-critical component (as much as its cultural-nationalism dimension) had to provide my students with constructive access points to a consideration of Canadian historical development and attitudes.

What emerged from the teaching of the course was that *Survival* did help students explore Canadian imaginative writing, but more for the book's thematic classifications than for its readings of individual literary works. Three of Atwood's themes proved particularly useful for organizing the course's literary materials: "Nature the Monster," "First People: Indians and Eskimos as Symbols" (called "Early People" in the table of contents), and "Ancestral Totems: Explorers—Settlers." *Survival* did more, however, than merely help me group readings under convenient thematic umbrellas; these three chapters steered students toward a wide range of literary and philosophical works not mentioned by Atwood and helped focus their attention on political and ideological issues from a variety of Canadian historical eras.

The appearance of both Susanna Moodie's *Roughing It in the Bush* (1852) and Atwood's own response to it, *The Journals of Susanna Moodie* (1970), at the top of the course reading list presumed that an examination of Canadian attitudes toward nature through these literary works would be in order. I gave my students a supplementary reading list so that they could judge Moodie's attitudes in the context of mid-nineteenth-century accounts of nature, including essays, histories, and guides by William Dunlop, Samuel Thompson, Anne Langton, and Moodie's sister Catherine Parr Traill. I had my students read Atwood's chapter "Nature the Monster," which discusses Moodie very briefly, and both her afterword to *The Journals of Susanna Moodie* and her valuable introduction to the Beacon-Virago edition of *Roughing It in the Bush.* In all three places, Atwood stresses Moodie's "double-minded attitude towards Canada" (*Survival* 51), the conflict between her idealized notions of nature as healer and source of transcendent inspiration and the reality of nature in Canada, a reality that Atwood identifies as a "tension between expectation and actuality" (51): "the conflict between what Mrs. Moodie felt she ought to think and feel and what she actually did think and feel" ("Introduction," *Roughing It* viii). Atwood also identifies a dichotomy in Moodie between the sublime view of nature at a distance and the "disagreeable things in her immediate foreground, such as bugs, swamps, tree roots and other immigrants" (51). My students recognized that Atwood probably derived this idea from what Frye theorizes as "the presbyoptic sense in Canadian culture" ("National Consciousness" 50), the "sense of probing into the distance, of fixing the eyes on the skyline" (*Bush Garden* 222), which Frye sees both in the paintings of Tom Thomson and in the poetry of Charles G. D. Roberts (223).

For a practical application of Atwood's thinking about Canadian artistic expression and national attitudes toward nature, the class examined a number of nineteenth-century poems that express conflicts between nature and civilization, colony and "motherland," change and permanence. In addition to the poems by Roberts, Bliss Carman, Alexander McLachlan, and Isabella Valancy Crawford that Atwood specifically mentions, I assigned readings from earlier in the century, especially occasional poems I thought of as more precanonical literary examples. I took many of these other poems from E. H. Dewart's *Selections from Canadian Poets* (1864), one of the earliest anthologies of Canadian poetry. When the class read such poems as McLachlan's "Britannia," Charles Sangster's "Brock" and "The Plains of Abraham," William Kirby's "Approach to Quebec" (all in Dewart), Crawford's "Said the Canoe" (in Atwood, *New Oxford*), and Oliver Goldsmith's "The Rising Village" (in Sinclair), I used Atwood's critique of Moodie as a starting point. I asked the students whether Moodie's "double voice" (as Atwood characterizes it in *The Journals of Susanna Moodie*) expresses the general sentiment of British immigrant poets in that period. It was instructive to see how a class study of these poems, both those alluded to by Atwood and those from Dewart's anthology, profited from Atwood's thematic readings in chapter 2 of *Survival.* What students discovered through Atwood's critical approach was less a consistent, definitive nineteenth-century Canadian attitude toward nature in the poetry than a perspective, marked by distinctive characteristics (especially unresolved ambivalences), that seems to persist throughout contemporary accounts of life in the period and pre- and post-Confederation literary expression.

This classroom exercise was repeated using chapter 4 of *Survival*, "First People," as a guide to the literary works that depict native peoples, particularly those that use "Indians" in symbolic ways. Again, I assigned works both referred to and omitted by Atwood: the Micmac sections of Joseph Howe's epic poem *Acadia* (Sinclair), John Newlove's "The Pride" (Atwood, *New Oxford*), Al Purdy's "Lament for the Dorsets" (Brown and Bennett, vol. 2), Charles Mair's "Song from *The Last Bison*" and A. M. Klein's "Indian Reservation: Caughnawaga" (Atwood, *New Oxford*), and Margaret Laurence's *The Diviners*. The almost twenty years that had elapsed between the publication of *Survival* and my teaching of this Canadian studies course were nowhere more apparent than in the discussion of First Peoples. In fact, by the second year of the course, I had added two important works that provided students with First Peoples' perspectives on European exploration and conquest of North America: the first, an anthology of speeches and documents of native peoples, Penny Petrone's *First People, First Voices*, which provides a counterhistory to those of the European explorers and colonizers; the second, an anthology of native short fiction, Thomas King's *All My Relations*, which introduces students to the depiction of First Peoples from a native perspective. Both works helped my class understand that the Canadian imagination is neither unitary nor born exclusively of European notions of time, history, and nature. Students learn to see "Indians" and "Eskimos" (terms that again date Atwood's writing) not merely as symbols, as "projections of something in the white Canadian psyche, a fear or a wish" (*Survival* 91), but also as imaginative articulators of their own cultural identity and of the diminishing effects of traditional literary symbolization. Supplementing Atwood's reading list with these works by First Peoples, I discovered, doesn't invalidate her thematic category; it expands its scope.

The other chapter of *Survival* I used in the classroom to great effect was "Ancestral Totems," Atwood's analysis of the theme of exploration and settlement in Canadian literature. I assigned the students selections from the journals of Samuel Hearne and David Thompson (Brown and Bennett, vol. 1) and discussed the forms, techniques, and purposes of exploration literature; in addition, I had students read literary works that deal with exploration, including poems that explicitly link mapping, geography, and discovery with their metaphorical correlatives in personal psychology: Douglas LePan's "A Country without a Mythology," John Newlove's "Samuel Hearne in Wintertime," Gwendolyn MacEwen's "The Discovery" and "Dark Pines under Water" (all in Atwood, *New Oxford*), and Miriam Waddington's "Voyagers" (in *Driving Home*). Atwood's discussion of literature about explorers in *Survival* (113–20), along with her characterization of Canada as "unknown territory" and her assertion that literature "is also a map, a geography of the mind" in her preface (18–19), helped my students think about exploration and discovery as themes that have persisted in Canadian literature. As Atwood points out in one of her 1991 Clarendon lectures at Oxford University ("Concerning Franklin"), a key moment in the exploration of Canada—the Franklin expedition—has provided abundant source material for Canadian imaginative writing: Atwood herself in "The Age of Lead" (*Wilderness Tips*), Mordecai Richler in *Solomon Gursky Was Here*, and, more recently, Rudy Wiebe's *A Discovery of Strangers*. A presentation by one of my students, using Stan Rogers's folk song "The Northwest Passage" to examine themes of exploration in the Canadian creative imagination, proved, to me at least, that the thematic approach expressed in *Survival* can encourage students to think analytically and interdisciplinarily.

What of the status of *Survival* and of thematic criticism itself? Many critics who decry the oversimplification of Atwood's survival thesis and describe the four basic victim positions as an odd blend of Frygian archetypal criticism and the *Games People Play* pop psychology of the 1960s (Steele 77) admit that *Survival* is a valuable guide to Atwood's creative writing. Both Woodcock and Steele show ways in which Atwood's criticism dovetails with her poetry and, in Woodcock's case, her novel *Surfacing*. "Atwood's criticism probably reveals more about the poetic world-vision of Margaret Atwood than about the structural principles of Canadian literature. Her criticism, in fact, is in many ways an extension of her poetry," says Steele (80), who thus effectively consigns *Survival* to the status of personal, almost solipsistic, vision. As Russell Brown notes in a recent paper (2), there has been a curious persistence in the antithematic stance of Canadian criticism since the early detractors of what Brown sees as the four books that define the thematic movement in Canada—D. G. Jones's *Butterfly on Rock: A Study of Themes and Images in Canadian Literature* (1970), John Moss's *Patterns of Isolation in English Canadian Fiction* (1974), *The Bush Garden*, and *Survival*. As if English Canadian thematics and its adherents still lurked disturbingly on the margins of respectable criticism, periodic attacks on these works, particularly *Survival*, have become routine.

Recently, too, Alan Lawson has taken *Survival* to task for what he calls its "illusion of totality"; he identifies Atwood's book with the "totalizing impulse" of all 1970s critical studies and, most pointedly, condemns Atwood's mimetic approach to Canadian literature. Lawson derides the "nation-as-author" conceit Atwood expresses in *Survival*: "I've treated the books as though they were written by Canada" (12). However, he fails to mention the important rider she adds immediately afterward, "a fiction I hope you'll go along with temporarily." I would agree with Lawson that literary texts are not reflections of life, just as a nation's literature does not necessarily reflect public attitudes or act as a reliable mirror of national sentiment; however, literary works do (particularly when they are elevated to the literary-historical and pedagogical canon) exert some influence on the way the country perceives its historical, intellectual, and imaginative development. *Survival* itself has become equally influential, especially as a model of Canadian cultural criticism. It gave rise to a flurry of thematic critical work in the 1970s, intended for a whole generation of students of Canadian literature. Two are of particular note: the Macmillan series of thematic studies, under the general editorship of poet-critic David Arnason, and the Writers' Development Trust project, which provides high school teachers with resource materials, classified and organized by theme, on Canadian literature.

My experience with *Survival* in the classroom has convinced me that there is a place for its type of theme-based literary criticism, specifically in interdisciplinary courses. In his introduction to a collection of essays on thematic criticism, Werner Sollors states:

> Interdisciplinary work that includes literature may, for obvious reasons, be particularly drawn to thematic approaches, as literary texts may be asked questions relating to historical, social, or cultural themes.
>
> (xiv)

Sollors argues that a new thematic critical approach is needed, one that goes beyond old-fashioned, theme-oriented literary explication, especially, in Sollors's words, "its long use in pedestrian high school textbooks" (xiii). *Survival*, despite its "necessary fiction" of naive mimesis, seems to fulfill Sollors's criteria precisely because it provides students in Canadian studies courses with the framework for a wide-ranging interrogation of Canadian literary texts. Beyond this, using *Survival* permits students to recognize imaginative literary works not only as discrete linguistic units of personal expression but also as essential mediators of a national culture.

Themes of Identity in Atwood's Poems and "Rape Fantasies": Using *The Norton Anthology of Literature by Women*

Sally A. Jacobsen

Margaret Atwood's poems and short story in Sandra Gilbert and Susan Gubar's *The Norton Anthology of Literature by Women* (1985) lend themselves to themes of identity that may be discussed in a women's studies or a general studies literature course. My course, American Women Poets, is a women's studies course, but a majority of students of both sexes enroll because it carries general studies credit. Because Northern Kentucky University is largely a commuter college, the average age of students is twenty-six. Displaced homemakers and the occasional grandmother leaven the ideas of recent high school graduates, making class discussions a yeasty mix. Focusing on themes of identity fosters a lively involvement with literature, since students are already engaged in carving out their own identities—whether they were attracted to the course because they are interested in women's studies or want the general studies credit. While poems in *The Norton Anthology of Literature by Women* explore identities brought to the fore in the women's movement—like "wife," "mother," "daughter," and "feminist activist"—it is easy to give these identities more universal names—like "spouse," "parent," "child," and "political activist"—so that men in the class see the relevance of these categories to their quests for identity, too. At the same time, men who may not have intended to enroll in a women's studies course benefit from having their consciousness raised to feminist concerns. Male students say that they are gratified by an increased understanding of women that the course gives them.

Every week students select from the assigned reading the poem or story about which they wish to write. The written responses are based on their choice of one of seven identities they feel the work expresses: identity as a parent or child; a spouse, lover, or friend; a "mover and shaker" (political activist); a spiritual being; an artist or worker; a sufferer; or a loner. The "identities" approach leads to intense discussion of the nuances of the works when students read their responses, either to the class or to a small group responsible for leading the discussion of particular poems. Students keep their responses in a journal to review before examinations, and they submit a few of the weekly writings for evaluation. Students may later trace one of these identities through the work of several writers as an essay choice in examinations or as a term paper topic. Hence, I mention here other poems in *The Norton Anthology of Literature by Women* with which Atwood's may be compared, but these themes of identity would also be useful in taking up Atwood's works in connection with others' in an introduction to literature course. Articulation of these particular identities as topics to explore expands such literary elements as the quest motif, bildungsroman, and antihero— patterns in literature that, as traditionally taught, bear little relevance to the patterns of women students' lives. The identities offer enough variety to speak to the experience and concerns of many kinds of students.

In my class, Atwood's most popular poem is "This Story Was Told to Me by Another Traveller," from "Circe/Mud Poems" (*Norton Anthology* 2297). Some students respond to "This Story Was Told to Me" on the identities of wives or lovers and sufferers, because two boys in the poem shape a mud torso of a woman with whom to "mate"; in forming their mud sculpture, the boys dehumanize the woman by sticking "to the essentials," emphasizing breasts and genitalia. Other students respond on the identity of "movers and shakers," because they believe that Circe, who narrates the poem, implies outrage at this male stereotype of women as she repeats the story. Most women students see the poem as a political protest against many men's ideal of a woman who is silent, listens intently to them, and allows them to use her unconditionally. A few mention men's resentment of the demands women make on them—something the mud woman cannot do. Male students in the enlightened 1990s, by contrast, see themselves as superior in maturity to the *boys* in the poem, who seem to be answering Atwood's implied question "Is this what men really want?" by saying, "No woman since has compared to my mud woman." One male concludes that the boys grew into men "forgetting that women have minds, just as they 'forgot' the head on their mud woman."

Most students enjoy the ironic tone of "This Story Was Told to Me by Another Traveller." The poem is funny because it pictures boys during puberty taking several steps further the crude drawings of female sex organs that adolescent boys often surreptitiously make in school notebooks, and because Circe nonchalantly adopts the uncritical point of view of the male "other Traveller" in telling the story. Her jaded view of men is amusing in being understated—for example, in her irony in saying, "they stuck to the essentials." For a few women students, however, the humor disqualifies the poem as a political protest. They have an indulgent attitude toward the boys "learning their sexuality through something as natural as the earth." Others see no humor and strive for a transition to the prose poem that follows, "It's the Story That Counts," in which Circe anticipates a painful separation of her identity from Odysseus's upon abandonment: "when you leave will you give me back the words?" (2298) These students credit Atwood with "revising the myth" by giving "the silenced perspective of women who've been seduced and abandoned" (the sufferers' identity). The poems are cathartic for students in articulating their pain. The works can sensitize the class to deep feelings about gender relations and thus increase students' respect for the power of literature to express what really matters to them—how the "story counts." A very brief poem, "You fit into me" (2296; from *Power Politics*), continues the discussion of lovers' identities, with its shock effect of a cuddling, affectionate love transformed into an oppressor-victim relationship.

Another poem, "The Animals in That Country," relates to students' activism on behalf of the environment, or, paired with "Procedures for Underground," it speaks to their identities as spiritual beings. Students argue whether the animals embroidered with "the faces of people" in the tapestry in "that country" are given more respect than the realistic "faces of animals" in "this country" (2293). Those who see nobility in the embroidered animals' faces bring up Elizabeth Bishop's "The Fish" (1745–46). Some identify "that country" as England, "this country" as Canada, with its emphasis on survival. Appropriate to this discussion is lecture material from *Survival*, in which Atwood distinguishes between the romantic personification of animals in British (and United States) stories and their realistic portrayal as "victims" in Canadian stories (71–85). For some students the political meaning centers on the cruelty of killing for sport, whereas others focus on Deep Ecology's indifference to merely human interests. One student says, "Atwood is trying to get us to realize that animals have just as much right to live on this planet as we do." (McKibben's *The End of Nature* and Devall and Sessions's *Deep Ecology: Living as If Nature Mattered* are useful Deep Ecology references.) Both the anticruelty and the Deep Ecology interpretations are enriched by the connection Atwood draws in *Survival* between writers in an expansionist, profiteering country who portray animals "heroically" and those in a less powerful nation who see more realistically that animal and human fate is bound up with nature's (74, 78–80). Students express amazed admiration for Atwood's subtlety in developing these political meanings.

Students inevitably recognize a spiritual identity in "The Animals in That Country" and "Procedures for Underground" (2293–94), and when they do, I introduce the literary notion that nature poetry is traditionally concerned with humanity's relationship to deity. I draw on Kathryn VanSpanckeren's article "Shamanism in the Works of Margaret Atwood," in *Margaret Atwood: Vision and Forms*. One student thinks that animals in "That Country" are at least seen as "sacred" in the tapestry. The Native American view that spirits of the dead inhabit nature pervades "Procedures for Underground," and a student notices that the poem "portrays respect" for the natural world and "the strength that Nature imparts to those who inherit it." Students draw connections between a shamanistic approach to the spiritual and the fact that the Native Americans who practiced such an approach were respectful of nature.

Although "This Is a Photograph of Me" (2292–93) at first appears to be another nature poem, with details of a woodsy natural setting, the poem focuses on the speaker, ironically absent from the "photograph," and students respond by writing about suffering and about feminist political identity. The poem startles readers by revealing in the fourth stanza that the speaker is drowned, leading one student to articulate the speaker's suffering: "The photograph is faded, as depression has faded or 'erased' the life and personality of the subject." Politically, another says, the poem "can apply to every woman. The sense of distortion of her body is in fact the distortion of her mind." Most women picture an ideal of their physical selves, says this student, "but until you find your inner self, you can't be seen in that picture." Both identities invite comparison with Adrienne Rich's "Snapshots of a Daughter-in-Law" (*Norton Anthology* 2026–29).

"This Is a Photograph of Me" gives an opportunity to mention Atwood's novels that many students are unlikely to have read—*Surfacing*, on the depression and quest-for-identity themes, and *The Edible Woman*, in relation to body images and anorexia nervosa. Because students may write a term paper on a novel, short fiction, or unassigned poetry by a course author or an unassigned author (comparing the work, if they wish, with assigned works), they are on the lookout for fiction that relates to identities discussed in class. "This Is a Photograph of Me" encapsulates several nuances of "drowning" developed in *Surfacing*, and a student who has read *Surfacing* in an introduction to women's literature course may speak up enthusiastically enough to persuade someone else to read the novel. The class interaction fostered by the identities discussions also makes students receptive to the professor's recommendations. Besides giving thumbnail descriptions of ways in which the quest for identity is treated in *The Edible Woman* and in *Lady Oracle*, I mention that these are short and very *funny* novels. At least one student will be drawn to *The Edible Woman* because of private agony about an eating disorder. Kim Chernin's *The Hungry Self* can be recommended as a resource, along with Elspeth Cameron's "Famininity" and Barbara Hill Rigney's *Margaret Atwood*.

To return to works in *The Norton Anthology of Literature by Women*, I find "The Landlady" (2294–95) a funny portrait of a grotesque meddler, useful in introducing Atwood's humor to students intimidated by poetry. One student, a fervent Christian, sees the poem as a classical opposition of the flesh and the spirit, comparable to the dichotomies developed by Anne Bradstreet and Emily Dickinson. For this student, the "landlady" is the speaker's material self, so solid she must be reckoned with: "She controls every facet of the woman's soul, what she lets in and what she allows out." In this reading, the conscience, traditionally the insubstantial part of the self, has developed into a tyrannical material self required by society, blocking spiritual self-realization. Both the simple humor of her grotesqueness and the symbolic tyranny of the "landlady" in forcing conformity make her a precursor of Mrs. Smeath in *Cat's Eye*, I point out.

Another kind of inner conflict emerges in "Spelling," the conflict between women's identities as mothers and as artists (2298–99). Mothers can pass to their daughters the power of the word, the art of resisting the oppression of women. Atwood's play on "spelling" and "making spells" and her powerful "metaphor" of the tortured witch invite comparison with Circe as creator (and, in fact, with the mud-sculpting boys as "makers"). Denise Levertov's "The Son," Louise Glück's "Illuminations," and Audre Lorde's "Now That I Am Forever with Child" (*Norton Anthology* 1949–50, 2359, and 2251–52) are terrific to compare with "Spelling" on the conflicted motherhood and artistic identities, while the dark side of women's suffering at the hands of patriarchy alluded to in "Spelling" is developed as a father-daughter oppression, both by Sylvia Plath in "Daddy" and by Anne Sexton in "The Moss of His Skin" (2207–09, 1993).

Atwood's story "Rape Fantasies" explores female sexual fantasy, a variant of the "wives and lovers" identity, and the perversion of that identity in rape. The story is valuable in opening discussion of these sensitive topics; both have intense interest for students, and rape is a particularly troubling subject for both sexes. (*The Norton Anthology of Literature by Women* is the most readily available source for "Rape Fantasies" in the United States, because the story was omitted from the United States edition of Atwood's collection *Dancing Girls*.) Students agree that the term *rape fantasy* is dangerous, for it fosters the mistaken perception that women want to be attacked and "ask for it" in dress or behavior. Students credit Atwood with dramatizing the absurdity of the idea that women desire rape.

In the story, four working-class women discuss a "rape fantasies" quiz in a woman's magazine. Estelle, a wisecracking nonconformist, objects to the quiz's use of the word *rape* to refer to fantasies of erotic encounters with strangers. That isn't rape, she says; "It's just some guy you haven't met formally. . . . Rape is when they've got a knife or something and you don't want to" (2302). Students wax eloquent on behalf of Atwood's point about erotic fantasy: "Atwood shows us the intriguing quality of fantasy and how we are in total control. Many women have been raised to view their sexuality as wrong" and "feel comfortable if they can imagine being satisfied without being responsible for it." One writer quotes an "anonymous" source: "I can't want sex and still be a good person. It should be his idea—he could even force it on me, gently of course and mostly for my pleasure. After all, it's my fantasy."

As the story progresses, Estelle humorously tries to fantasize genuine "rape," in which a sense of the threat of rape exists. In each episode, she maneuvers herself out of the victim position by taking power back from the rapist. She identifies in each assailant an element of common humanity— the first displaying gallantry, the second suffering from a winter cold, and the third experiencing mad delusions—and forms a conversational bond with them that allows her to trick them and escape. Many students do not understand that Estelle is performing an intellectual exercise, or devising a heuristic, to demonstrate the impossibility of a female "rape fantasy"— showing that rape is an act of power, not of sexual attraction, and that one can refuse "victimhood." Several students think that because Estelle "wants to have conversations with these 'perverts,' " she must be an exceptionally lonely person ("Even in her fantasies she doesn't meet Mr. Right")—or, in the case of the rapist with a cold, that she is impelled to "mother" in a love relationship. (The idea of the victim "mothering" a rapist is really very funny, most students recognize.) I help students past misunderstandings of the story by outlining the four basic victim positions defined by Atwood in *Survival* (36–39). Because Estelle takes action to minimize her victimization, she starts each fantasy in Atwood's "Position Three," "To acknowledge . . . that you are a victim" but to decide how much of the victimization "could be changed if you made the effort"—a "dynamic position" in which anger is applied to effect change (37–38). Part of the humor of the story is Estelle's easy success in prevailing over the rapists, her movement to "Position Four": "To be a creative non-victim," in which position the "role of Victim . . . is no longer a temptation" (38–39). In real life one cannot move to "Position Four" so easily, but there is satisfaction in refusing as much of the victim role as possible.

As in discussions of any aspect of female sexuality portrayed in the works studied, the men in the class sit in gratified silence, drinking in details for their sex education, while women students draw distinctions between "erotic" fantasy and "rape." Male students will join the discussion of rape if they are asked the question with which one student concluded his response to the story: "What about a man fantasizing about rape?" The instructor can remind students of the locker-room bragging in J. D. Salinger's *Catcher in the Rye* and ask if they have witnessed similar boasting about planned rape exploits. Several of Atwood's points about the dangers of indiscriminate use of the term *rape* were driven home in my class when one man answered, "Yes. There is a type of man who, if he is rejected sexually by a woman, will grumble to his friends about what he plans to do to her, the next time he gets her alone—but I assume that's 'just talk.' " The two sexes stared bleakly across the classroom at each other, in a shock of recognition. Even so, students may not see the irony in the ending of "Rape Fantasies" unless their attention is drawn to it. Estelle concludes, "Like, how could a fellow do that to a person he's just had a long conversation with, . . . I don't see how they could go ahead with it, right? I mean, I know it happens but I just don't understand it" (2307). This is exactly the situation in "date rape," the most insidious form of sexual assault threatening students. Estelle has built her entire fantasy defense on the establishment of conversational rapport with rapists. Atwood here acknowledges that such rapport is no defense. A further irony lies in Estelle's revelation, at the end of the story, that she has "fantasized" these heuristic rape incidents in a bar, perhaps telling them to a new acquaintance, a potential rapist.

My undergraduate students' responses reveal the value they find in Margaret Atwood's works, in that the works speak to what really matters to them, and the students' writings demonstrate Atwood's ability to involve readers in literature, a new experience for some of my students. *The Norton Anthology of Literature by Women* (now in its second edition) is the best collection I know for including Atwood in a survey course in the United States. If, for a general studies course, a teacher wants an anthology that includes male authors, X. J. Kennedy's *Literature: An Introduction to Fiction, Poetry, and Drama* is a good choice. The 1991 edition adds to Atwood's "You fit into me" her ecological and spiritual poem "All Bread" and a story from *Dancing Girls*, "The Sin Eater." A more generous number of works by Atwood appear in *The Norton Anthology of Literature by Women*, however, and this is its greatest strength for all the authors in my course. The weakness of the anthology, if there is one, is that in their eagerness to include works relevant to the concerns of the women's movement, the editors sometimes scant concerns of the authors themselves. For example, one would not want to sacrifice any of the sixteen of Denise Levertov's poems included, dealing with varieties of the goddess and women's spiritual identity, artistry and its connections with both spiritual identity and physical passion, and women's identities as lovers, spouses, mothers, and sisters. But that leaves no space for any of Levertov's poems exploring pacifism or environmental issues, and this is a shame, particularly when the poems omitted deal with concerns of intense interest to students. A partial solution is to have students submit proposed topics and works to be considered in their term papers. Then the instructor can alert students to works by authors whose inclusion in Gilbert and Gubar gives no hint of the writers' interest in the topics.

Happily, Margaret Atwood's selections have escaped this occasional narrowness of editorial focus, and the variety of Atwood's concerns is well represented in the anthology, as the diversity of subjects about which my students respond suggests. Other strengths of *The Norton Anthology of Literature by Women* are the informative introductions to the authors, which help students get their bearings (such information is often lacking in introductory anthologies following the New Critical model), and Gilbert and Gubar's "Selected Bibliographies" on the authors and their work. Their bibliography on Atwood judiciously balances Canadian and United States scholars (2392). Some might view the sheer bulk of the volume, in its inclusion of United States, British, and Commonwealth authors, as a drawback, but I consider this inclusiveness to be an asset. Even though I assign less than a third of the material in the volume, students browsing through their books become interested in authors of whom they have never heard, and fostering this literary curiosity is a prime purpose of an introductory course. Occasionally a student asks to write a term paper comparing a United States author's portrayals of a subject with those of one of her British contemporaries represented in the anthology. This sort of experience can lead a student to declare an English major.

The Trickster Text: Teaching Atwood's Works in Creative Writing Classes

Kathryn VanSpanckeren

I have used Margaret Atwood's works in creative writing workshops at several universities and have found them to be powerful models for creative writing students. Her dazzling style, subtle wit, and penetrating social criticism inspire my students, as do the changes she rings on traditional material such as the initiation quest in *Surfacing*, the romance in *Lady Oracle*, or the Bluebeard fairy tale in *Bluebeard's Egg*. These topics have been treated by many scholars, however. Here I want to focus on what students can learn about viewpoint, speaker, and audience from what I call Atwood's "trickster texts."

Tricks—contradictions, puzzles, mazes, deconstructions, and impossible assertions—sparkle throughout Atwood's work. They are almost her signature. Generally, though, the trick is only part of a larger whole. For example, the tricky ending of *The Handmaid's Tale* reveals that the novel is a series of tapes. First-time readers get halfway through *Surfacing* before grasping that the narrator is untrustworthy. Other examples are *Lady Oracle*'s mazed versions of selves and peculiar ending, and *Bodily Harm*'s two radically different readings (in one, the whole takes place on the operating table during a mastectomy). Such long, complex works depict fictive realities apart from the reading process; the characters and situations outlive the books and dwell richly in our imaginations.

Trickster texts are different. They are short. As Poe urged for the short story, they make a single impression. They may be poems or stories. Their essential feature is that they are almost wholly a trick—usually a trap—and that they primarily concern the communication process. We do not remember them for their imaginative worlds but rather for our response to them. Experiencing them, the reader becomes one of the protagonists (generally the victim). They are among Atwood's most appreciated and anthologized short works. Examples include the poems "This Is a Photograph of Me" and "Siren Song" and the story "Rape Fantasies."

Atwood's trickster texts demonstrate the power of viewpoint and the pitfalls inherent in any single point of view. Her earliest trickster text, "This Is a Photograph of Me," shows that viewpoint is not a simple, static entity:

> It was taken some time ago.
> At first it seems to be
> a smeared
> print: blurred lines and grey flecks
> blended with the paper;

then, as you scan
it, you see in the left-hand corner
a thing that is like a branch: part of a tree
(balsam or spruce) emerging
and, to the right, halfway up
what ought to be a gentle
slope, a small frame house.

In the background there is a lake,
and beyond that, some low hills.

(The photograph was taken
the day after I drowned.

I am in the lake, in the center
of the picture, just under the surface.

It is difficult to say where
precisely, or to say
how large or small I am:
the effect of water
on light is a distortion

but if you look long enough,
eventually
you will be able to see me.)
            (*Selected Poems*, Oxford UP and Houghton, 8)

Atwood is not speaking; the "I" is a mask or persona. Similarly, the poem
is not about a photograph or a landscape. Rather, the poem's subject is
poetry's complex mediations between reader, text, and "reality." The poem
works because we discover its subject only at the end.

Communication theorists such as Larry Samovar and Richard Porter have
shown that communication is a "dynamic transactional behavior-affecting
process" in which meaning is complete only when the audience perceives
and reacts (17). Response is integral to meaning. Meaning is a two-way cycle,
not a unidirectional, linear construct. Atwood's trickster texts, such as this
one, function in the hyperspace of deferred meaning between sender and
recipient by elaborating on the collaborative nature of "reality."

This sense of address accounts for the force of the poem. Though only
one person (or persona) is speaking, the poem does not feel like a dramatic
monologue, since it draws the reader in through the detailed description of
the photograph. We are given the background—"a lake," "low hills"—and
expect to be given the subject as well. This expectation is abruptly shattered
by the second half of the poem, which deconstructs the first.

Atwood's trickster texts duplicate the main problem in intercultural communication—"error in social perception brought about by cultural varia-

tions" (Samovar and Porter 23–24). Our cultural backgrounds as readers lead us to expect one sort of outcome. Atwood's failure to give us that outcome, and her substitution of another outcome, not only make her poem original and interesting—the substitution and its implications constitute the heart of the poem. Herein lies the seriousness of the trickster texts: they are demonstrations of how preconceptions about the persona or "other" blind us to messages. The texts have important implications for intercultural and intergender understanding.

Parallels for the pedagogy I am describing exist in the teaching of multicultural studies. The main thrust of multicultural pedagogy is to encourage students to enter the subject position of the "other" in order to maximize intercultural communication. Methods include role playing, oral history, autobiography, and creative writing. Cortland Auser, among others, has devised techniques in which students assume masks or personae that allow them to deal creatively with new cultural paradigms. His teaching builds on the work of Walker Gibson, while Margaret Bedrosian uses the ideas of Paulo Freire. She defines her interactive, student-centered class discussions as a radical alternative to the classic "banking concept of education" made up of a "narrating Subject (teacher) and a listening Object (student)" (Tu-Smith 18). My method—derived from my work as a poet, folklorist, and teacher of multicultural literature—consists of initial student-centered, highly participatory discussions followed by guided self-explorations in which students assume the subject position of an "other." Discussions make use of the communication model, beginning with the speaker, moving to the recipient (reader), and concluding with reflections on the process as meaning.

Discussions begin with the speaker. In "This Is a Photograph of Me," if the speaker drowned yesterday, how can she be speaking today? Is she a ghost? Parallels between the creative unconscious and the underworld may be noted; Pluto ruled over treasures such as gold mines, for example, as well as over the underworld. Dead souls undergo a night-sea journey on Charon's ferry, but the night-sea journey is also an image of birth and a stage in the archetypal heroic quest. The artist's dive into the unconscious is a risky departure from ordinary life. The perspective from the depths may be so radically new that it looks like death. Yet the poem ends with the word "me." Identity is affirmed in the creative process.

Regarding the audience, or "you," does the wording "look long enough, / eventually" to "be able to see me" represent an invitation to reread the poem? Is this reflexivity—the poem telling the reader to reread itself—a comment on the nature of all poetry? Does the smudged granular photograph suggest the printed page? The speaker's assumption that the reader will want to identify her becomes a self-fulfilling prophecy. If the first half is a set of instructions—beginning with "first" in stanza 1, followed by "then" in stanza 2—the last half (in parentheses) may be read as an almost magical consequence. There is a distinct air of mediumship about this poem, as if the concentration demanded in the first half called up a spirit.

The third area of discussion involves the communication strategy of the poem as a trap or mirror for self-reflection. Students note how the second half deconstructs the first by introducing the dead "I" and the notion that reality isn't what one can see (the house, lake, and hills) but rather what one cannot see (what is under the lake). Ordinary reality conceals as much as it reveals. The second half is about seeing: how water distorts light, for example. The context always affects its subject. Nevertheless, some transmission of meaning is possible, given the will to penetrate beyond appearances—even if the meaning is only, or mainly, the absence of meaning.

Discussion shows the interconnectedness of the speaker, reader, and message. For instance, the poem starts with the word "It," an indefinite reference that paradoxically implies that the reader already knows what is meant. This is a minute example of the poem as a whole, since it erases itself in its own statement. Similarly, the early, foregrounded details—"tree / (balsam or spruce)" and the "small frame house"—dwindle to insignificance while the process of looking assumes new meaning. Ultimately the text collapses like a black hole in space: viewpoint is to subject as speaker is to poem. They are all one. The poem should be reread for proper appreciation. The ending, "I am in the lake, in the center / of the picture, just under the surface. . . . but if you look long enough, / eventually / you will be able to see me" takes on haunting new resonance.

The first in Atwood's *Selected Poems*, "This Is a Photograph of Me" functions as an introduction, not only to *The Circle Game*, the volume in which it originally appeared, but to the longer collection. Other poems in the *Selected* volume work in similar ways, particularly "Procedures for Underground" and the last poems from *The Journals of Susanna Moodie* ("Thoughts from Underground," "Alternate Thoughts from Underground," "Resurrection," and "A Bus along St. Clair: December"). Dualities are set up between many opposed elements: life and death, self and other, past and present, appearance and reality. Atwood extends her scope to include male versus female and United States versus Canada in *Power Politics*, and to incorporate myth/propaganda versus experience/truth in *You Are Happy*, selections from which end *Selected Poems*. But the operations and techniques of her poetry as a whole are inherent in the first poem.

The clearest, simplest example of what Atwood can do (and what students can learn from her) is "Siren Song," which appears about midway through *You Are Happy*, in the "Songs of the Transformed" (all of which are written as songs of the dead or of animals).

> This is the one song everyone
> would like to learn: the song
> that is irresistible:

the song that forces men
to leap overboard in squadrons
even though they see the beached skulls

the song nobody knows
because anyone who has heard it
is dead, and the others can't remember.

Shall I tell you the secret
and if I do, will you get me
out of this bird suit?

I don't enjoy it here
squatting on this island
looking picturesque and mythical

with these two feathery maniacs,
I don't enjoy singing
this trio, fatal and valuable.

I will tell the secret to you,
to you, only to you.
Come closer. This song

is a cry for help: Help me!
Only you, only you can,
you are unique

at last. Alas
it is a boring song
but it works every time.
          (*Selected Poems*, Oxford UP and Houghton, 195–96)

The poem seduces the reader into destruction. The line break before the last stanza reenacts the reader's fall, as does the witty internal rhyme "at last" and "Alas."

The tricky "I" need not be a shamanic voice or siren; it can inhabit a mindless suburbanite, as in the story "Rape Fantasies." At first this story seems a comic reverie; the speaker is evidently a single working woman given to imagined rape scenes in which her talk disarms rapists. She is the spinster of cliché, a would-be Scheherazade. Only at the end of this shaggy dog of a story does the reader become aware of crucial details. The woman is in a restaurant, not alone. We are not hearing a dramatic monologue or reverie; this is nervous, perhaps drunken, babble directed to an unknown man (a potential rapist). The story ends:

Like, how could a fellow do that to a person he's just had a long conversation with, once you let them know you're human, you have a

life too, I don't see how they could go ahead with it, right? I mean, I
know it happens but I just don't understand it, that's the part I really
don't understand.   (*Dancing Girls*, McClelland, 104)

The hapless reader is thrust into a painful, ambiguous role as a voyeur; the
woman speaking is transformed from a comic featherbrain to an isolated,
desperately lonely victim. As the story's message changes, so does the audience. Unexpectedly elided with the listening "you" (the potential rapist),
we unwittingly become unstable, unreliable readers.

Since the man does not appear in the story, interpretation depends on
the reader's assumptions. Would the woman's prattle placate or inflame?
Who is the man likely to be? How can one avoid culture-bound interpretation? Am I, a United States reader, projecting violence onto a peaceful
Canadian story? In a 1980s study, Geert Hofstede has found that people in
Canada and the United States are similar, except that the United States
scores higher in "masculinity," associated with violence, assertiveness, and
materialism, as opposed to a "feminine" concern for life and the well-being
of others (Lustig 57). A careful reader from the States might want to explore
Canadian readings.

Atwood's trickster texts contain a faint, oddly welcome didactic element.
They are moral fables. In them, blindness leads to a fall, though particulars
vary. Careful, even wary observation and discrimination are always called
for. In "Siren Song," the speaker turns us into victims, but only because we
fall for her flattering blandishments. "Rape Fantasies" demonstrates, with
devastating accuracy, how a potential victim might invite her own demise.
The tricky viewpoint is used in both works almost as a setting. The texts
begin with close-ups, slowly drawing back cinematically to give us more
context—an establishing shot—only at the end.

Through assignments in guided self-discovery, creative writing students
learn from Atwood's examples to enter new viewpoints and to grasp the
inadequacy of essentializing, monocentric views and uncritical "realism."
Specific assignments put the points of the discussion into practice. Students
are given topics for writing poems or stories:

1. Select one poem or story and critique it using the communication
    model, identifying subject and object positions and looking for meaning
    as process.
2. Write a reflexive poem or story.
3. Write a story told by a liar. Use the first person.
4. Write from the viewpoint of the opposite sex.
5. Write your own funeral elegy.
6. Become a historical figure. Write what you want to say to people
    today—an explanation? a warning? The *Susanna Moodie* poems are
    good models.

7.   Write a story, poem, or essay in which an unexpected audience is only gradually revealed. "Rape Fantasies" is a model.
8.   Write a piece that denies what it is by describing a place somewhere else, characters who are not there, and an action that did not happen.
9.   Describe the other world (underworld).
10.   Write from the viewpoint of an animal.

These assignments enable students to experience how viewpoint determines meaning. The assignments can also be used to sensitize an increasingly multicultural student population to the crucial importance of subject position. They enhance an appreciation of Atwood's work and of contemporary writing by showing how trickster elements can elicit, from a work, new dimensions of meaning.

Until recently, as ethnic scholars such as Henry Louis Gates (Editor's Introduction 1) and Thomas E. Sanders and Walter W. Peek (68) have noted, the trickster tale was dismissed as a low level of narrative found among tribal peoples. Only since the mid-1980s have seminal works by ethnic scholars, such as *The Signifying Monkey* by Gates and *The Sacred Hoop* by Paula Gunn Allen, revealed the extraordinary richness and centrality of the trickster. Prometheus, Odysseus, Jason, and other classic culture heroes were tricksters. In European, African, and Native American tradition, tricksters are also creators; the spirits of art and experiment are one.

Margaret Atwood is the trickster or culture hero of her own fictional worlds. Her tricks are acts of creation. In their pure, simple form as trickster texts they are cautionary tales, arguments for polycentric vision. They are also brilliant jokes, paradoxes, hoaxes. Reading them, one recalls her unfinished doctoral dissertation on fantasy, her love of fairy tales and mythical monsters, and her esteem for science, which is forever reminding us that there is more to almost everything than meets the eye. In her trickster texts, Atwood becomes the postmodern fabulist par excellence, summoning up an interactive simulacrum of reality at once compelling and patently false. She shows herself to be the heir of Poe and Borges.

Reading as Rehearsal in a Communication Class: Comic Voicings in Atwood's Poetry

Carol L. Benton

Scholars who have noted comic moments throughout Atwood's short stories and novels have often overlooked or denied the impulse toward comedy within her poetic texts (e.g., Fulford, L. B. Thompson, Wagner). I have defined a comic impulse as "a poetic moment made incongruous by language, sense imagery, or any other discrepancy between what is expected and what is given" (Benton 26). After writing my dissertation and several papers on Atwood's comic impulse, as well as performing a one-woman show of her works, I turned to the challenge of weaving her texts into classroom teaching. This discussion focuses on how I use Atwood's poems to supplement my interpersonal communication course—particularly how interpersonal themes such as self-perception, relationship progression, and conflict management can be effectively explored with texts from *Power Politics* and *You Are Happy*.

I have seen Atwood's poems used successfully in communication courses such as interpretation of literature or performance studies, gender and communication, and family communication and have discovered that her poems are especially suited for use in basic or general studies communication courses. The works are accessible to listeners, since many of Atwood's poems allow a comic reading of serious interpersonal themes and topics. Using such texts within the communication classroom can therefore be an entertaining and effective means of engaging students in serious critical discourse. I rely on Atwood's comic poems to initiate in-class discussions about interpersonal issues and principles.

At our four-year liberal arts university, virtually all of the 12,000 students registered are obligated to fulfill an oral communication requirement before graduation. While most individuals enroll in Public Speaking, some choose the interpersonal communication course (IPC), since they are convinced that it must be less painful than standing up and giving a speech. Thus, few students taking communication courses demonstrate genuine enthusiasm for the subject, as they are there under duress. It is not uncommon for instructors of IPC to rely on literary texts as a path of entry into interpersonal concepts. Literature by such diverse authors as Diane Wakoski, Robert Frost, Maya Angelou, Erma Bombeck, Alice Walker, and Langston Hughes can stimulate interesting discussions of IPC theories. By contrast, I rely exclusively on Margaret Atwood's texts.

In my IPC course, I highlight theories and include modules on such concepts as self-awareness and self-concept, appropriate self-disclosure, critical listening skills, symbolic interaction, language and perception, gender and relationship issues, symbolic competence, assertiveness training, and conflict management; I include a variety of topics and exercises in class sessions to overcome students' resistance to active participation. For instance, I may have students read dialogues about an imaginary family or couple, or I may read one of Atwood's poems aloud. In either case, I then draw students into full-class discussions by asking them to explain how interpersonal concepts (i.e., self-esteem, assertive versus aggressive communication, disconfirming talk within relationships) or principles (i.e., interpersonal communication as an irreversible, inevitable process) can be practically applied or viewed through the dialogue or poem. Ideally, students should be able to articulate how such texts depict interpersonal concepts.

The composition of students enrolled in IPC varies significantly from semester to semester. Although the course is labeled as a third-year class, it includes first- through fourth-year students scrambling to enroll in the two dozen sections we offer annually. Each class is limited to twenty-six students. About sixty percent of the course is devoted to theories, and all students are expected to apply theory through participation in classroom activities and exercises. As background, it is beneficial to turn to the theoretical assumptions that inform the way I use Atwood's poems in class.

In Atwood's poems, text as script and reader as performer may come together to establish a comic interpretation. Reading may be profitably viewed as a rehearsal process. Active reading has a performance dimension that allows students to try on various interpretations for textual appropriateness. Since there is no one "correct" final performance, each reading may be thought of as a possible rehearsal. The simile "reading as rehearsal" demands the active participation of a reader *with* the text; she or he becomes the necessary agent for lifting language off the page and making it sensuously, somatically alive. A theoretical precedent for this approach can be found in the reader-centered phenomenological theories of Roman Ingarden, Georges Poulet, and, specifically, Wolfgang Iser. Originally, the approach of reading as rehearsal was intended to inform and explicate the silent reader's engagement with a given text. However, in the classroom the phrase is less a theoretical concept and more a descriptive comparison. I am the sole performer for my IPC audience. I read selected poems aloud to the class and use the presentation to activate discussion. Occasionally, I even present alternative or conflicting rehearsal versions of a poem. I have read the same text aloud several different ways (sarcastic, depressed, bitter, disgusted), in order to point up the layers of emotional meaning possible within a text and, thus, within an individual. I label my performance as "rehearsal" so that the students feel comfortable not only exploring various meanings and alternative enactments but also critiquing the texts as well as my performance of a poem.

Primarily, I select poems that allow a comic reading, or rehearsal. If a text supports a comic interpretation, then serious concepts can be introduced without putting the students on the defensive. By relying on a comic voice, I can link interpersonal themes to intimate relationships less stridently and with more chance of being heard by the students. A number of Atwood's poems can illustrate interpersonal concepts and can serve as a point of departure for extended full-class discussion; this essay is limited to several texts to which I am partial as a performer.

A couple of areas in IPC are enhanced by looking at Atwood's poems. It is fruitful to read "This Is a Photograph of Me" (*Selected Poems*, Oxford UP and Houghton, 8) when examining the issues of perception and the nature of reality. After the title, the persona's game is heightened if the reader responds with a comic voice. The poem's speaker is a cunning, manipulative, and controlling persona who plays a perceptual game of hide-and-seek. In the beginning, I present a matter-of-fact tone of voice. As the poem progresses, I adopt a sarcastic, haughty, or even unexpectedly casual vocal quality. This shift reflects the more covert and controlling nuances of the section of the poem located within parentheses. The comic tone emphasizes the poem's ironic features. After rehearsing one possible reading for the class, I present a series of probes intended to spark class discussion:

1. Who is the speaker (persona) and how does she feel toward her audience?
2. How does the concept of perception operate within this text?
3. Do you think she is hiding from something or someone? If so, why?
4. What are some other ways that this poem might be read? Can you demonstrate how you might read a couple of lines using your insights?
5. What does this poem have to do with IPC?

Most students are willing to suggest alternative rehearsal possibilities.

The main area in IPC that benefits from an in-class reading is relationship progression. One goal for students who take my sections of IPC is to become aware of the effects of relationships on individuals—including physical and sexual changes—as people initiate and develop personal ties. I can assess whether students have achieved this goal by having them explain and interrogate particular relationship issues in poetic texts. A number of Atwood's poems explore female and male interactions, romantic myths, conflict, and relationship deterioration, all of which are linked to the progression of intimacy. I find it constructive to perform one or more of the following texts when teaching units on primary relationships and conflict.

Female and male gender dynamics are placed in the foreground of "Tricks with Mirrors" (*Selected Poems* 183). This five-part poem is uttered by a persona who adopts the role of mirror reflecting the "other's" vain male attitudes. When reading this poem, I try to heighten the sense that the persona is poking fun at her lover. The impulse toward comedy occurs because of a juxtaposition between controlling persona and her detached voice. Since the persona refers to herself as a mirror, door, and pool, it is crucial to ask the students what they think these metaphors might mean. It is particularly useful to ask both female and male students how they respond to the text. Often it seems that the women in my classes identify with the mirror, responsible for reflecting the "attractive" image. The men frequently react to what the women in class say and resist engaging directly with the poem. When this happens, I ask the students to think about what is *really* going on. By this point, students are usually eager to talk. This text lends itself to a classroom discussion that blends relationship and gender issues, perception, and self-concept.

The theme of gender dynamics is especially engaging in the class, since many students identify with the ironic challenges that make up the dance of romance. The parodying of romantic love, while a theme in many of Atwood's texts, is nowhere more evident than in *Power Politics*. In this collection, the theme of war between the sexes is depicted by a persona who describes the eventual crumbling of a relationship. The impulse toward comedy may be found in words, stanzas, and images, as well as in the voicing of passages. The persona's voice may be rehearsed with a coy, sarcastic, seductive, wry, self-deprecating, and mocking tone.

Entrance to *Power Politics* is provided by a poem that foreshadows the sexual violence woven through the volume:

> you fit into me
> like a hook into an eye
>
> a fish hook
> an open eye   (1; *Selected Poems* 141)

This short text is difficult for students to hear as anything but terrorizing. A comic reading is not funny but relies on incongruous or unexpected vocalizing to point up irony. I examine the relationship between the way conflict is exhibited and the construction of male and female gender roles by asking students such questions as:

1. What do the "hook" and "eye" images symbolize?
2. Why does this text reflect an unproductive conflict strategy?
3. Who (speaker or other) has the coercive power within this poem?
4. What type of relationship roles are defined for the speaker and other?

After a brief analysis of this text, it is helpful to move quickly to a more overtly comic selection.

The persona continues mocking romantic conventions in "He Reappears" and "You take my hand and." In this second poem, the love relationship is compared to a bad movie, and romance is likened to climbing in the wrong window. My students respond enthusiastically to this poem, with someone almost always asking whether this speaker is a "love addict." The poem provides an entrance into a discussion of the problems of addictive behavior. Although this is a stretch from what I take to be the text's meaning, such an interpretation can facilitate an understanding of the troubling interpersonal dynamics of addictive and compulsive behaviors.

Most of the time I use some aspect of an Atwood poem in my daily lesson plan. However, occasionally I have performed a poem just to see what would happen. An instance occurred the first time I brought "They Eat Out" into the classroom. I think that this text is one of the wittiest and most accessible poems in *Power Politics*. I quickly discovered that the text provides a number of points of departure for discussions related to IPC. Note the following excerpt:

> the ceiling opens
> a voice sings Love Is A Many
>
> Splendoured Thing
> you hang suspended above the city
>
> in blue tights and a red cape,
> your eyes flashing in unison.
>
> The other diners regard you
> some with awe, some only with boredom:
>
> they cannot decide if you are a new weapon
> or only a new advertisement.   (5; *Selected Poems* 144)

Here the familiar popular-song title, the lover as superman, and the references to media advertising are powerful colloquial reminders of contemporary sexual assumptions embedded in North American culture. To bring out the wit of the poem, I use a sarcastic tone of voice. Discussion questions after reading this text may include these:

1. What are the conflict strategies used by the speaker of this poem?
2. Does this poem display a stage of relationship deterioration? Which stage?
3. Is the speaker leaving, maintaining, or manipulating the relationship?
4. What myths of love and romance are being parodied?
5. What are the realities of being in an intimate relationship?

An oral rehearsal reading ought to run the gamut from sarcastic detachment to expansive hyperbole. This poem is now a part of my regular IPC performance agenda.

Although I have been discussing the advantages in using Atwood in sections of IPC, her comic poems create some problems in the classroom. Students initially appear to resist interactive learning approaches. They often seem more comfortable taking notes from a teacher they perceive as expert. When I bring in and perform literary texts, educational responsibility shifts from teacher to student. Through performance I open myself up to critique, a shift that is uncomfortable for some of the students. Finally, I wonder about the ethics of using Atwood's comic poetry in the IPC class. In a sense I may be distorting Atwood for the student audience; not all her poems are comic, yet hearing them enacted as such may set up students to "misread" Atwood's other works. I have not resolved this dilemma. These difficulties, while a challenge, do not outweigh the many benefits and opportunities for interaction her poems offer.

Throughout Atwood's canon there are many poems that can be used to help elaborate interpersonal concepts and theories. There are several reasons that Atwood tends to work in IPC. First, supplementing textbook and theoretical material with poetic texts provides the students with a variety of illustrations for interpersonal subject areas. Students frequently remember a poem longer than related textbook material. Also, the comic possibilities of the poems I include make them, perhaps, less threatening and more engaging for the students. Finally, my own excitement and knowledge undoubtedly influence the quality of the classroom learning experience. I believe that Margaret Atwood's poems can be used as stimulating vehicles to help illustrate interpersonal principles, because they allow for a comic interpretation of important relationship themes.

A Practical Exercise: Popular Culture and Gender Construction in *Surfacing* and *Bodily Harm*

Garry Leonard

Atwood's characters—both male and female—often discover that supposedly ephemeral items designed to be quickly consumed actually exert more of an influence on their identity than those things that pose as permanent. After all, the Commander in *The Handmaid's Tale* was formerly a market researcher. His skill at uncovering, detailing, and eventually cataloging the hopes, fears, and hypocrisies of consumers in order to sell people what they would not otherwise think to buy turns out to be perfect training for managing a political administration dedicated to the systematic control of human sexuality. The Market Researcher easily becomes a Commander because knowledge of how an individual experiences desire and identity in a given cultural and historical context can be used either to evoke persistent feelings of a happiness forever about to be purchased or to impose forbidding moral strictures that seem to bear the divinely sanctioned imprimatur of universal truth.

Atwood does not cite individual advertisements, and the general discourse of advertising, merely in pursuit of static "realism." On the contrary, she presents the dynamic of advertising, as well as the broader social phenomenon of what we might call "commodity culture," to demonstrate the extent to which social relations, gender, and even subjectivity itself all depend on the simulated universe of consumerism. For Atwood's men, both "reality" and "masculinity" are always cultural constructs, but it is not they who understand this; it is her women. When David follows the narrator of *Surfacing* into the woods, expecting her to accept him as a sexual partner because Joe, her lover, has already slept with Anna, David's wife, she is struck by his mechanical and antiseptic approach: "Geometrical sex, he needed me for an abstract principle; it would be enough for him if our genitals could be detached like two kitchen appliances and copulate in mid-air" (Fawcett, 179; ch. 18).

Capitalizing on this insight, she successfully parries his argument with a mechanical objection: "I'm sorry, but you don't turn me on." Curiously, the phrase "you don't turn me on" or "you do turn me on" became sexual clichés of the so-called sexual revolution as part of the supposedly power-neutral gender discourse, but Atwood draws forth the implicit mechanical metaphor in this phrase: human beings as so many blenders and toasters waiting for someone to push their buttons and activate the culturally constructed circuit board of desire (making sex not a gender bender but a gender blender!). The narrator's rejection of David turns out to be so aptly phrased, so unanticipated by him, that he is momentarily unable to pose as "masculine," and the power equation shifts entirely away from him. The narrator tells us "the power flowed into my eyes, I could see into him, he was an impostor, a pastiche, layers of political handbills, pages from magazines, affiches, verbs and nouns glued on to him and shredding away, the original surface littered with fragments and tatters" (179). What I might call the postindustrial self no longer breaks down; it peels, like the billboards equating trivial objects of mass production with essential sensations of coherence and identity. Often in Atwood's fiction, to be is to consume. What one is—that is to say, what one imagines one is—depends on what and how one consumes.

Advertisements constantly provide students with the latest dance steps for the waltz of misrecognition between the "masculine" and "feminine" subject. Furthermore, they are more skilled at reading the encoding of gender than they realize. Nearly all of Atwood's work concerns itself with popular culture in one way or another, but my classroom exercise has been particularly useful in sparking discussions about gender as a social construct in *Surfacing*, *The Handmaid's Tale*, and *Bodily Harm*. For the purposes of this essay, I confine my examples primarily to *Bodily Harm*, with occasional reference to *Surfacing*. The reader is invited to think about the exercise I outline in relation to any number of Atwood's works, including the poetry.

In the class meeting just before the actual exercise, I arbitrarily divide the class in half and then ask one half to bring in a man's cologne advertisement and the other half to bring in an advertisement for a woman's perfume. In class I ask students to write for about five minutes on how the advertisement tries to make the product desirable to the potential consumer.

My own thesis, which I keep to myself, is that, in the case of cologne and perfume, what is being marketed is roughly the same: a scent of one sort or another contained in a bottle. Because the differences that exist between the products are minute, advertisements must make them attractive to the consumer by sustaining cultural myths of "masculinity" and "femininity." In essence, men's cologne advertisements offer the "masculine" consumer reassurance that he is innately a man, just as perfume ads reassure a woman she is innately "feminine." The paradox, of course, is that this appeal to biological essentialism can be conducted only by marketing the product as a guarantor of culturally—and psychologically—determined gender constructs. The radically different marketing technique for cologne and perfume (i.e., the shape of the bottle, advertising copy, images, layout) can be fairly regarded as a rich source of cultural assumptions about the "masculine" and "feminine" self.

Typical name brands for men's cologne include, for example, Monogram, Boss, and Member's Only. Name brands for women's perfume include Masquerade, Enigma, Poison, and Windsong. Even at first glance, there is a clear contrast between certitude, power, and privilege versus uncertainty, mystery, potential treachery, and disorientation. In the context of Atwood's fiction, my point is that she is frequently preoccupied with the tension women feel between their own impulses and what society dictates these impulses should be. But Atwood is also a student of the social construction of "masculinity," and if her women are often tired of pretending to be what men need, the men are often presented as desperately trying to appear authentic and unified. But the manner in which they do so (making a film entitled "Random Shots," for example, in *Surfacing*) only serves to highlight the very sense of fragmentation they are anxious to keep at bay. More important, she also illustrates in her fiction the interdependence of these two cultural constructs. A woman masquerades as feminine in order to make a man believe his performance as "masculine" is somehow genuine and natural. Contrary to Freud, anatomy is not destiny; it is, rather, a starting point for generating two mutually defining symbolic constructs.

The juxtaposition between a man's cologne, Pour Lui; and a woman's perfume, called Masquerade, particularly caught the attention of the class. The Pour Lui advertisement showed a man in a three-piece suit leaning forward and regarding the viewer with unflinching challenge. The copy reads, "[a] Man's fragrance projects his power of pure style." The Masquerade advertisement showed a woman at a costume ball, wearing a mask, and being passionately embraced by a man. The copy reads, "Unleash your fantasies." Members of the class discussed how the ad for the cologne presumed that men knew who they were—and that this fragrance would confirm their self-sufficient autonomy—while the Masquerade advertisement emphasized the need for the woman to perform, to costume herself, to package herself as a fantasy for the man (the man is shown easing down the zipper of her dress as though he were unwrapping a package). The woman's successful "unleashing" of fantasy—or herself as a fantasy for the man—is then consumed by him. The paradox, for the "masculine" subject, is that in searching for the "feminine" principle that will authenticate him, he is looking for confirmation of his identity from the very fantasy/masquerade that his own need for unity has generated! This fantasy (that is to say, the woman herself, masquerading as "feminine" for his benefit) appears to resolve this conflict, but in fact she embodies it.

When I steered the attention of the class back to two deodorants they brought in, Secret and Brut, they now saw a similar juxtaposition and dynamic, one in which the "masculine" deodorant is autonomous and powerful, while the "feminine" deodorant needs to suggest flexibility, mystery, and the ability to transform rapidly into something else if necessary. Other advertisements seemed to leap out to add to this discovery, notably one perfume ad whose copy says, "Want him to be more of a man, try being more of a woman." Another cologne ad, for Monogram, featured a bottle, embossed with a monogram, placed on a desk with other personal items such as an engraved pocket watch and expensive pen. Next to this, the succession of women's perfume ads touting Enigma, My Sin, Windsong, and Deception all suggested the need for a woman to perform as "feminine" in order for a man to feel "masculine." In short, the contrast between self-assured identity in the cologne advertisements, and complex masquerading in the perfume advertisements, was evident in many sets of advertisements. At this point, I was able to illustrate the interdependence of the imagery: the men in the cologne advertisements wished to see their identity as natural, and the women in the perfume ads were experimenting with self-conscious performative modes that might permit and strengthen this basic "masculine" fantasy.

An interviewer challenged Atwood by asking, "[a]re you suggesting that the masculine image is counterfeit?" Her response is both unequivocal and thoughtfully modulated: "Certainly it's a counterfeit. But then you have to say, 'Counterfeit of what?' . . . I would say 'fraud,' or 'mask,' or 'a costume.' Probably 'costume,' because there is something about a costume and it does mean something. It just isn't the same as what's underneath it" (Ingersoll, *Conversations* 31). Because the men in Atwood's fiction are usually "counterfeit" in one way or another, many of the women learn to masquerade as something they are not, in order to confirm the authenticity of a "masculine" subjectivity. Of course this "authenticated" subjectivity remains a fictional construct, albeit one the man refuses to recognize. Certainly this is the role of Anna relative to David in *Surfacing*: she gets up early every morning to put on her makeup—her mask—before David gets up. As I will suggest, Rennie Wilford, in *Bodily Harm*, is also persuaded to act out a part necessary for the preservation of Jake's illusions about his "masculinity." One major change we witness in Rennie is her movement away from masquerading as "feminine," a movement brutally initiated when she must undergo a mastectomy. The operation unsuits her for her role, and she becomes aware of its falseness for the first time: "A secure woman is not threatened by her partner's fantasies, Rennie told herself. As long as there is trust. She'd even written that . . . in a piece on the comeback of satin lingerie and fancy garter belts. And she was not threatened, not for some time" (Bantam, 106; ch. 2). The incertitude of "masculinity" is directly related to the impossibility of being genuinely "feminine"—which is the binary opposition that masculinity depends on in order to authenticate its (spurious) unity and coherence.

Although students respond to the juxtaposition of men's cologne and women's perfume ads, they are sometimes slow to respond to the novels themselves. Indeed, one positive dimension of my classroom exercise is that the class first explores the social construction of gender in the "neutral" domain of advertisements—a medium they often see as "natural"—before we turn to Atwood's brilliant problematizing of the same issue. Students who feel they have either no right, or no inclination, to comment on Atwood, nonetheless consider themselves to be experts on popular culture, and they offer their "readings" with much less hesitation and self-censorship. I find it easy to move from the juxtaposed image of the advertisements to the fiction itself because similar "gender juxtapositions" abound throughout Atwood's novels. There is the description of the narrator's childhood notebook in *Surfacing*, for instance, full of cut-out images of women, from magazines, in different forms of dress: "They were ladies, all kinds: holding up cans of cleanser, knitting, smiling. . . . A lady was what you dressed up as on Halloween when you couldn't think of anything else and didn't want to be a ghost" (105; ch. 10). Her brother's scrapbook is presented as a direct contrast: "[E]xplosions in red and orange, soldiers dismembering in the air, planes and tanks" (104).

In *Bodily Harm*, this juxtaposition appears again, not between two advertisements but between two magazines—the "masculine" one called *Crusoe* (once again suggesting exploration, self-reliance, and mastery) and the other, *Pandora* (suggesting enigmatic and dangerous mystery). Rennie writes an article for each. In *Pandora*, the article is titled "Relationships," and it offers advice to a woman who is being bored to death by her date: "Study his tie, she recommended. If you're stuck, make an imaginary earlobe collection and add his. Watch his Adam's apple move up and down. Keep smiling" (19; ch. 1). The burden is not on the man to be engaging; instead it is expected, despite considerable difficulty, that the woman will masquerade as interested. The way for her to gauge the success of the masquerade is to observe that the man assumes the pose to be "natural." Rennie's magazine advice would be implicitly reinforced by the perfume ads that would no doubt accompany her text. What a man falls in love with is a successful masquerade of "femininity." "He can't seem to forget you," begins one famous perfume ad; but then the "you" drops out of the equation: "Your Windsong stays on his mind." As I read this, the "you" he can't forget is the performance by the woman of something she is not: her Windsong. Conversely, the essay for *Crusoe* is entitled "How to Read Her Mind." Note the two different magazine titles; one cites an imperialist conqueror, the other a mythical woman whose treacherous curiosity introduced sin into the world. Rennie's article for men in *Crusoe* simply inverts her advice given to women in *Pandora*: "If she's looking too hard at your earlobes or watching your Adam's apple go up and down, change the subject" (19; ch. 1).

As John Berger notes, in *Ways of Seeing*, men act and women appear; men look at women and women watch themselves being looked at by men. In *Bodily Harm* we see the masquerade of heterosexual desire that promotes posturing in order to elicit a presumably inherent passion and eroticism. The advice given to women on how to look is then exposed in *Crusoe* as a code to discover what the woman is "really" thinking. There is rich irony in the fact that Rennie writes both articles. One form of posturing decodes another form of posturing, and this decoding masquerades as the truth. The encoding of gender becomes more specific and more personal when extended to individual commodities, but the formula is the same. "Look in the medicine cabinet," a seasoned interviewer tells the narrator of *Bodily Harm*. "It

matters what they roll on under their arms, Arid or Love, it makes a difference" (67; ch. 1). If deodorant can imply one's attitude about romance—in
this case, cynical or sentimental—it can also offer a spurious authentication
of "masculine" or "feminine" gender. Men who read *Crusoe* may well see
advertised in it, and thus they may purchase, a deodorant called Brut.
Women who read *Pandora* will be urged to buy one called Secret, which is
"strong enough for a man" but—for reasons never specified—"made for a
woman."

In *Bodily Harm*, Atwood's principal strategy for delineating the difference
between living in the"First World" and living in the "Third World" is to
show Rennie Wilford as a woman who has defined herself by what she buys,
by the trends she adheres to, and by her detailed knowledge of the latest
style. After her operation, her body has been "cut" in a fashion that will
never be in style. Her hastily conceived response is to seek relief by fleeing
the First World and removing herself to a Third World market where com-
modified femininity is not yet a product exported or imported into the
country. Once there, she begins to question who she is in this environment
that offers no props in the form of commodities, and no stage on which to
perform the masquerade of femininity. Before the operation, she involved
herself in the production of a "lifestyle." After the operation, she feels like
damaged goods, and such a performance of life seems impossible.

Of course, because Rennie makes her living writing lightly ironic articles
on "lifestyle," she views the dynamic of creating a "lifestyle" with be-
musement: "Rennie was working on a piece about drain-chain jewellery. . . .
It was the latest Queen Street thing, she wrote. . . . In fact it wasn't. . . .
Sometimes Rennie liked to write pieces about trends that didn't really exist,
to see if she could make them exist by writing about them. . . . People
would do anything not to be outmoded" (23–25; ch. 1). Her observation that
"people would do anything not to be outmoded" becomes all too applicable
to her when, after her operation, she flees the First World and attempts to
lose herself in the Third. Atwood makes clear, then, that despite Rennie's
ironic distance from the process of "fashioning" both gender and identity,
Rennie cannot help but see that, in the First World, style is power.

Indeed, she is initially attracted to Jake because he, too, is an expert on
producing a "lifestyle" through the packaging and exhibition of one's self as
though one were a commodity on the open market: "He was a designer of
labels, not just labels but the total package: the label, the container, the
visuals for the advertising. . . . He decided how things would look and what
context they would be placed in, which meant what people would feel about
them. He knew the importance of style" (103; ch. 2). One of the things he
packages, of course, is Rennie. He scrupulously decorates their apartment
in a style he finds appropriate, and buys her lingerie in an attempt to make
her a "product" appealing to him. Not content with merely dressing Rennie
for her part as his lover, however, Jake must also position her on the bed

as the incarnation of a *Playboy* centerfold: "Put your arms over your head, Jake said, it lifts the breasts. Move your legs apart, just a little. Raise your left knee. You look fantastic" (106). No longer a "whole" woman in a male-defined sense, Rennie is "damaged goods." In the context of the juxtaposed advertisements, the class can see more clearly the reasons for the rapid failure of Rennie's and Jake's relationship after—and even just before—she undergoes a mastectomy.

When they decide to make love again for the first time since the operation, she looks over the "packaging" he has purchased for her: "He liked buying her things like that. Bad taste. Garters, merry widows, red bikini pants with gold spangles, wired half-cup hooker brassieres that squeezed and pushed up the breasts. The real you, he'd say, with irony and hope." A wardrobe that had been merely "bad taste" is now literally unwearable, and she turns away from it: "In the end she wore nothing" (20; ch. 1). Whereas Jake once served as the director of her "feminine" masquerade, setting the scene and coaching her performance, the impending operation makes all his attentions feel intolerably alien to Rennie. Jake may be "a designer of labels," but he has no label for Rennie—indeed, for any woman—who is unable to perform as "feminine." When Rennie refuses to wear the costume Jake bought to make her "real" for him, and instead offers herself without props or adornment, this abandonment of gender masquerade produces a sexual encounter devoid of all sensation: "Her body was nerveless, slack, as if she was already under the anaesthetic. . . . At last she faked it. That was another vow she'd made once: never to fake it" (21). The irony, of course, is that she has been "faking it" all along—outfitting herself in costumes she finds in "bad taste"— in order to make her relationship with Jake appear "real" to him. If he feels completed and fulfilled by her masquerade, then she is free to enjoy the fantasy of herself as "feminine."

Understanding Rennie's postoperative status as "damaged goods" also suggests to the class why she compulsively engineers a sexual relationship with Daniel, the surgeon who performed the operation. In stark contrast to Jake, Daniel is a man completely devoid of style, and a man equally unable to detect its presence in other people: "The people she knew spoke of themselves as bottoming out and going through changes and getting it together. The first time she'd used these phrases with Daniel, she'd had to translate. . . . This was the difference between Daniel and the people she knew: Daniel didn't think of himself" (140; ch. 3). But Daniel is a poor solution for the disenchanted Rennie, not only because he is married but also because the culture he lives in is still one in which to be is to be seen. To a woman no longer able, or no longer willing, to subscribe to a masquerade of "femininity," the result is a painful sense of invisibility, or of having been discarded as unmarketable.

And so it is only in the uncommodified "Third World" that Atwood's novel becomes self-consciously political. Rennie has the unexamined imperialist expectation that she will feel better once she travels out of the "First World" because she will somehow be superior to her surroundings. As tourist and observer, she can experience whatever she wishes while remaining immune to entanglements or consequences. Instead of being the one consumed as a fantasy object by others, she hopes to become a consumer herself. But by literally becoming a tourist, Rennie must face the extent to which she has been, metaphorically, a tourist in her own life. She has even processed her breast cancer and subsequent operation into cute titles that would make the painful details of her life "easy reading" for someone else. Indeed, one sign of her reawakening is that she slowly weans herself from her automatic habit of envisioning everything that happens to her as the topic for a snappily titled "lifestyle" piece. As Sharon Wilson has argued more generally, "[Atwood's] characters and personas often seem to view life . . . themselves, the past, and other people as photographic trophies or the raw material for popular journalistic pieces on life-styles" (Wilson, "Turning Life" 136). It is as if Rennie had wandered away from the glitzy aisle in the department store of the "First World" only to stumble into the back room where the degradation and exploitation that make this world possible are everywhere on display.

Atwood organizes the contrast between the two worlds around the concept of lifestyle when the politician Dr. Minnow, running for office, tries to enlist Rennie's aid in her capacity as a journalist of the "first world":

> "It's not my thing," she says. "I just don't do that kind of thing. I do lifestyles. . . . You know, what people wear, what they eat, where they go for their vacations, what they've got in their living rooms, things like that," says Rennie, as lightly as she can.
> Dr. Minnow considers this for a moment. Then he gives her an angelic smile. "You might say that I also am concerned with life-styles. . . . It is our duty, to be concerned with lifestyles. What the people eat, what they wear, this is what I want you to write about."
> (136; ch. 3)

Dr. Minnow knows that he is using Rennie's own term against her. In her definition, "lifestyle" is a strategy for insulating one's self from events, and from any responsibilities those events might engender. It is a way to weave together a fabricated identity through the process of consumption. The events of one's personal life, once packaged as a "lifestyle," become just another commodity, as Rennie herself notes: "The people she knew . . . would have regarded it all as an experience. Experiences were like other collectables, you kept adding them to your set. Then you traded them with your friends. Show and tell" (143; ch. 3). When "style" becomes "life," the result is simulation and performance. Identity becomes a package ("what people wear, what they eat") and the home itself becomes a stage with props ("what they've got in their living rooms"). Dr. Minnow ignores the emphasis on "style" and focuses attention on the social and political inequities of life, inequities that are glossed over by pursuing a "lifestyle."

In a subsequent class, students—unprompted by me—came forward with tourist advertisements and travel pieces of the sort Rennie might have written. They saw them as particularly appropriate to the latter half of the book, in which Rennie's search for an uncommodified identity and meaning has branched out from what it means to be a woman to what it means to be a citizen of the "first world." The advertisements offer escape, sexual release, and relief from the "hustle and bustle." They assure tourists that the places they visit will have no relation to where they have come from, and therefore will serve as a way to get away from it all.

Let me conclude on a note of caution. I do not offer this classroom exercise as the only or final approach to Atwood. Many of the results of the exercise are difficult to quantify, but I have a clear sense that something both simple and profound occurred: *Bodily Harm* became important to students. It moved, in a sense, from being a part of my syllabus to being a part of their lives. As readers and teachers, we sometimes, for the sake of "clarity" or "comprehensiveness," minimize the disturbing challenge to our reality that writers in general, and Atwood in particular, make. This exercise in bringing popular culture into the classroom produces open-endedness rather than closure. But to my mind, the greatest teaching does not so much present resolution as generate an atmosphere in which the student and, inevitably, the teacher, too, experience more fully both the impossibility of an unproblematic truth and the automatic uncertainty of any ideological premise that is confidently labeled as a given. The problem with popular culture—and thus the reason for bringing it into the classroom—is not just that we need to learn more about it but that we think we know more than we do. Increasingly, I find that my role as a teacher is not to facilitate comprehension in the students but rather to make problematic their own eagerness for "answers."

"Hypocrite Lecteuse! Ma Semblable! Ma Soeur!": On Teaching *Murder in the Dark*

Patricia Merivale

What is in all likelihood Atwood's most critically neglected text, *Murder in the Dark: Short Fictions and Prose Poems* (1983), is, by the same token, one of her most difficult, challenging, and rewarding. But I think the Approach Direct, or throwing the students in to sink or swim, which I recommend with most Atwood texts, needs to be supplemented, for this text, with several versions of the Approach Oblique. To that end I suggest a number of approaches, methodological and intertextual, designed to enrich the close readings (excellent ones, by Christl Verduyn, Pierre Spriet, Lorna Irvine, and Sherrill Grace are already in print) that each seminar will want to make for itself. Any or all of Atwood's prose poems—but I particularly recommend *Murder in the Dark*—can be key texts, not only in a graduate seminar on Atwood, or on modern women poets, but also in a comparative literature seminar on the genre of the prose poem. Her prose poems hold their own even in the presence of Baudelaire, essentially the originator of the modern prose poem, as of so much else in modern and postmodern literature; they work particularly well in a comparative Canadian context, teamed with the rich body of Québécois prose poems.

Murder in the Dark shares many of its puzzling properties with other examples, indeed with the entire tradition, of the relatively unfamiliar genre to which it belongs—the prose poem. That the prose poem tradition is, as it happens, almost exclusively French invites a somewhat more comparative approach than is usual in Atwood studies.

Twenty-seven of Atwood's prose poems are found in *Murder in the Dark*; another ten are scattered among her lyric collections. *Good Bones* (1992) contains twenty-six examples of what I am calling "prose poems"; the blurb writer calls them "parable, monologue, mini-romance and mini-biography, speculative fiction, prose lyric, outrageous recipe and reconfigured fairy tale." My own title, *"Hypocrite Lecteuse! Ma Semblable! Ma Soeur!,"* is taken from "Let Us Now Praise Stupid Women" (*Good Bones* 37); it is Atwood's own regendered (mis)appropriation of Charles Baudelaire's famous line "Hypocrite lecteur,—mon semblable,—mon frére!" ("Hypocritical reader,—my double,—my brother!") (*Les fleurs du mal* 6). It is widely known, also, of course, through T. S. Eliot's quotation of it in *The Waste Land* (76).

The genre itself has always posed critical problems, starting with the basic definition: a short text of lyric intensity set out as prose, with justified right margins to the edge of the page. Prose poems are commonly as elliptical as lyric poems by the same poet; indeed, in Atwood's case, often even more so. But prose poems also contain the teasing promise of a narrative structure, a miniature story, a setup culminating in an epiphany—that is, a concentrated, intense perception, not unlike that which concludes a Joyce or Mansfield or Atwood short story. Yet a prose poem is not narrative but pseudonarrative, a complex and often self-reflexive emotion-cum-perception, allegorized, as it were, into a narrative pattern. Because Atwood is consciously working in this generic tradition, a few examples from other prose poets (probably French-language writers, but see Michael Benedikt's useful paperback anthology for international representation) will make the generic codes she is following clearer and will enhance one's respect for her abilities in a highly cosmopolitan genre, one that few other Anglo-Canadians have even attempted.

Some strategies for defining and analyzing the prose poem, developed chiefly by recent critics of Baudelaire, such as Mary Ann Caws, Marie Maclean, and Edward Kaplan, turn out to be very helpful in working with Atwood. These critics find that a multiplicity of generic allusions, to different kinds of prose narratives, seems characteristic of the prose poem. it is an intensely, because abbreviatedly, metafictional genre. "These texts include in perfect but minimal form," says Maclean of Baudelaire's prose poems, "the *Märchen* or wonder-tale, the *Sage* or anecdote, the fable, the allegory, the cautionary tale, the tale-telling contest, the short story, the dialogue, the novella, the narrated dream," all forms "deterritorialized" and then "recontextualized" in the prose poem for new poetic purposes (45).

Atwood's texts, likewise, tend to be marked by explicit relationship to, even miniaturizing parody of, specified narrative genres: "True Romances" (in *True Stories*), "Adventure Story" (in *Selected Poems II*, Oxford UP), "Horror Comics," "Women's Novels" (both in *Murder in the Dark*). Titles such as these play a key role in establishing the contract between author and reader of prose poems, a promise of performance, as it were. They set up protopatterns for each individual poem, while reinforcing the oxymoronic nature of the "prose poem," inherent in that very designation. Note the blending of "form" and "content" in the equally oxymoronic title—as the argument of the poem itself demonstrates—of the poem "Happy Endings," which, like "Women's Novels," is a comic skit on the literary anesthetics available for female readers wounded in the sex war. Among the key formal properties of prose poems are such titles as "Before the War," "Raw Materials" (both in *Murder in the Dark*), or "True Romances," picked up in openings, repeated in endings, and turned into punning refrains that thereby constitute frames for the poems.

The prose poems of Baudelaire's sequence *Spleen de Paris* (1869) were, like Atwood's, first published individually. Baudelaire himself described them as interconnected by theme rather than by plot, as readable in any order, and as autonomous units that could be either detached from the whole or kaleidoscopically rearranged within it, at the reader's pleasure, to yield another "reading" of the whole sequence (see Maclean 44).

Thus a viable "context" for any one poem in *Murder in the Dark* could be made from any or all of the other twenty-six. One could also examine the abridged sequence of thirteen poems from *Murder in the Dark* that Atwood published in *Selected Poems II* (1986). It contains all but one ("Liking Men") of the twelve poems in section 4, plus "Bread" and "The Page" from section 3, but none of the first thirteen poems. I particularly regret the omission of "Autobiography" and "Murder in the Dark," but also of "Women's Novels" and "Happy Endings." Or, conversely, one could enlarge the sequence by adding Atwood's other prose poems, which bracket *Murder in the Dark* chronologically. The most important, besides those in *Good Bones*, are the five prose poems in the "Circe/Mud" sequence of twenty-four poems (*You Are Happy*, 1974), the twelve-part prose poem "Marrying the Hangman" (*Two-Headed Poems*, 1978), the five-part prose-poem sequence "True Romances" (*True Stories*, 1981), and the three prose poems, "An Angel," "Men at Sea," and "Adventure Story," first collected in *Selected Poems II* and reprinted in *Good Bones*.

The title of the opening poem of *Murder in the Dark*, "Autobiography," seems at first somewhat cryptic for a prose poem that poses as, if anything, a painterly description of landscape. But it turns out to be an appropriate title poem for the seven other poems of the first section, all of which are plainly, literally, "autobiographical," though doubtless fictionally so. All eight are epiphanic, "Autobiography" more compactly and obliquely, the others more narratively, in the manner of sharply abridged modernist short stories of growing up. The smell of rust, "a whiff of the future" ("Boyfriends" 14), prefigures the liminal experiences yielding, in each poem, "sudden knowledge" of wickedness, violence, aging, death, unfairness, suffering, and the shallow falsities of romance, sentimentality, and idealism: "a small face streaming with tears and red berries" ("Making Poison" 10); "pure hatred, real after all" ("Horror Comics" 13); "the body up there was actual, it was aging . . . *like us* it was caught in time" ("The Victory Burlesk" 15; my emphasis); and the finest, defining, as well as prefacing, the other epiphanies, "the half-eaten carcass of a deer, which smelled like iron, like rust . . . the point at which the landscape dissolves, ceases to be a landscape and becomes something else" ("Autobiography" 9).

The prose poem "Raw Materials," whose five parts constitute the whole of the second section, suggests samples of supposedly actual "raw materials" for "touristic" texts like the poems "Postcard" and "Petit Nevis" (*True Stories*), the short stories "A Travel Piece," "The Resplendent Quetzal" (*Dancing Girls*), and "Scarlet Ibis" (*Bluebeard's Egg*), and the novel of the same period, *Bodily Harm* (1981). But sections 3, 4, and 5, at least, of "Raw Materials," amplifying the pun lurking in its title—"raw" as painful, like a scraped wound; "raw" as sexually or otherwise indecorous—achieve prose-poem effects, as distinguished from the fictional or lyrical effects of what they, or recollections like them, were turned into. "Real experience" is the tourist-poet's ever-retreating goal, which arrives, if it ever does, in blurred and ambiguous versions of the "sudden knowledge" of the childhood epiphanies.

"Murder in the Dark," the lead poem of the six in the third section, is a mini-metaphysical detective story, and thus a self-reflexive text, playing on the paradox of the "Cretan Liar": "by the rules of the game, I must always lie. / Now: do you believe me?" (30). Embedded in the poem are two "performances," one of the child's game and one of its adult variants, which are, says the speaker, "not as much fun" (29). Metacritically, "you can play games with this game" (30), but Atwood explicitly scorns this relatively trivial option. The poem is like "Making Poison" in its unsparing look at the latent violence and hostility in "I," the narrator—not just in masculine "others," as often seems the case in Atwood's "sex-war" poems, nor just in adults, but in female children (cf. especially *Cat's Eye*), from their earliest years. But the poem's real interest lies in the parable of the artist, working "in the dark," with murderous "designs on you," the reader (30). Crimes in litera-ture, including sexual ones, resemble crimes of jurisprudence in that, as Baudelaire put it, they are "crime[s] where an accomplice is indispensable" (qtd. in Maclean 129).

The first thirteen prose poems are only intermittently self-reflexive; are these the "short fictions" offered in Atwood's subtitle? Perhaps so, but by analogy with Baudelaire's equally anecdotal prose poems, they too should be read as poems. But Atwood's retaining only the *second* half of *Murder in the Dark* for her *Selected Poems* suggests that she may find the more satisfying representatives of the prose-poem genre to be those in which the power of imagination, which can extend the power of vision beyond the limits of language, provides "increasingly disturbing" (Grace, "Stories" 70) texts with all the compact subtlety of her best poems in the lyric mode.

"Him," "Worship," and "Iconography" blend self-reflexiveness with the politics of the sex war: "he's just landed and you are the land" ("Him" 56); "When you're being worshipped there isn't much to say" ("Worship" 51); "He has the last word. He has the word" ("Iconography" 52). These are neat inversions of the misogynistic patterns in Baudelaire's poems of Woman reified by the Poet; in Atwood the Poet watches the man reify her. "Liking Men" achieves an almost Baudelairean symmetrical structure of balanced halves; the first part attempts to portray domestic or personal affirmation, as the woman caresses the tender feet of a man. The poem swivels on the line "You don't want to go on but you can't stop yourself" (53) into the balancing political negations of men's boots stamping on women's faces and bodies.

Perhaps, through its fairy-tale allusive patterns, "She" links the visionary world and the sex-war world. "Hand," a moving piece of "raw material" for

Bodily Harm, certainly links the world of politically caused suffering with the worlds of human empathy and of poetic vision—seemingly via sisterhood, as in the novel. "Strawberries" and "Everlasting" use more traditional natural, indeed botanic, extended metaphors to suggest epiphany, while "Instructions for the Third Eye" allegorizes in anatomical metaphor the operations of the poetic imagination, in order to, as Grace puts it, provide "instructions on how to read [*Murder in the Dark*]" ("Stories" 69).

"Mute" and "The Page," which repay the closest of close readings, are the two finest poems in the collection. Along with the aptly named "A Parable," they are the culmination of Atwood's artist parables in the prose-poem form. The title motif of "Mute," "muteness," the innate or enforced inability to speak, is of course one found everywhere in Atwood's other works (e.g., "The Sin Eater" [*Bluebeard's Egg*], "Training" [*Dancing Girls*], numbers 7, 13 in "Small Poems for the Winter Solstice" [*True Stories*], and elsewhere, especially in *True Stories*), as are, to a lesser degree, the motifs of deafness and blindness. "Mute" brings these three privative images together to form the familiar iconic triad—but here it is an aesthetic as well as an ethical one: "see no evil, speak no evil, hear no evil."

"The Page" is perhaps the only Atwood prose poem to resemble the symbolist, or at least Mallarméan, abstraction of "whiteness," a corporeal textuality, indeed a "texte-corps" (text-body), comparable to those in the poems of contemporary Québécois feminists, writers inevitably closer both to the Paris of Mallarmé and the symbolists and to the Paris of Kristeva. Which doesn't make it a better poem than those I have been willing to compare with Baudelaire's but does make it an intensely interesting chord in Atwood's "duet with two deaf singers" ("Two-Headed Poems," *Selected Poems II* 36).

Except for "The Page," the *Murder in the Dark* poems are far closer to Baudelaire's typology of pseudonarratives than to the more cryptic, in- or anticoherent prose poems of Mallarmé, Rimbaud, or the French surrealists. But Grace makes a pertinent comparison, not with surrealist prose poems per se but between the surrealist paintings of, for instance, Magritte and Remedios Varo ("Stories" 71) and the painterly strategies of Atwood's verbal collages (69), crossdisciplinary intertexts that merit further exploration.

In addition to this diachronic or generic-historical approach, prose poems like Atwood's can, and should, be examined synchronically—placed on a generic spectrum with Atwood's other works. Here Atwood's writing is a gift to the student of the genre, for recognizably the same lyric voice, though even more joky, astringent, and blackly humorous, can be heard in her prose poems as in her verse lyrics. The same twists and turns of event are recognizable as in her fiction, although the "events" in the prose poems are on a different, more linguistic, more self-referential level than those in her short stories. Of course there are places in her novels, foci of descriptive intensity closely comparable to prose poems, where "description" turns out, on close examination, to be the psychic projection of her perceiving, often narrating, central consciousness. The prose poem "The Page," the lyric "This Is a Photograph of Me," and some suitably watery paragraph from *Surfacing* or, better, the conclusion to the short story "Death by Landscape" (*Wilderness Tips*, 1991) all show Atwood exorcising, not necessarily for the last time, her archetypically Canadian theme of the death by drowning of the poet, the poet-persona, the poetical alter ego, or the poet's beloved. Any number of analogous transgeneric triads from her works, like the travel topos, the muteness motif, and such recurrent images as bread or hands, would lend themselves to this synchronic critical approach.

Key rhetorical devices include the persistent reification of words and language by simile—"words fall away from me like shed clothing" ("Last Poem," *True Stories* 74)—or metaphor, as in the "bruised" nouns and "wound-up vowels" of "Mute" (49). Writing itself is reified—that is, made into a tale or narrative allegorical of, or with a "scene" of, the writing (telling) or the reading (listening) process. Gender is allegorized into some of the many possible ways of telling stories about gender, sometimes almost as recipes, in the tone of mock instructions to a creative writing class.

All Atwood's prose poems are built on *mises en abyme*, or inner duplications, whether static inner artifacts like *The Boys' Own Annual* and horror comics, or dynamic ones, comparable to Baudelairean inner performances, like the Victory Burlesk, the children's games, and especially the storytellings, enacted throughout, that textualize events by making them *into* stories. Atwood has a strong sense of the colloquial oral traditions of contemporary feminine subcultures: see, for instance, the telephone dialogue in "True Romances" number 3. She characteristically updates folktales and fairy tales into stories like those that women tell to themselves or to each other.

The methods of narratological criticism offer some of the most exciting routes into Atwood's prose poems. Her "narrative performances," frequently describable in the earlier critical language of the dramatic monologue, have complex structures of tellers and hearers and concomitantly strong roles for readers, both real and implied. Atwood's pronouns provide clues throughout: "I" is a strong narrative persona, of course, but "you" can be, by way of a pseudovague colloquialism, "one," everyone, anyone, "you" as a strongly defined female reader, presumed to be on "I's" wavelength, or even "you" as a shifty equivalent to "I," speaking to herself. Do male readers feel excluded from the implied readership of these poems? Or pushed, in the sex-war poems and stories, into *being* the masculine "you," the antagonist? Female readers of Baudelaire, by authorial intention, I fear, often do.

There are two other narrative modes in which the prose poems of *Murder in the Dark* participate: the metaphysical detective story and the artist parable. Both lend themselves to analysis as postmodern genres, and of course they are not mutually exclusive; in my view, indeed, most metaphysical detective stories *are*, like "Murder in the Dark," artist parables, though

not vice versa. Any prose poem with strong epistemological elements—
following, shadowing, poking about in order to find out, as, for instance, in
Atwood's versions of the Bluebeard theme, that one *is* the person one has
been shadowing—tells us that, as Umberto Eco puts it, "*we* are the guilty
party" (81; my emphasis); the major relationship in *Cat's Eye* provides a
novelistic parallel. Such patterns provide quasi-allegorical narrative proposi-
tions about the relationship of art, life, and text—that is, artist parables—
as in *Lady Oracle, Cat's Eye*, and, of course, any number of Atwood's self-
reflexive poems in both prose and verse.

Another problem, that of genre and gender, might well, in many classrooms, take precedence over a diachronic inquiry into the genre of the prose
poem, or even synchronic readings of Atwood's oeuvre. The three modes,
artist parable, metaphysical detective story, and prose poem, singly or in
combination, have been notably masculine ones, thus challenging Atwood's
ability to persuade genres to change gender. There is work to be done at
the borderline where genre and gender meet.

Even female lyric poets have been little given to writing prose poems,
although the contemporary women poets of Quebec (see Brossard) are, significantly, perhaps the major exception. "The Page," "A Parable," and
"Mute" can be usefully juxtaposed with the prose poems of Nicole Brossard,
Madeleine Gagnon, and France Théoret, exemplifying the French philosophical branch of feminism, with its somewhat abstract concern for the
barely corporeal text-body. "La peau m'est venue d'une histoire"; "meutris-
sures de bleu ou de lexique" ("my skin came to me from a story"; "bruises,
blue or lexical": Brossard 150, 154), "des mots qui avaient besoin de l'eau
pour vivre" ("words which needed water to live": Gagnon, in Brossard 248),
and much else on films, surfaces, margins, and the processes of writing are
allegorized in terms of the body, with its skin, its wounds, and especially
its wounded skin.

However, more characteristic of Atwood is an acerbically political kind of
feminism. Atwood's prose poems of the sex wars invert or subvert the misogyny, bordering on highbrow pornography, of Baudelaire's prose poems,
while maintaining, but recontextualizing, in her lyrical transvestism, the
irony of the Baudelairean narrative voice. In that whole misogynist repertory,
whose most powerfully intelligent exponent is Charles Baudelaire, woman,
reified and dangerously idealized, is seen as perfect only insofar as she
reflects the man to himself. Compare his prose poem "Le galant tireur"
("The Gallant Marksman"; *Spleen de Paris*) with three Atwood lyrics (*Selected
Poems II*): "the doll / I made of you . . . holding in its plaster hand / your
doll of me" ("Five Poems for Dolls" 7); "the hole *No* makes / in the center
of her forehead" ("Nomads" 124); and on woman as "Subject to / depiction"
("Squaw Lilies: Some Notes" 171).

Atwood's deployment of bodily images and metaphors in her prose poems
links the elliptical corporealities of her lyric poems with the more explicit

corporealities of her novels. The fragmentation of the body, the incessant taking of parts, sometimes grotesquely fractured—either literally or textually or both—for the whole, such as the "hands" of such texts as "Hand," or the "scorched faces" of "Hopeless," marks all her works. The body as grotesquely subject to the erosions of time brings poems like "Autobiography" and "The Victory Burlesk" into closer relationship to Baudelaire's classical odes to "Time the Devourer," and to its correlative, the ambiguous, dangerous powers of art and the artist, seen in "Mute" and "The Third Eye," than to the highbrow pornography that mars even so fine a Baudelairean artist parable as "Une Charogne" ("A Carrion"; *Les fleurs du mal*). Such comparisons both confirm and elucidate our sense of the self-reflexive and the metafictional as the dominant mode of Atwood's complex but rewarding texts, and help to establish them, individually, as among her finest artist parables and, collectively, as among her finest poetic sequences.

But "The Page" could perhaps serve all by itself for this analysis; body and text weave in and out of each other in a neo-Gothic artist parable of the perils of life conjoined to art: "the page is not a pool but a skin" (45).

Over to you, "hypocrites lecteuses! mes semblables! mes soeurs!"

Overview

Respondents to our questionnaire wrote that the main rewards of teaching *The Handmaid's Tale* are its readability and accessibility and its success at engaging students virtually unanimously, even the most inexperienced readers, through characterization, plot, and relevant social themes such as gender politics and fundamentalist religions. The central challenges, in contrast, have been to create appreciation for the novel's structural and stylistic complexities, especially the figurative language, narrative voice, and "Historical Notes," and to place it generically as a feminist critique of the dystopian tradition.

In addition to the strategies for teaching Atwood noted in the "Backgrounds" section, questionnaire respondents suggested approaches that get at the novel's stylistic complexity and those that probe beneath obvious themes. In the exploration of style, teachers can ask students to open the novel to a random point and free-write for two pages about Atwood's attention to detail in a particular paragraph or paragraphs, then make a list of the most evocative details; presumably, discussion about how Atwood succeeds in re-creating vivid detail will ensue. Students might pay attention to changes in verb tense patterns in chosen passages. Larger writing assignments on matters of style or craft include constructing an alternative ending to the novel, pretending that the "Historical Notes" section has been lost; composing one's own autobiography as Offred does; redesigning the script for the film version of *The Handmaid's Tale*; and, for creative writers, comparing specific differences between one's own techniques in creating science fiction and Atwood's techniques.

Assignments that probe thematic issues include asking questions to which students must prepare written responses in or out of class: Is Moira a hero? Why are books forbidden in Gilead? Why is there no laughter? no love? Who is in power? Fuller discussions might result from comparing Atwood's vision with that of Margaret Laurence, or comparing Hawthorne's *The Scarlet Letter* with *The Handmaid's Tale*. An in-class tactic that might prove especially provocative is the following: divide students into groups according to the groups in the novel (Econowives, Commanders, etc.); give each group fifteen to twenty minutes to prepare and present a justification of the group's importance to the Republic of Gilead; finally, have all the groups question one another. Such a wealth of strategies attests to the many interpretive possibilities the novel allows.

Similarly, the essays in "A Case Study: *The Handmaid's Tale*" together suggest an explanation of the book's attraction, for each one links Atwood's work with another literary mode or another discipline, or indeed with other Atwoodian fiction. The novel thus seems to speak to concerns not merely literary. Pamela Hewitt shows the value of Atwood's science-fiction novel, and its film adaptation, in a sociology class in which sex roles are analyzed. Ruud Teeuwen discusses Atwood's play with the utopian/dystopian tradition within the context of his interdisciplinary course on utopias. J. Brooks Bouson connects *The Handmaid's Tale* with psychoanalytic theory, especially the Freudian family drama in which a young girl wishes to displace her mother and marry her father. Carol L. Beran compares *The Handmaid's Tale* with *Life before Man* to show that *Life before Man*, a realistic novel, can be read as a foreshadowing of specific social critiques that appear under the guise of science fiction in the later novel. Kathleen E. B. Manley juxtaposes "Little Red Riding Hood" and *The Handmaid's Tale* in her treatment of folkloric echoes in that novel and "Bluebeard's Egg." Mary K. Kirtz continues the discussion of book-to-film translations in her study of *Surfacing* and *The Handmaid's Tale*, arguing that sloppy filmic treatments of novels actually encourage closer readings of the novels. In forging so many connections between Atwood's most-often-taught novel and other modes or disciplines, these critics bear witness to and partially explain the book's wide appeal, an appeal further attested to by the wealth of scholarly articles published annually on it (see the *Newsletter of the Margaret Atwood Society*).

SH

Understanding Contemporary American Culture through *The Handmaid's Tale*: A Sociology Class

Pamela Hewitt

In both book and film form, Margaret Atwood's *The Handmaid's Tale* provides a creative teaching and learning tool for a course in the sociology of gender. As the Handmaid's story unfolds, students discover a futuristic dystopian version of American culture reified by its pseudodocumentary framing (Murphy 25).

By contrasting the unfamiliar with the familiar, science fiction can provide a medium for the growth of creative thinking about present and future social worlds (Milstead et al. xii). While a number of other social science-fiction stories and novels demonstrate more specific aspects of sex roles, *The Handmaid's Tale* offers a unique opportunity to explore the full spectrum of gender issues. Atwood's novel presents the reader with a retrospective individual narration of a life experience that is gendered, but not thematically unidimensional, and the film adaptation adds a different storytelling mode as well as rich comparative possibilities.

Institutional analysis, concept application, and book-to-film comparison are three useful pedagogical approaches to *The Handmaid's Tale*. Because social institution is a central concept in sociology, cross-institutional analyses of *The Handmaid's Tale* can work well in most lower-level sociology courses. As sets of consensus-based behavior rules reflecting cultural imperatives, the five institutions generally recognized by sociologists as the building blocks of the social structure are education, polity, religion, economy, and family, and these consensus-based, culturally determined institutions provide a systematic way for students to interpret *The Handmaid's Tale*. Students in groups representing the five basic social institutions can contrast Gilead with contemporary culture as an in-class discussion project. They can also be assigned papers on institutional norms or institutional change, or write about their conception of a postrevolution Gilead society.

For upper-level substantively oriented sociology courses, focusing on a single social institution may be more appropriate. The major social institution encompassing sex-role norms in reproduction is the family. In most societies reproduction is carried out in the context of marriage and the family, along with such related functions as economic support, socialization of children, and intimacy. In *The Handmaid's Tale* Atwood creates an elaborate social context for reproduction, involving the designation of a specialist class of fertile women who serve as portable wombs. In Gilead other traditional family functions take place in a separate family group that enjoys the status and prestige of a legitimized social institution. The Handmaid is only technically a physical extension of the wife as reflected in the roles played in reproductive sex. Although the Handmaid's presence is necessary, she doesn't really exist as a human being, and she lives on the fringe of the family system, easily replaced and discarded. The reproductive function is thus removed from the family; new family members are obtained in the same way one might order a tulip bulb through the mail, plant it, pick the bloom, and take the credit for growing it.

Applying abstract concepts to concrete situations reifies their meaning. *The Handmaid's Tale* provides a rich source for the application of gender concepts. Following are examples of concepts appearing in most textbooks used in courses in the sociology of sex roles, along with a sample description of their application.

Sexual objectification. This concept involves the transformation of a human being into a one-dimensional sexual entity. One especially memorable illustration of this concept in *The Handmaid's Tale* occurs at Jezebel's, an underground nightclub populated by women who serve as sexual playthings for a clientele of powerful Gilead men. Attired in antique pre-Gilead outfits that reflect their sexual objectification (lingerie, baby-doll pajamas, bikinis, sexy exercise clothes, and cheerleader costumes), these women enact a pathetic nightly drama truly scripting them as shameless and abandoned jezebels (Houghton, 235; ch. 37).

Patriarchy. This concept refers to a male-dominated social system. In a patriarchal family, the male head of the household controls most aspects of family life. A good example of patriarchal control in *The Handmaid's Tale* is the ritualistic reading of the Bible by the aptly named Commander. In this ritual preceding the reproductive ceremony, selected Judeo-Christian biblical passages are read to the household group to provide a religious mandate for the Gilead version of reproduction (87–88; ch. 15).

Gender stratification. This form of social stratification reflects differential access to cultural resources based on gender. Cultural resources include a variety of rewards such as occupational prestige, respect, and self-esteem, as well as money and goods. An interesting example of gender stratification in *The Handmaid's Tale* occurs in the context of a pre-Gilead flashback. Offred/Kate describes the transitional period when women's access to employment and money began to be taken away. One day she found her "Compubank" account closed and her employment terminated because the government decided that women would no longer be allowed to earn or handle money. Any female's existing funds were transferred to the Compubank account of her husband or "male next of kin" (178; ch. 28).

Additional concepts that can be productively applied to *The Handmaid's Tale* include androgyny, gender stereotyping, homophobia, the Cult of True Womanhood, gender, the gender gap, gender identity, feminism, women's liberation movements, sexual orientation, sexism, gender socialization, pornography, rape, sex-typing, social control, social change, machismo, and nonconscious ideology. Concept application can be used in several different ways in the classroom. Students can be asked to apply these concepts to examples from *The Handmaid's Tale* either as part of a classroom presentation, as a group class project, or as an individual written assignment. The application of central course concepts to another culture helps students develop a deeper understanding of the meaning and personal relevance of these constructs.

The transformation of novel to film should entail creation rather than simply duplication. Although Atwood was heavily involved in overseeing the book-film translation (Johnson, "Uphill Battle"), the movie treatment of *The Handmaid's Tale* differs in distinct ways from the book. A film provides a more focused story and is selective in what it presents in the time allotted. Stuart McDougal, in a discussion of book-to-film adaptation, which he calls the "metamorphic art," describes the required contraction as due to two factors: time constraints (a two-hour on-screen maximum) and the difficulty the audience has incorporating too many characters (3–4). The differences between the book and the film versions of *The Handmaid's Tale* can provide the basis for a challenging classroom project that encourages students to think about the demands of their culture, especially in terms of mass-media economics. Producing a financially successful film involves taking into account the perceived interests and needs of the viewing public (Kaminsky 3). McDougal points out how a profit-driven film industry often dictates the character of the product (5).

Students in my sex-roles courses were asked to read the book before viewing the film. Several subsequent classes were devoted to discussions of the book, using institutional and conceptual analysis. Then the film was shown during the next two classroom meetings. In the following session the class discussed how the translation of the book to film changed the story in particular ways that reflected public preferences. Students interpreted the book-film discrepancies in the light of cultural requirements, particularly the criteria for successful revenue-producing films. Asking students to engage in this task encourages critical thinking in a number of beneficial ways. To contrast the book and the movie, students must be familiar with both, not merely in the descriptive sense of knowing the character and plot, but analytically, in understanding the difference between the two modes of storytelling. Comprehending the "why" of the book-film translation requires students to demonstrate an objective cultural awareness as well as knowledge of mass-media demands. Focused class discussion usually results in a consensus that five concepts differentiate the novel from the film adaptation: sexualization, plot smoothing, simplification, thrill seeking, and resolution. The film adaptation literature documents these characteristics (Bone and Johnson 214; McDougal 1–7).

Sexualization. Sex in United States cinema is a marketing strategy reflecting the larger culture, especially the mass media. Sex is frequently used to sell products, maintain and focus interest, and tap a common cultural theme. We see this in the prominence of sex and the objectification of female sexuality in popular music, advertising themes, television and radio programming, best-selling books and popular magazines, and of course films. The film version of *The Handmaid's Tale* represents this cultural focus. At the Berlin premiere of the film, the journalist Brian Johnson noted the critic Marcia Pally's comment that the sex and violence in the story had been beefed up, and the politics toned down ("Hollywood Meets the New Europe" 40). The novel describes the Handmaids as asexual beings who function only as biological instruments of reproduction. Their dress, demeanor, and behavior requirements preserve this asexuality. In the film, however, their mandatory veils are not the bulky "flying nun" head appendages that the book describes (8–9; ch. 2) but, rather, more enticing "peekaboo" head ornaments. The downcast eyes required of the Handmaids in the novel symbolize their subservience (28; ch. 5). In the film, the same orbital mandate takes on a flirtatious significance.

The posters advertising the film in the United States feature the protagonist in her red outfit offering an alluring full-lipped pout and direct, sexually challenging gaze. Had she engaged in such behavior in the "real" Gilead, she would have been sent to sweep up radioactive waste in "the Colonies" or perhaps been assigned to the sex servant caste of her friend Moira. Many more instances of sexualization emerge during class discussion. The instructor has only to observe the embarrassed squirming and smirking of students during "the ceremony" scene to figure out that the film inspires sexual interest, tension, and reflection.

Plot smoothing. The Handmaid's Tale (the book) appears choppy because the plot does not unfold in a continuous, historical manner; rather, it is interrupted by numerous flashbacks that appear without warning and often without logical context. In the United States, popular films generally present their plots in a more predictable and temporally linear fashion. The film version of *The Handmaid's Tale* offers a more simplified unfolding of the story, emphasizing events and visual cues instead of the feelings and perceptions focused on in the novel.

Simplification. Because of the limited time allotted to movies shown in theaters in the United States, a great deal of condensing of the book must occur. Thus a film omits much of what may be regarded as details and unnecessary side trips from the main plot. In a review of the movie, Johnson points out that the emphasis, by the screenwriter (Harold Pinter) and the director (Volker Schlondorff), on the ceremonial aspects of the story results in a "dangerously spare" plot ("Fascism's Handmaid").

Thrill seeking. Many successful films are fast-paced affairs with standard thrill-provoking effects intertwined into the scene sequences. We expect some adventure in film, and the easiest way to incorporate it is to add graphic "blood and guts" scenes—for example, a car chase. The film version of *The Handmaid's Tale* manages to satisfy these requirements by turning Offred's house getaway into a *Psycho* knife scene, with accompanying suspense tricks, and adding an exciting van chase sequence in the "cops and robbers" mode.

Resolution. Hollywood loves happy endings. Although contemporary films are less likely to incorporate the traditional "family values" happy ending— boy gets girl; they walk off into the sunset and get married—usually an acceptable plot resolution that provides the requisite closure and cognitive order for the viewing public is required. The film treatment of *The Handmaid's Tale* has a finish that is nothing like the one in the final book chapter ("Historical Notes"). Rather than end the story with a technical report containing the scientific guesses about Gilead society by dusty academic archaeologists, the movie features a peaceful, hopeful, maternal, and pregnant ex-Offred gazing into the distant wilderness, waiting at the home front for her man's return.

In addition to the suggested oral class exercise, there are other ways to use the book-film comparison. Students can write papers providing their own interpretations of the book-film discrepancies or conduct a content analysis using either analytical areas specified by the instructor or those that emerge in class discussion.

The Handmaid's Tale is a pedagogical gold mine. It is a book that students say they can't put down, and a film they find to be a gripping social morality tale with a discomforting contemporary cultural relevance. Embedded in the story are a wide variety of gender-relevant social issues useful for classroom interpretation and analysis. These issues come alive for students in the novel and film presentations of a simultaneously inspiring and terrifying futuristic vision of America. In an interview with Johnson at the Berlin world premiere of the movie ("Returning to a New Berlin" 45), Atwood commented that the reaction to the story in the United States was "How long have we got?"

Dystopia's Point of No Return:
A Team-Taught Utopia Class

Ruud Teeuwen

The utopia course in which I teach *The Handmaid's Tale* is a contribution of the comparative literature department to a new liberal arts program at the University of Utrecht. I teach the course together with two senior colleagues, one a scholar of Greek, the other a scholar of Latin. We have ordered the course chronologically, with *The Handmaid's Tale* coming at the very end. Before we get to *The Handmaid's Tale*, the Greek scholar first takes the students through Plato's *Republic* and through a challenging comparison between Plato's ideas and Karl Popper's criticisms in *The Open Society and Its Enemies*. The Latin scholar introduces students next to representations of idyllic nature and to myths of a golden age in Roman literature, and to the amalgamation of those ideas with Christian motifs in Augustine's *The City of God*. It is then my turn, with Thomas More's *Utopia*, Voltaire's utopian parody *Candide*, and excerpts from nineteenth- and early twentieth-century utopias such as Charlotte Perkins Gilman's *Herland* and Edward Bellamy's *Looking Backward: 2000–1887*. In the final two weeks of the course, we turn to dystopias. In the first of those weeks we discuss the chilling depiction of a technocratic communist society in either George Orwell's *Nineteen Eighty-Four* or in the short novel *Blokken* (*Blocks*, 1931) by the Dutch author Ferdinand Bordewijk. Then, in the final week, it is on to *The Handmaid's Tale*.

Much of the course's eye-opening power, students' evaluations reveal, hinges on our ability to show utopia as a genre with an amazingly small but strong fund of ideas, recombined in ever-new ways. Because *The Handmaid's Tale* is the last and latest of the reading assignments for the course, the novel becomes, in our class, the *culmination* of the utopian themes, motifs, and problems. In the two class meetings I devote to *The Handmaid's Tale*, students are excited by their own intellectual mastery of a generic tradition. This mastery allows them to recognize and appreciate Margaret Atwood's imaginative employment of utopian and dystopian situations and concerns.

Our students—freshmen and sophomores all, and usually more than forty to a class—are generally unfamiliar with the traditions of utopia as a genre of literature and of thought. Before the Greek scholar begins our chronological discussion of texts, I therefore open the course with a backgrounds lecture on the philosophical and generic problems that utopia poses. We keep returning to these problems in later classes. Because the points we discuss in the opening lecture and advert to throughout the course come to a head in class discussions of *The Handmaid's Tale*, I need to sketch them briefly here.

The main philosophical assumption we establish explains why so little *happens* in utopias. Utopias deal in ideal societies; the closer a society is to perfection, the less room it will allow for change, because change from perfection can only be a detraction from it. I then point out that this assumption of perfection determines to a large extent the shape of utopia as a literary genre. How does one write about perfection? Is not perfection the death of plot? A bright student may bring up that perfection, although uneventful on principle, can be delineated and its origins can be described. This descriptive tendency in utopian fiction (or, for that matter, in the nonfictional utopian blueprint that such fiction often claims to be) contrasts with the plausible narrative, careful plotting, specified time and place, and individualized psychology one hopes for in realistic novels. Change and conflict are the stuff of novels, and expectation and remembrance the mental operations of their protagonists. Utopia, by contrast, is the genre of enthusiastic description rather than narration of events, and inhabitants of utopian societies fulfill their tasks or leisure without much mental reference to anything beyond a timeless present. Morally, utopia is the genre of noble absolutism that provides a standard of behavior for each and all, whereas morality in the novel is a much more character-specific, muddled, and context-dependent affair. Structurally, utopias are diptychs. One panel shows the flawed world of injustice, greed, and inequality, of baffling questions and inhibiting complications (book 1 of More's *Utopia*). The other panel shows the perfect answer, a socioeconomic system of indubitable fairness (book 2). Utopian expositors offer to guide us, listeners *in* the book and readers *holding* it, out of our sorry existence, and to teach us the grammar of perfection.

Many of the generic assumptions and characteristics of utopia I discuss in class (and have pointed out here) are described with great clarity in chapters 3 and 4 of Gary Saul Morson's *The Boundaries of Genre*. Morson also, quite persuasively, describes the utopian plot as a reenactment of the allegory of the cave in the seventh book of Plato's *Republic* (Morson 89). We are the cave dwellers, and someone who escaped from the cave has come back to fetch us. That which we took for reality was only shadows, the escaped prisoner tells us, and he or she knows the way to true reality. What do we do: follow the lead of the one who got away or stay put?

Utopia is a genre that makes an uncomfortably direct and intense appeal to the reader. Utopian descriptions of happiness and freedom are prospectuses for an ideal world, and utopian expositors press us for an affirmative response. They will not take qualms or second thoughts, and least of all literary criticism and appraisal, for an answer. So shall we come out of the shadow and into the light then, leaving our copies of *Utopia, Herland, The City of God, Looking Backward*, or *Walden* on our desks for, say, the course on literature and madness that meets later in this same classroom? It is tempting. But to which light should we turn: the light of a feminist society, of an agrarian, socialist, or Christian one, the light of Boston in the year 2000? Preutopia is a marketplace strewn with utopian prospectuses! The sheer number of ideal worlds makes the act of choosing less clear-cut than utopian expositors make it out to be. Let us therefore mobilize our opinions on the plethora of social, political, and economic reforms proposed and think them through. This decision to study and deliberate will disappoint each of the expositors, but who can afford a heedless embrace of a single perfection if perfection comes in such variety?

This hedged answering to ardent questioning is a prominent feature in the tradition of utopia as a literary genre itself. Thomas More marks his distance to Hythloday's enthusiastic account of Utopia by his aloof politeness to the zealous reformer. Voltaire's answer in *Candide* is a sardonic exposé of utopian faults of logic. Dystopias—*The Handmaid's Tale* among them— utterly distrust utopian proposals and never allow utopias to be embodiments of "the principle of hope" (as Ernst Bloch, in *The Principle of Hope*, has argued utopias are), revealing potentials for a better order hidden in existing social realities. Instead, dystopias make a particular utopia's unfitness for human habitation palpable by a novelistic imagination of a human being's life there. And even forthright utopian expositors are not really absolute beginners: they usually answer to tradition by mixing and matching perfections outlined in the two ur-utopias, Plato's *Republic* and More's *Utopia*. Plato is answerable for utopian hostility toward literature and fiction (*Republic*, books 2 and 3); for the position of women as a utopian issue, together with such topics as rationalized procreation, eugenics, the disposal of defective births, and the reform of families into "households" (book 5); for the division of labor and the installation of a division of professional guardians (book 2). Thomas More adds the *topoi* of the end of fashion; the usefulness of colonies; the end of privacy; euthanasia; free time as a problem; and functionality, austerity, and the "natural" as principles of utopian virtue and happiness.

This (incomplete) catalog of utopiana makes it plain that Margaret Atwood, in *The Handmaid's Tale*, does not cheat the tradition of utopia out of many of its favorite themes and motifs. But in the pages of the novel, these utopian elements do not congeal into a static configuration. *The Handmaid's Tale* is, indeed, a novel, and my students recognize that Atwood's dynamic play with utopian themes and motifs (and with their disengagement from Offred's private longings and remembrances) constitutes and fuels the plot that makes *The Handmaid's Tale* a novel.

Dystopia is a countergenre to utopia (and it is this point that I stress in the course), but it is also a genre in its own right. This is to say that dystopia has its own tradition of illustrious precursors, its own repertoire of images and situations, and a generic logic of its own that steers a specific, somber view of the world. It is as a separate genre, much more than as a countergenre, that dystopia is already familiar to my students. Fresh from a reading (which often is a rereading) of *Nineteen Eighty-Four*, they will not feel as if they enter on entirely new territory when they follow Offred in her restricted life in Gilead. Indeed, Gilead is initially more familiar to the reader than to Offred. Orwell's postrevolutionary London also knows color-coded overalls, a past abolished by a continuous rewriting of it, show trials and public hangings, Hate Weeks and labor camps, reeducation sessions and private nostalgia. Winston Smith also thinks of suicide, sex, books, and privacy. With the unavailability of independent information, there is a breakdown of "objective reality" (as Orwell calls it) that makes Oceania, like Gilead, a rather abstract notion in the minds of its inhabitants. In Oceania, as in Gilead, interminable wars with shadowy enemies yield ever-more victories, and ever-tighter rations of surrogate coffee, chocolate, and sugar. The atmosphere of terror leads one to adopt inscrutable facial expressions and behaviors in both Gilead and Oceania, and to entertain, against one's better judgment, the possibility that one would be much worse off anywhere else but right here.

For all the parallels to that powerful precursor *Nineteen Eighty-Four*, *The Handmaid's Tale* is a work with an entirely different scope and feel. Dystopian novels generally attempt to strike a balance between explaining the design of a certain utopia's terror and describing the experience of living under it. Attention to design makes dystopias political novels, admonitory imaginings of still-avoidable futures. A concentration on experience makes dystopias, like all novels, potential sources of knowledge and insight in human nature. In Orwell's book, compared with Atwood's, the emphasis falls rather heavier on design than on experience. Readers of *Nineteen Eighty-Four*, along with Winston, read considerable portions from the book by Emmanuel Goldstein that sets out the theory and practice of oligarchical collectivism—the book that puts Julia to sleep when Winston reads it aloud to her. There is also the appendix on Newspeak, and O'Brien's educating Winston toward orthodoxy. *The Handmaid's Tale* can leave much of the ways and means of a totalitarian society implicit: such knowledge has become part of readers' cultural and generic awareness. It is by rather casual references that Atwood establishes Gilead's specific character as a puritanical-Christian utopia, backdrop to Offred's alarming new life.

Atwood's emphasis falls on that alarming life, on being a woman in Gilead, and on remembering the times before Gilead. Remembrance is a much vaguer presence in *Nineteen Eighty-Four*: Oceania has been in place for decades at the time we join Winston's life in it, and memories of prerevolutionary life have, for the most part, lost the intensity of the personal. Gilead exists for just three years: Offred's daughter, taken away when she was five, must be eight now, Offred muses (Seal, 59–60; ch. 12). In *The Handmaid's Tale* memories are still suffused with detail. Where despair is a dull presence in Winston's life, it is an acute pain in Offred's.

The Twelfth Symposium on Gileadean Studies is the only sustained explicative reflection, in *The Handmaid's Tale*, on the new society that came and went. In his lecture at this conference, Professor James Pieixoto of

Cambridge University invokes the historical wisdom that "no new system can impose itself upon a previous one without incorporating many of the elements to be found in the latter" (287; "Historical Notes"). Gilead, indeed, is hardly an invitational utopia, with cave dwellers persuaded by a passionate expositor. People are rounded up and made part of Gilead's diverse collection of elements imported from the time before. It is the job of Gilead's rulers to sever all these constituent elements—buildings, clothing, economic systems, as well as people and much more—from the irrelevance of their original contexts and forge them into the single new context that is based on Gilead's principles of organization. The new way in which all elements hang together should eventually gain the authority of the commonplace. This authority, however, Gilead cannot hope to acquire without a transitional phase of rigorous repression of the memories, desires, and idiosyncrasies that point to old, original contexts and that hamper the development of the single new one.

It is this being taken up in a new context that Offred resists, and one can see why: Gilead does away with the idea of the human being as inviolable basic unit of its social structure. Gilead's essential units are smaller than the human body, and women's bodies especially are carefully divided up. "For our purposes," Aunt Lydia explains to the Handmaids, "your feet and your hands are not essential" (87; ch. 15). It is the womb that is essential, and Offred imagines her essence reduced to that pear-shaped organ, with her monthly cycle the motive force of a whole cosmology in which hope changes into dark despair each time the moon of ovulation wanes (see 69–70; ch. 13). This cosmology paces and dictates the activities of the Marthas, doctor, Wife, and Commander of her household and yet, for all the synchronized activity it produces, there is no interaction of lives. All possibility of that is counteracted by elaborate ceremoniousness, body veiling, and biblical allusiveness that accompany solicitations of the body's reproductive function. Gilead has introduced the austere functionality of utopias, but not the attribute that can redeem a utopian society: the full participation it offers everyone in safe and benign communal life.

In one of the study questions to *The Handmaid's Tale* distributed in the course's bulk pack, I ask students to link Offred's observations that she lives in "reduced circumstances" (8, 99, 104; chs. 2, 18, 19) and that "context is all" (136, 180; chs. 24, 30) to the nature of the novel's plot. Students understand that as Gilead does not accord Offred a satisfying context, Offred has to fashion it herself. Offred's creation of context makes up most of what happens in *The Handmaid's Tale*. My question of how exactly Offred does this usually elicits the answer that Offred weaves her life into a plot of opposition to Gilead, a plot of smaller and greater subversions and clandestine actions that alleviate her imprisonment in Gilead's uneventfulness. It is the plot of sex over procreation, adventure over ceremony, Scrabble over Prayvaganzas. In this plot, Offred moves her hips when Guardians watch, hoards butter, makes love to Nick both with and without Serena Joy's complicity, commits the act of reading, visits Jezebel's, and knows about Mayday. Subversion brings Offred the excitement of danger and love, and this makes it, in effect, also a force of reconciliation to her lot.

In another study question, I ask students to check how much of the dialogue in *The Handmaid's Tale* consists of clauses given in quotation marks, indications of direct discourse. Not much of the dialogue does, and dialogue is not often a record of direct exchange between separate consciousnesses. On pages 195–96 (ch. 32), for instance, the reader witnesses the conversation between Offred and Rita, as Rita gives Offred a match for the cigarette she got from Serena Joy. Then, on page 196, Offred goes upstairs with match and cigarette and thinks back on how, the night before, she was tempted to ask the Commander for a cigarette. Quotation marks disappear as dialogue gives way to recalled conversation. One of my students will conclude that much of the novel takes place in Offred's lonely mental withdrawal from Gilead. In the long hours she spends in "her" room, she thinks of the time before or goes over the day's events, adding and deleting things. If no student spontaneously makes the next connection, I take refuge in rhetorical questions: "Isn't this mental withdrawal also a method by which Offred creates context for herself?" "Isn't withdrawal as much a part of the novel's plot as opposition is?" The discussion that ensues about the nature, causes, and effects of the plot of withdrawal can be the most exciting one of the entire course. Seeing this withdrawal in the self as a consequence of a society's refusal to offer context to its constituents, students suddenly seem able to voice their indignation at a system that inflicts such forlornness.

In *The Handmaid's Tale* the utopian master plot of the escape from the cave is inverted into a dystopian longing for a *return* to the cave of shadows. Offred is "a blank, here, between parentheses," "a refugee from the past," marooned "without valid passport" in the wrong world, the wrong genre (210, 213, ch. 35). But to what exactly does Offred long to return? Aren't the Aunts right in characterizing pre-Gilead as a place where women cannot go out alone, where rape and pornography are rampant? Students realize that pre-Gilead is the period in which they themselves live, and, much like Offred, they feel again the direct and uncomfortable appeal of the Aunts, Gilead's expositors. Some students, secure in their faraway Dutch classroom, elude this appeal by pleading exemption from being American. After all, they contend, pre-Gilead is the present United States, the country that brings all human vices to a head. If the United States did not indeed have this special claim to excessiveness, they argue, Atwood would not have chosen to situate pre-Gilead to the south of her own country. Others argue along with Offred that one must not let one's view of a society be guided by its excesses. But isn't Offred too quick in dismissing those "excesses"? In the mirror of her recollection, pre-Gilead appears as happy family life, well-stocked supermarkets, intense college friendships, and an unassuming job. It is a woman's world of sheer pantyhose, Opium perfume, high-heeled shoes, kitchen-table talk, mother-daughter irritations, and magazines. Offred knows the stories that the Aunts stress, but "We lived in the gaps between the stories" (53; ch. 10).

The desire to live in gaps between stories is a longing for uneventfulness, but an uneventfulness of a kind different from Gilead's. It is the uneventfulness of being taken up in full, quotidian context, of completely fitting one's time and place. It is the uneventfulness that the fine-meshed fabric of ordinary life confers on those who participate in it. In her hours of reflective withdrawal, Offred has been keeping this quotidian context intact for herself, setting off her own life against the brighter and braver lives of her mother and Moira, women who refuse to seek shelter "in the gaps between the stories" and lead lives of struggle and politics.

In Offred's nostalgic gaze, pre-Gilead acquires an idyllic quality. The sensation of idyll (Joachim von der Thüsen suggests in an essay on the topic) is that of entering a place one has never visited before and that yet feels like home. It is when she visits Jezebel's that Offred comes to realize that pre-Gilead is not that welcoming place that always is home. Offred realizes that she has been to Jezebel's before ("It was a hotel, then"; 220; ch. 37), but her visit there now does not feel like a return. To Offred's Commander, however, entering Jezebel's is "like walking into the past" (221; ch. 37). Offred recognizes that, in the eyes of her Commander and many like him, a clear continuity exists between pre-Gilead and Gilead. This perception of continuity in those who supposedly made a clean break indicates to Offred that a return to pre-Gilead cannot offer a complete escape from Gilead. Seeing Jezebel's through the eyes of her pleased Commander, Offred acknowledges the "excessive" pre-Gilead she has always played down.

Offred's recognition is disheartening: there is no idyllic past to return to. Dystopia has reached its point of no return. After her visit to Jezebel's, Offred throws herself into her dangerous liaison with Nick. She decides to make a cave out of the crannies that the plot of opposition pried into Gilead's sides: "Being here with him is safety: it's a cave" (253; ch. 41). The plot of withdrawal gives way to one of desperate risks and reckless abandon, the beginning of an end that is not a return.

Students realize that the blocked return is a comment on their own times. Often the dystopian plot of a return to the cave is a tonic for the reader, because the society longed for in the book is the mirror image of the reader's own. *The Handmaid's Tale* is unwilling to fall in with this dystopian exit into an unchanged past. *The Handmaid's Tale* frustrates readers in their desire to congratulate themselves on their times. The postutopian "Historical Notes" does little to comfort the distressed reader. The atmosphere of tired jokes and innuendo at the conference on Gilead suggests the past of the mid–twentieth century rather than a glorious late-twenty-second-century modernity that has supplanted Gilead's backwardness. Gilead turns out not to have been a break with history, wisely abandoned, but a stage in history from which there is no retreat and that has made a significant mark on the future.

A Feminist and Psychoanalytic Approach in a Women's College

J. Brooks Bouson

Commenting that when she reads a woman writer, she feels she is "reading something closer to home," Margaret Atwood admits that "things that are closer to home have the power to make you a lot more nervous and anxious than things that are more remote" (Lyons 72). As I have discovered in teaching *The Handmaid's Tale* at a women's college to both traditional-age and returning adult students, Atwood's novel has the power to make women readers anxious. And it also brings home the truth of the dictum that for women "the personal is political."

Despite *The Handmaid's Tale*'s painful subject matter, many of my women students report in their response statements that they feel compelled to read the novel. "I could barely put the book down," one student comments. "I was riveted to it with terror and pain. When I would put the book down, I'd have to force myself to get back to reality." Another student, who describes *The Handmaid's Tale* as "one of the most fascinating and compelling novels" she had ever read, remarks that she became "so wrapped up in" the novel that she found it difficult to "put the novel down," and she felt she was "alongside" Offred, "experiencing everything" that Atwood's character was "going through." Since women readers can readily identify with Offred, and since their own, often unacknowledged, anxieties about sexual exploitation may be stirred by Atwood's novel, reading *The Handmaid's Tale* can be an emotionally wrenching experience for many student-readers. "I felt disgust, anger, fear, and sadness while reading this novel," remarks one student. "I became outraged for Offred but at the same time defeated with her," writes another student.

Responding with great passion to the plight of Atwood's character, students also pay heed to the political implications of *The Handmaid's Tale*. "It literally gave me chills not only to read this story but to really believe that something like this can happen [in the United States]," comments a student who "did not believe for a minute" that Atwood's novel was "pure fantasy." Aware of the conservative backlash against feminism and the political agenda of the New Right fundamentalists, she found it difficult to dismiss the book. "I'm fearful that in many subtle ways some similar things are already happening; I'm frustrated and angry, and I don't know what to do with these overwhelming feelings." "Once the remote possibility of Offred's fate is internalized by the reader, it becomes necessary to take time out to consider the magnitude of it," writes another student. "This incredibly sterile, oppressed society is not beyond rational comprehension given the realities of Nazi Germany, for example. It is an extremely unsettling realization that such a fate could actually befall contemporary women."

Because *The Handmaid's Tale* provokes such a passionate response from women students, who are anxious to talk about and make sense of what they have experienced, I find it easy to lead them into a more formal discussion of the feminist and psychoanalytic concerns at the thematic center of the novel. To help situate students, I provide an overview of Freud's theory of female development, focusing particular attention on the oedipal drama, in which the girl becomes attached to her father and views her mother as a rival for the father's affection. I begin my analysis of *The Handmaid's Tale* by concentrating on the novel's family—and female oedipal—drama, showing how the novel makes visible the pattern of desire laid down during female oedipal development and how it stages the female oedipal fantasy, in which the girl wishes to take the place of the mother and marry the father. "If female readers of a particular culture share certain fantasies, it is because particular child-raising patterns, shared across a culture, embed common fantasy structures in their daughters," remarks Jean Wyatt (20). Not only are family relations "the principal conduits between cultural ideology and the individual unconscious," but cultural ideology "is most subtle and insidious when it comes in the form of interpersonal relations in the family" (104). In female oedipal development, the daughter's relationship to her father "trains her to idealize a distant and mysterious figure whose absences she can fill with glamorous projections." Some of the behaviors that "speak directly to the quirks of a female unconscious patterned by life in a patriarchal family are waiting, flirting, and the oedipal triangle," writes Wyatt. Because the "father's homecoming" is the "exciting event of a child's day," the waiting daughter comes to associate novelty and stimulation with the arrival of the father—a behavior that is repeated later in the romance scenario in which "lover and waiting woman assume the active and passive roles first played out by father and daughter" (27, 28). Enacting an important developmental role by "diverting his daughter's erotic impulses, first oriented toward her mother, into heterosexual channels," the father also engages in "sexual flirtation" with the daughter but does not follow through because of the incest taboo (29).

Providing a thinly disguised dramatization of the female oedipal situation, in which the daughter views the mother as a rival and is drawn to the father, *The Handmaid's Tale*, as I point out to my students, presents Serena Joy as a "malicious and vengeful woman" and the Commander as "not an unkind man" (Fawcett, 208, 330; chs. 26, 39). And the narrative also enacts the "waiting" and "flirting" behavior typical of the father-daughter relationship. When asked to meet secretly with the Commander in his study, Offred finds that these visits give her "something to do" and "to think about" (210; ch. 26) and thus relieve the tedium of her life of passive waiting. But she also realizes that she is "only a whim" for the Commander (205; ch. 25), who likes it when she distinguishes herself, showing "precocity, like an attentive pet, prick-eared and eager to perform. . . . [H]e is positively daddyish. He likes to think I am being entertained; and I am, I am" (238; ch. 29). But what is culturally repressed in this developmental scenario—because of the taboo against incest—is acted out in the novel's staging of the monthly insemination ceremony.

In essence victimizing readers by positioning them as voyeurs and subjecting them to the obscene spectacle of the Ceremony, the narrative partially conceals what it reveals as it minimizes the horror of what is being described. For Offred protectively distances herself from what she is experiencing: she "detaches" herself, she "describes," she finds "something hilarious" about the impregnation ritual (123; ch. 16). Similarly, at least one critic claims to find a "humorous correspondence" between Atwood's description of the Ceremony and its biblical source in the Rachel and Bilhah story alluded to in one of the epigraphs to the novel (Freibert 283). If readers, in being encouraged to locate the connections between the Gileadean Ceremony and its biblical counterpart, participate in the narrative's defenses, this pornographic—and voyeuristic—scene is, nevertheless, profoundly disturbing. The fact that students typically omit direct references to the Ceremony in their response statements and are uncomfortable discussing it in class reveals just how disturbing this central scene is.

As Offred lies between the legs of the Commander's Wife, "my head on her stomach, her pubic bone under the base of my skull, her thighs on either side of me," the Commander services Offred. "What he is fucking is the lower part of my body. I do not say making love, because this is not what he's doing. Copulating too would be inaccurate, because it would imply two people and only one is involved. Nor does rape cover it . . ." (121; ch. 16). Despite the text's denial, this passage dramatizes a terrible kind of rape. Because the Handmaid takes on the role of the dutiful child-daughter in the Commander-father's household, the Ceremony, with its degrading oedipal flesh triangle, is presented as a thinly disguised incest drama. In the displaced drama of Janine, the narrative makes explicit reference to the forbidden theme of incest. "So well behaved. . . . More like a daughter to you. . . . One of the family," Offred imagines the Wives saying when the pregnant Janine is "paraded" before them. "Little whores, all of them," is the remark made when Janine has left the room (147; ch. 19). Although *The Handmaid's Tale* deliberately stages an incest drama, it also defends against it by focusing attention on Offred's involvement in an all "too banal" plot. In her relationship with the Commander she has become the mistress of a man whose wife doesn't understand him (203; ch. 25).

A character that students find both puzzling and troubling, the Commander is figured as both a protector and a persecutor. For although he wants to make Offred's life more bearable, he also affirms the masculinist ideology that subordinates and sexually enslaves women. In Gileade, he claims, women are "protected" so that they "can fulfill their biological destinies in peace" (284; ch. 34). Teresa de Lauretis, in her description of "Freud's story of femininity," remarks that for Freud the "difficult journey of the female child to womanhood . . . leads to the fulfillment of her biological destiny, to reproduction." Freud's notion that "reproduction is 'to some extent independent of women's consent' makes us pause," remarks de Lauretis. "While 'the aim of biology' may be accomplished independently of women's consent, the aim of desire (heterosexual male desire, that is) may not. In other words, women *must either* consent *or* be seduced into consenting to femininity" (131, 132, 134). Focusing on women's "consent" to femininity, *The Handmaid's Tale* reveals that what lies behind the benevolent paternalism of the Commander and the culturally conservative ideal of protected womanhood is a rigid belief in male authority and in the hierarchical arrangement of the sexes. In Gilead, women are stripped of their individual identities and transformed into replaceable objects in a phallocentric economy. Bound in a master-slave relationship, the Handmaids are sexual objects for male consumption.

"How numbed Offred's feelings are," remarks one of my students, "yet (thank God), they finally begin writhing under the surface. Her fear which is so powerful at the beginning gives way to defiance." If *The Handmaid's Tale* concerns itself with the troubling issues of incest and forced sex, it also incorporates a feminist retaliatory speech, which partially contains and masters the female fears it dramatizes. Describing how this tactic works, Offred thinks that "there is something powerful in the whispering of obscenities, about those in power. . . . It's like a spell, of sorts. It deflates them, reduces them to the common denominator where they can be dealt with" (287–88; ch. 34). Indulging in a form of penis ridicule, Offred likens the Commander's penis to a "stub," an extra "thumb," a "tentacle," a "stalked slug's eye" (113; ch. 15). Attending a Gileadean group wedding, she imagines the impressive-looking Commander, who is officiating, in bed with his Wife and Handmaid. "Fertilizing away like mad" and "pretending to take no pleasure in it," he is "like a rutting salmon," in her view. "When the Lord said be fruitful and multiply, did he mean this man?" (282; ch. 34). And she imagines sex among the Angels and their new brides as "momentous grunts and sweating, damp furry encounters; or, better, ignominious failures, cocks like three-week-old carrots, anguished fumblings upon flesh cold and unresponding as uncooked fish" (288; ch. 34).

Externally compliant, Offred expresses her defiance through her "inner jeering" at the Commander (177; ch. 23). And yet, despite Offred's cynical inner voice, her anger remains largely censored. Claiming, at one point in her narrative reconstruction of events, that she fantasizes stabbing the Commander when he first asks her to kiss him—"I think about the blood coming out of him, hot as soup, sexual, over my hands"—she subsequently denies this impulse. "In fact I don't think about anything of the kind. I put

it in only afterwards. . . . As I said, this is a reconstruction" (181; ch. 23).
Although Offred fantasizes killing the Commander, she acts out her killing
rage against her male oppressors only in the displaced drama of the state-
sanctioned Particicution ceremony. When a man accused of rape is thrown
at the mercy of a group of Handmaids, he is mobbed and brutally killed.
"There is a bloodlust; I want to tear, gouge, rend," as Offred describes it
(358; ch. 43). On the fringes of her tale there is the partially expressed drama
of female rage. But in the film version's rewriting of *The Handmaid's Tale*,
as my students and I discuss, Offred's angry fantasy of killing the Commander
is, indeed, enacted.

If the text's rage is acted out in the film version, the novel, in contrast,
intertwines its increasing anger about male oppression, which culminates in
the Particicution ceremony, with Offred and Nick's love affair. Predictably,
some students take comfort in the novel's invocation of romance, which
provides Offred—and readers—a temporary escape from the sexually re-
pressive world of Gilead. But students are also open to my analysis of how
the novel both uses and subverts the traditional romance plot and romantic
discourse.

Although Offred's love affair with Nick is presented as a form of female
opposition to the state, the novel's use of the conventional romance plot
may appear, at first glance, to present a culturally conservative message to
women readers—namely, that only in a love relationship can a woman reach
self-fulfillment. And yet if the narrative recuperates the romance plot, it
also interrupts it by having Offred tell two radically different versions of her
initial sexual encounter with Nick. The first version is erotic. "His mouth is
on me, his hands, I can't wait and he's moving, already, love, it's been so
long, I'm alive in my skin, again, arms around him, falling and water softly
everywhere, never-ending." Claiming that she invented this version of
events, Offred then relates another story, which actively undercuts the erotic
discourse of the first description. In a telling role reversal, Nick becomes
the sexual object and commodity. When he tells her that he could "just
squirt it into a bottle" and she could "pour it in," she thinks that perhaps
he wants something from her, "some emotion, some acknowledgment that
he too is human, is more than just a seedpod" (338–39; ch. 40). That Offred
subsequently admits that it "didn't happen that way either" (340) points to
the narrative's reluctance to commit itself to the romance plot. And if Offred's
sexual relationship with Nick is presented as an important act of defiance
against the Gilead regime, it is also entrapping. For when Nick becomes
Offred's lover, she loses her desire to escape Gilead. Above all else, she
wants to be near Nick; with him she feels she can make some kind of life
for herself. "Humanity is so adaptable, my mother would say. Truly amazing,
what people can get used to, as long as there are a few compensations" (349;
ch. 41).

Because of the novel's troubling descriptions of women's sexual exploitation and degradation, which one student reports touched off her own "feelings of being powerless," it is not surprising that student-readers want Offred "to be saved." But if *The Handmaid's Tale* generates a powerful wish to see Offred rescued, it also intentionally leaves the reader in a state of suspense. For as the Eyes help Offred into the black van, she is uncertain whether she is going to her "end" or a "new beginning," whether she is stepping up "into the darkness within; or else the light" (378; ch. 46). Although Offred's fate is left hanging in the balance at the end of her narrative, the "Historical Notes" section appended to her tale acts out the rescue fantasy generated by the narrative. Speculating on what probably happened to her, Professor Pieixoto, the twenty-second-century historian who transcribes Offred's tapes, comments that while her "ultimate fate" (393) is unknown, the weight of evidence suggests that Nick engineered her escape. And her narrative, he claims, has "a certain reflective quality. . . . It has a whiff of emotion recollected, if not in tranquillity, at least *post facto*" (384).

Because many of my students find the "Historical Notes" both jarring and confusing, I spend some time discussing the content and function of this appended material and also commenting on Atwood's presentation, in the character of her pedantic, misogynistic professor, of a "bad" reader, someone who can decode textual puzzles but remains strangely out of touch with the text he is reading. Suggesting that there are appropriate and inappropriate ways of responding to literary texts in the "Historical Notes," Atwood dramatizes her desire to save her novel from those readers who, like her fictional professor, would treat the text as a verbal artifact to be coldly dissected and ultimately dismissed.

"*Come with me*, the writer is saying to the reader," writes Atwood. "*There is a story I have to tell you, there is something you need to know*" ("An End to Audience?" in *Second Words*, Beacon, 348). As Atwood reads and interprets women's lives in *The Handmaid's Tale*, she tells a story she wants her women readers to hear and respond to. A novel that women readers find difficult to dismiss, *The Handmaid's Tale* both involves readers emotionally and forces them to pay heed to Atwood's feminist critique of the gender and power politics that drive masculinist culture.

The End of the World and Other Things:
Life before Man and *The Handmaid's Tale*
Carol L. Beran

Toward the end of Margaret Atwood's *The Handmaid's Tale*, the narrator describes the Handmaids at a Particicution: "There's a surge forward, like a crowd at a rock concert in the former time, when the doors opened, that urgency coming like a wave through us" (Fawcett 359; ch. 43). The simile forces us to compare—rather than contrast—our culture with the most horrifying scene we are shown in the Republic of Gilead. Students reading Atwood's dystopia readily develop contrasts between its society and ours; the connections between the present and Atwood's vision of the future, my students tell me, make the book "scary." Readers quickly identify surrogate motherhood, capital punishment, and toxic wastes as current issues that are taken to horrific extremes in Atwood's dystopia. Concerns such as class prejudice, the devaluing of older women, and the survival of the human species, however, generally seem to them more relevant to the Republic of Gilead than to the present. Studying *The Handmaid's Tale* in conjunction with *Life before Man* (1979) creates a context in which students can become more aware of Atwood's specific social critiques of the present.

Atwood's statement that *Life before Man* begins a new trilogy (FitzGerald and Crabbe 136) implies that *The Handmaid's Tale* would be the final volume of the trilogy. It makes sense, therefore, to study the dystopia in comparison with one of the earlier novels in the trilogy. Disenchanted with first-year composition readers and anthologies for introduction to literature courses or women writers courses because these volumes too often contain only snippets, I now include longer works of literature to generate richer discussions and written responses of greater depth. I find that using more than one work by an author provides a context that allows students at Saint Mary's College to form more informed perceptions of each work and gives them a clearer sense of the writer's themes and techniques than a single work can offer. Because *The Handmaid's Tale* generally has greater immediate appeal to undergraduates than *Life before Man* does, I suggest assigning it first. Questions regarding the connections between Gilead and the present can initiate a comparative study of the novels, beginning with Atwood's presentation of major political, social, and environmental themes in the two books.

In *Life before Man*, Atwood includes discussions of Quebec separatism that point to political tensions in Canada during the 1970s. Although widespread apathy concerning the Quebec election surprises Nate, he finds his mother's work for causes like Amnesty International irrelevant. By the end of the novel, his political awareness is heightened sufficiently that he can solicit signatures on a petition about wrongdoing by the Royal Canadian Mounted

Police. Readers of the two novels realize that continued insensitivity toward minorities and unexamined policies for preserving law and order could result in a police state like that in *The Handmaid's Tale*. In Gilead, government forces combat Baptists in Appalachia, and Quakers have become hunted subversives. The Eyes, with the help of the Guardians, unresisted even by petition signers denouncing their activities, exercise unlimited police power, while the Commanders control everything from women's fashions to sex. Yet, by the end of *The Handmaid's Tale*, all the major characters have been revealed to be thwarting the rules of their society: Ofglen and Nick apparently belong to the subversive Mayday network, Moira's activities at Jezebel's undercut the system, and Serena Joy and the Commander both incite Offred to act illegally. By portraying characters working against oppression or behaving subversively, Atwood expresses hope for a better future and demonstrates actions that may bring it into being.

My students find the hierarchical social structure of Gilead appalling. They believe that modern society is free of stratification. Looking at Atwood's presentation of the relationship between ethnic background and social class in *Life before Man* reveals that social stratification is in fact a current problem. Auntie Muriel classifies all ethnic minorities "on a descending scale, graded according to skin color and religion" (Warner, 122; Elizabeth, 15 Jan. 1977), creating her own Great Chain of Being. Lesje feels isolated because of her Lithuanian Jewish and Ukrainian background; she believes that her ethnicity is responsible for her unmarried, childless, marginalized status, since men perceive her as exotic rather than as a potential wife and mother of their children (see Beran, "Canadian Mosaic" 60–64). Similarly, Offred's status as a Handmaid is privileged (Handmaids are "precious national resources" [107; ch. 14]) yet frowned upon by Marthas like Rita ("it's the red dress she disapproves of, and what it stands for" [12–13; ch. 2]) and scowled at by the Econowives (who "do not like us" [59; ch. 8]). Nevertheless, both novels offer hope for the future. By the end of *Life before Man*, Lesje decides to have a baby whether or not Nate assents, and accepts that her position at the museum indicates that "she belongs" (283; Lesje, 18 Aug. 1978). The "Historical Notes" section at the end of *The Handmaid's Tale* not only assures us that the social structure of Gilead does not persist indefinitely but also indicates that women and native peoples have prominent positions in the world of 2195.

In both *The Handmaid's Tale* and *Life before Man*, Atwood foregrounds serious environmental concerns. William's predictions of fetal mutation, drowning in garbage, and extinction of the human species in the earlier novel foreshadow conditions depicted in the later work. The employment of Unwomen to clean up huge quantities of toxic wastes, the scarcity of food, Gilead's declining birthrate, and the Unbaby born to Janine show what could happen. Specific passages invite direct comparison:

> She would have a throwback, a reptile, a mutant of some kind with
> scales and a little horn on the snout.
>
> (*Life before Man* 270; Lesje, 30 May 1978)
>
> . . . an Unbaby, with a pinhead or a snout like a dog's, or two bodies,
> or a hole in its heart or no arms, or webbed hands and feet?
>
> (*The Handmaid's Tale* 143; ch. 19)

However, at the end of *Life before Man,* Nate's increasing social consciousness, Lesje's decision against abortion, and Elizabeth's vision of people helping each other in an idealized China that as yet exists only in propaganda
posters all offer hope that the human race may not suffer the fate of the
dinosaurs. Although the situation in *The Handmaid's Tale* is presented more
bleakly than that in *Life before Man,* the "Historical Notes" with which the
later book ends imply that the human species survives until 2195 and that
people can again enjoy fresh seafood unavailable at Loaves and Fishes. The
factors that make survival possible in *The Handmaid's Tale* are similar to
those offering limited hope in *Life before Man*: Offred's connection with a
subversive group, her bid to continue the human race by mating with Nick,
and her attempt to survive emotionally by relating to Nick indicate ways an
individual contributes to the preservation of life on earth.

Human reactions to possible ultimate devastation illustrate strikingly the
victim positions that Atwood describes in *Survival.* Introducing key ideas
from *Survival* enables students to compare character development in the
two novels. For example, victims in Position Two blame their plight on
overpowering ideas like Fate or Biology (*Survival* 37; ch. 1). Lesje, conscious
of the possibility that the human race, like the dinosaurs, could become
extinct, confronts one of these powerful concepts. The Gileadean theocracy
imprisons Offred in a role based on her biological processes. When she hears
that Ofglen has hanged herself, she gives up: "I resign my body freely, to
the uses of others" (*Handmaid's Tale* 368; ch. 45). Victims in Position Three
refuse to accept the role as inevitable, an attitude that may enable them to
move toward Position Four, becoming creative nonvictims (37–38). When
anger prompts Lesje to try to become pregnant, she moves into Position
Three; her decision to become a single mother if necessary marks her as a
creative nonvictim who may give birth to a child who will symbolize the
continuation of the human race. Offred's defiance of the rules in her affair
with Nick marks her passage through Position Three. Like Lesje, she believes she is pregnant, though Offred calls it "wishful thinking" (348; ch.
41). Whether she gives birth to a baby becomes less significant than her
creation of the narrative that bears witness to her existence. Her words
empower her as a creative nonvictim (see Beran, "Images" 70–72).

Life before Man and The Handmaid's Tale are alike in that, besides warning us, they suggest that by being creative nonvictims, we can prevent
doomsday and devise a more acceptable future. To emphasize the hope-

fulness of the two books, students can make a series of specific comparisons of recurring motifs. I begin by asking students to prepare, from the day's reading assignment, two or more examples of something that repeats, together with a tentative analysis of their function and significance. After one student has presented a motif, I ask if others have additional examples of that motif or examples of a related motif. A complex weave of images soon becomes apparent. Introducing the second novel allows the class to focus on patterns found in both books, in order to compare and contrast Atwood's use of the recurring materials. The motifs of a woman contemplating the ceiling, of a woman locked in a bathroom, of cigarettes, and of people helping each other reward detailed comparative analysis.

At the beginning of *Life before Man*, Elizabeth is looking at the ceiling:

> A small crack runs across her field of vision, a smaller crack branching out from it. Nothing will happen, nothing will open, the crack will not widen and split and nothing will come through it.
>
> (3; Elizabeth, 29 Oct. 1976)

Chapter 2 of *The Handmaid's Tale* begins with Offred describing the room at the top of the Commander's house:

> Above, on the white ceiling, a relief ornament in the shape of a wreath, and in the center of it a blank space, plastered over, like the place in a face where the eye has been taken out. There must have been a chandelier, once. They've removed anything you could tie a rope to.
>
> (9; ch. 2)

Offred associates the ceiling with suicide; the light fixture had been removed after the previous Handmaid hanged herself. Similarly, Elizabeth, pondering the ceiling, "knows about the vacuum on the other side of the ceiling" and fears she "could be pulled up and into it like smoke" (4; Elizabeth, 29 Oct. 1976). She imagines she "can see up through the dark ceiling" to "the place where there is nothing between her and nothing" (142; Elizabeth, 27 Jan. 1977) as she contemplates Chris's suicide.

Offred can "step sideways out of [her] own time" as she lies "under the plaster eye in the ceiling" (49; ch. 7), just as Elizabeth is "somewhere between her body, which is lying sedately on the bed, . . . and the ceiling with its hairline cracks" (4; Elizabeth, 29 Oct. 1976). Offred describes her experiences looking up at "the blind plaster eye in the ceiling" as "attacks of the past, like faintness, a wave sweeping over my head" (68; ch. 9). The ceiling decoration symbolizes present reality when she awakes from dreams and knows she is "really awake because there is the wreath, on the ceiling" (139; ch. 19), but it is also a source of visions: "In a minute the wreath will start to color and I will begin seeing things" (166; ch. 22). Visions on the ceiling can disembody women whose bodies are being used for sex: "When in doubt, when flat on your back, you can look at the ceiling. Who knows what you may see, up there?" (287; ch. 34).

In *Life before Man*, the complex series of associations that flow from the scenes in which Elizabeth contemplates the ceiling culminates when Elizabeth faints at her aunt's funeral: "A black vacuum sucks at her, there's a wind, a slow roar. . . . Elizabeth falls through space" (277; Elizabeth, 3 June 1978). She regains consciousness in two senses, recovering physically from the blackout and emotionally from the numbness she has experienced since Chris's suicide. Although she is aware she has "built a dwelling over the abyss," she begins to think "with anticipation" of everyday things like making peanut butter sandwiches or "her quiet living room with its empty bowls, pure grace, her kitchen table" (278). In *The Handmaid's Tale*, the motif climaxes as Offred waits in disgrace, contemplating suicide: "Behind me I feel her presence, my ancestress, my double, turning in midair under the chandelier." Rather than obey her predecessor's imagined command to "get it over" (375; ch. 46), Offred, like Lesje and Elizabeth, moves forward into an uncertain future: "And so I step up, into the darkness within; or else the light" (378). Her step is upward, her narrative ends with the word "light" rather than "dark"; in this uncertainty there is hope.

Tracing the motif of a woman locked in a bathroom demonstrates parallels between Lesje's experiences and Offred's. Three scenes in which Lesje locks herself in bathrooms reveal change as she moves from sheer escapism (her bathroom prehistoric fantasies at Elizabeth's party) through self-protection (her night in the bathroom after "the incident" with William) to resistance against victimization (destroying her birth control pills rather than committing suicide with a grapefruit knife).

For Offred, as for Lesje, bathrooms are scenes of subversive activity. Baths at the Commander's house are carefully monitored because "there were incidents in bathrooms at first: there were cuttings, drownings" (81; ch. 12). Offred's subversive activity in the bath consists of remembering the past. When Moira and Offred meet by prearranged signal in adjacent stalls in the restroom at the Rachel and Leah Re-education Center, Moira talks of escape, which she later effects by overpowering an Aunt in the washroom. In the ladies' lounge at Jezebel's, Moira narrates the story of her escape and recapture, foreshadowing a possible fate for Offred and foregrounding the problem of being a victim of an overpowering force. Yet the fact that Moira can tell her story presages Offred's narrative and implies that, as Offred says, "she knows there is a point" (316; ch. 38).

Comparing the frequent references to cigarettes in *Life before Man* and *The Handmaid's Tale* underscores the importance, for Atwood, of interpersonal relationships; analyzing the contrasts opens up questions about freedom and repression. Characters in both novels associate cigarettes with relationships. Lesje and Nate smoke in most of their encounters. When Nate lights her cigarette during their first lunch date, Lesje feels he is staring at her nose, "which makes her nervous" (57; Lesje, 15 Nov. 1976). In the hotel room, they sit on either side of the bed smoking, unable to connect. Lesje wonders why he doesn't "stub out his cigarette, stand up, take her in his arms?" (112; Lesje, 15 Jan. 1977). At the end of the novel, Lesje's longing to smoke a cigarette in the museum, and Nate's imagining that he will light one as he waits for her, signal the tenuous connectedness of the pair.

In *The Handmaid's Tale*, cigarettes again represent connections between people; however, as trivial objects that become valued because of scarcity and prohibition, they also represent freedom and pleasure. When the Commander asks Offred what she would like, she requests knowledge of "whatever there is to know" rather than "candy, cigarettes" (243; ch. 29), signaling her priorities. Offred was buying cigarettes when she discovered that her bank account had been canceled; her inability to purchase them symbolizes her loss of freedom. Smoking signals her connection with Moira, both in her memories of the past and in Jezebel's. Cigarette smoke symbolizes the Handmaid's unwanted connection with Serena Joy: "I smell the hot singe of the smoke, breathe it in" (105; ch. 14); later, Serena Joy gives Offred a cigarette to seal their pact to have Offred impregnated by Nick. Offred values the cigarette too much to smoke it, yet feels cheapened: "All you need to give them is a cigarette" (340; ch. 40). Offred's connection with Nick begins early in the novel with her desiring his cigarette; to her, his smoking represents his comparative freedom. He smokes as she enters his room in her descriptions of their sexual encounters, defining each of her versions of their relationship:

> I smell the smoke on him, in the warm air of the room, all over. I'd like to take off my clothes, bathe in it, rub it over my skin.
> (337; ch. 40)

> "Here," he says to me, "have a drag." No preliminaries, he knows why I'm here. . . . I take the cigarette from him, draw deeply in, hand it back. Our fingers hardly touch. (338)

> . . . he's holding a toothbrush, or a cigarette. . . . He's always got something in his hand, as if he's been going about his life as usual, not expecting me, not waiting. (345; ch. 41)

Atwood's presentation of relationships in terms of cigarettes is part of a larger recurring motif that pervades both *The Handmaid's Tale* and *Life before Man*: the image of people helping each other. The appearance of this motif in both novels suggests hope for the future. At the beginning of *Life before Man*, Elizabeth is unable to cook for her family; Nate makes tea for her and macaroni for the children. Repeated allusions to Kilmer's "Trees" mark Elizabeth's resistance to nurturing: "A tree whose hungry mouth is pressed. If you didn't want trees sucking at your sweet flowing breast why did you have children?" (229; Elizabeth, 9 July 1977). Her epiphany at her aunt's grave enables her to nurture her children again. However, Atwood juxtaposes this progression in Elizabeth's vision with complementary insights. The Lifeboat game at Elizabeth's dinner party initiates a series of experiences in which Elizabeth becomes increasingly aware of her marginalization as she celebrates her thirty-ninth birthday and approaches the end of her childbearing years. In the Republic of Gilead, she would be declared an Unwoman. Yet Elizabeth's epiphany in the final scenes in *Life before Man* expresses hope: she realizes that she is now alone with her children, who will soon no longer need her; nevertheless, the posters in the Chinese Exhibit enable her to envision an ideal world in which people no longer slander women and people help build each others' houses (see Beran, "Intertexts" 200–04).

In *The Handmaid's Tale*, the Mayday/*m'aidez* motif suggests a similar willingness of individuals to aid each other: "You can join us" (218; ch. 27), Ofglen says. Ofglen aids the condemned rapist at the Particicution, telling Offred, "He was one of ours. I knocked him out. Put him out of his misery" (360; ch. 43); her suicide protects Offred and the others in the Mayday network. At the end of Offred's narrative, Nick assures her that the people who take her away are Mayday. She, however, feels helpless: "I have given myself over into the hands of strangers, because it can't be helped" (378; ch. 46). The "Historical Notes" verify that the help Offred receives enables her to survive to record her story.

In a course on Margaret Atwood's fiction, the comparison could be expanded to include the middle novel of the trilogy, *Bodily Harm* (1981). Comparing just the two novels discussed here can culminate in an essay question that takes into account the additional novel: Now that you have studied the first and third novels of Atwood's second trilogy, what would you expect the middle novel to be like?

Although studying either *Life before Man* or *The Handmaid's Tale* can be rewarding, considering them together enriches the experience. Comparing the two novels heightens our sense of the applicability of Atwood's vision of a future society to contemporary life. Furthermore, the comparison reveals Atwood's increasing privileging of art: Offred's narrative replaces Lesje's baby as a symbol of the survival of the human race. Pairing the novels foregrounds the hopeful elements in both works, clarifying that *The Handmaid's Tale* is not just a warning but a call to action.

Atwood's Reconstruction of Folktales: *The Handmaid's Tale* and "Bluebeard's Egg"

Kathleen E. B. Manley

Teaching Margaret Atwood's *The Handmaid's Tale* and "Bluebeard's Egg" in a class on folklore and literature provides opportunities for exploration of a particular connection between the two disciplines. In this relationship, one which few folklorists and literary scholars address, the writer deconstructs a specific folktale and then constructs a literary text emphasizing a fragment or subtext of the tale. Discussion of such works increases students' understanding of the links between folklore and literature.

The three commonly recognized relationships between folklore and literature are these: first, writers may use folklore as *product*, often to provide verisimilitude, such as when they describe a traditional house or incorporate a folk belief; second, they may use folklore as *situation* (context), for instance, by including a storytelling session or the building of a traditional house; third, authors may use the folktale *medium*: the language and style of a *Märchen* (fairy tale) or tall tale (Lewis 345). A good example of a writer's use of folklore as product is Mark Twain's description of beliefs in witches in *Huckleberry Finn*. Henry James uses folklore as situation at the beginning of *The Turn of the Screw*, when the characters have been telling ghost stories. And as far as medium is concerned, Hans Christian Andersen is among many European writers who imitated the style of the *Märchen* following the publication of the Grimms' *Kinder- und Hausmärchen* in the early nineteenth century.

Folklorists debate the purity of the Grimms' tales as folklore, but reading these tales, discussing them, and referring to Max Lüthi's *Once upon a Time* (especially chapter 3) helps students recognize common folk motifs and plots. Students can then examine some texts that use folklore as product, situation, or medium: Shakespeare's *King Lear* or Welty's *The Robber Bridegroom*, for example. Atwood's approach, to deconstruct a *Märchen* and bring a fragment or subtext to the surface in a reconstruction of the tale, differs from the more commonly recognized uses of folklore. The plot of the reconstruction may deviate widely from the original, as in *The Handmaid's Tale*, or it may contain some similarities to the original plot, as is the case for "Bluebeard's Egg." These two texts provide students with excellent examples of the deconstructive-reconstructive relationship between folklore and literature.

The *Märchen* that forms the basis for "Bluebeard's Egg" is the Grimms' tale "Fitcher's Bird" (Grimm and Grimm 164–67). Atwood takes certain elements from the *Märchen* that she then uses, in new form, in her short story. She deconstructs the *Märchen* into the various components that interest her. Careful comparison between the tale and the story shows students that

Atwood's interests lie in the third sister's cleverness in destroying the wizard; the dismemberment of the first two sisters; the egg; the room in which the wizard keeps his dismembered victims; the wizard's magic; and the wizard's touch. These fragments suggest a subtext about relationships between women and men that Atwood brings to the surface in "Bluebeard's Egg."

Sally, in "Bluebeard's Egg," is the equivalent of the third sister in the tale; she is Ed's third wife, and her knowledge of the "actual fates" of the other two has "always been vague" (Fawcett, 165). Like the third sister in the tale, Sally is clever. She takes evening classes, presumably to be more interesting to her husband; but when it seems to make no difference to him, she keeps taking them anyway (157). Most of her cleverness, however, she uses to hide her true self even from herself. She makes Ed her world, belittling her night classes so that he will not think they are more important to her than he is; she also makes sure that the jobs she takes do not engage her completely and do not put her in a position of power (154–55). Only on the collapse of her world, when she sees Ed's hand on Marylynn's buttock, can one hope that she will use her brain, as the third sister in "Fitcher's Bird" does, to help herself. The golden pink egg she sees at the end of the story is a contrast to the insubstantial picture of her heart on Ed's machine; it may indicate that if she is courageous enough, she will become a person in her own right. She may, like the clever sister in "Fitcher's Bird," escape from the wizard. Atwood's creation of Sally as a reconstruction of the Grimms' third sister raises questions about women in female-male relationships; what pressures, Atwood asks, must exist before a woman refuses to subordinate her intelligence to her desire for steady male companionship?

Atwood's interest in the dismemberment of victims in "Fitcher's Bird" appears in the short story in the figure of Ed, the wizard character, a "heart man" who listens gravely to women's troubles with their hearts. Atwood also has her protagonist support her interest in dismemberment: *Trouble with your heart? Get it removed*, [Sally] thinks. *Then you'll have no more problems*" (153). The room in the Grimms' tale where the wizard keeps the dismembered bodies becomes, in Atwood's story, an examining room where Ed and the other "heart men" can see hearts through pictures provided by sound waves. Sally's curiosity, like that of the women in the Grimms' tale, leads her to the room; Ed dismembers her by showing her her own heart on a screen, a disembodied image in black and white (161). The scene clearly indicates, symbolically, Sally's fragmentation as a person. Again, Atwood's interest is in the female-male relationship: Sally's desire for closeness not only causes her to hide part of her cleverness but also results in an incomplete self in other respects; nothing outside of Ed engages her. "She knows she thinks about Ed too much" (168) and "everything is fascinating, but nothing enters her" (169).

Ed is both the wizard and the unbloodied egg of the Grimms' tale. As the egg, Ed is smooth and impenetrable, not giving up any secrets, not showing any emotion. He makes love the same way, time after time (162). Sally is aware of the irony of his being a heart man who, she thinks, knows nothing "about the workings of hearts, real hearts, the kind symbolized by red satin surrounded by lace and topped by pink bows" (152). Neither he nor Marylynn gives any sign that the hand Sally saw on Marylynn's buttock was real, yet the incident reveals to Sally that possibly Ed is, like the wizard, "enormously clever" (182). Like the Grimms' wizard, whose touch propels women into his basket, Ed's touch is dangerous. Sally experiences that danger in his touching Marylynn, in his almost touching "right there in Sally's living room" the women who say they have heart trouble (153), and in the cold precision with which he touches her in the examining room containing the heart machine. By bringing this fragment about touch to the surface in "Bluebeard's Egg," Atwood explores some aspects of this sense for women and men. Since Sally does not allow Ed to know her whole self, he does not "touch" her deeply, and his touching her in the examining room emphasizes her dismemberment; both she and he contribute to it. At the same time, his touching of others, and in particular a "member" of her friend Marylynn's body, threatens her world and, ultimately, sets in motion her questioning of her dismemberment.

In addition to Ed, Atwood places another egg, briefly mentioned above, in the story: the glowing golden pink one Sally sees at the end. A contrast to the bloodied egg in the Grimms' tale and related to the "real hearts" symbolized by red satin with pink and white trim, this egg indicates a possible birth of Sally's whole self; it does not reveal guilt in the way the egg in the Grimms' tale does. Sally's guilt has been lack of recognition of her whole self, and her fear of the egg shows that the birth of this whole self may not come to pass (184). She may instead remain a fragmented person with her heart on the outside. Using the components of the Grimms' tale that interest her—cleverness, magic, dismemberment, rooms, touch, and the egg—Atwood explores in "Bluebeard's Egg" a subtext of concerns about relationships between women and men, examining how those relationships affect women's construction of self.

In *The Handmaid's Tale*, Atwood deconstructs "Little Red Riding Hood" (Grimm and Grimm 102–05). In this tale she also finds fragments that call for reconstruction: the garden, the wolf, the grandmother, and Little Red Riding Hood herself. In the novel she explores the relationship of character traits and flowers to the subtext of sensuality she sees in the original tale.

The garden images Atwood uses in *The Handmaid's Tale* make a strong connection between flowers and sensuality, a connection Sharon Wilson suggests (*Sexual Politics* 283). The gardens in the novel, unlike the woods in the Grimms' tale, are regulated, civilized places; for the most part, the novel's grandmother figure, Serena Joy, controls them. Some of the gardens are even pale reminders of the real thing, such as the lilies on the pillow in the narrator's room (Fawcett, 75; ch. 10), the forget-me-not wallpaper in the bathroom (81; ch. 12), and the withered daffodils in the sitting room. Even these dried-up representatives of the garden, however, evoke in the narrator the danger of forbidden sensuality; one evening she risks leaving her room to steal a withered daffodil and instead kisses Nick, the chauffeur (126–27; ch. 17).

Serena Joy's real garden, like the woods in the Grimms' tale, presents danger in spite of its regulated, civilized nature; the Handmaid's function, to provide a child for the household, is supposed to be devoid of passion, yet "heat rises, from the flowers themselves," and walking through the garden makes her head swim. She realizes the garden has "something subversive" about it (196; ch. 25). Like the woods, the garden and its flowers suggest wildness, a lack of control just beneath control, and a temptation, like that for Red Riding Hood, to stray off the path. A further suggestion of this connection between flowers and lack of control occurs at the Salvaging; the narrator notices a dandelion (353; ch. 42), a response to her longing for one at the Prayvaganza, "rubbishy and insolently random and hard to get rid of and perennially yellow as the sun" (275; ch. 33). Significantly, at the Salvaging the women lose themselves, joining together to execute a political prisoner accused of rape. Although the narrator does not participate in the execution, or "Particicution," directly, she feels the bloodlust within her (357–60; ch. 43). The Handmaid insists that flowers are one of the "good things" in the story she is telling: "where would we be without them?" (344; ch. 41)

In spite of the ostensible control over gardens in the novel, then, flowers in both real and fake gardens symbolize sensuality, lack of control, and rebellion, all of which are, indeed, "good things" in the story. As a reconstruction of "Little Red Riding Hood," The Handmaid's Tale explores a subtext that Atwood found in the Grimms' tale; she brings the connection between flowers and sensuality to the surface and uses dead and controlled flowers in the novel to express Gilead's negative stance on sensuality.

Atwood's deconstruction of the traditional "Little Red Riding Hood" leads her to consider not only the sensuality lurking in the woods of the Grimms' tale but also particular traits of the characters. The narrator is obviously a reconstructed Little Red Riding Hood character (Wilson, Sexual Politics 271), and Atwood focuses on her naïveté. She wears red and carries a basket for shopping trips, returning to the "grandmother's" house with the basket full of provisions. She does not ask questions and, at least at the beginning of the novel, behaves as she is expected to behave (38–39; ch. 5). Like Red Riding Hood, her sensuality is just beneath the surface; gardens, even supposedly controlled ones, lead her astray, and so do wolves, reconstructed in the novel as Nick and the Commander.

Like the narrator, Nick and the Commander are fragmentations and reconstructions of the Grimms' characters; Nick represents the wolf's trait of animal sensuality and, because of his sensual and sexual nature, the wolf's persuasive power—it is the wolf, in the Grimms' tale, who draws Little Red Riding Hood's attention to the flowers (Grimm and Grimm 103). But Nick is a hunter figure as well, aiding in the narrator's rescue. Wilson suggests the Commander's role as wolf (*Sexual Politics* 279, 287), but unlike Nick, he remains a sinister wolf; his seeing the Handmaid alone, as he does, could lead to her death. Atwood thus emphasizes the trait of selfishness that she sees in the wolf of the Grimms' tale. At the same time, though, she makes the Commander a pathetic, impotent figure when he and the narrator have their night out at Jezebel's: "He's down to the shirt; then, under it, sadly, a little belly. Wisps of hair" (331; ch. 39). He is able to look only "worried and helpless" as, near the end of the novel, two men lead the Handmaid away (377; ch. 46). Through the gardens and the characters in this novel, Atwood explores sensuality and sexuality, subtexts that surfaced for her as a result of her deconstruction of the Grimms' "Little Red Riding Hood."

Teachers should not only make their students aware of Atwood's techniques of deconstruction and reconstruction. They should point out, in addition, her acute consciousness of the possibilities of the reconstruction of narrative and of the questions narrative raises vis-à-vis reality. Atwood discusses these ideas in an interview (Ingersoll, *Conversations* 209–11), and in the course of the novel the protagonist mentions several times that her story is a reconstruction, suggesting that one constructs reality through storytelling. For example:

> This is a reconstruction. All of it is a reconstruction. It's a reconstruction now, in my head, as I lie flat on my single bed rehearsing what I should or shouldn't have said, what I should or shouldn't have done, how I should have played it. If I ever get out of here—. . . .
> When I get out of here, if I'm ever able to set this down, in any form, even in the form of one voice to another, it will be a reconstruction then too, at yet another remove. (173; ch.23)

The narrator also gives several possible versions of what happened to her husband, Luke (132–35; ch. 18), and several versions of her first sexual encounter with Nick (337–40; ch. 40). Of the last she says, "All I can hope for is a reconstruction: the way love feels is always only approximate" (340). Through her narrator, then, Atwood indicates her interest in stories as ways to create different worlds; it is not surprising that the novelist herself uses *Märchen* as a basis for reconstructions that reflect subtexts she sees in the originals.

Atwood's "Bluebeard's Egg" and *The Handmaid's Tale* illustrate a relationship between folklore and literature that differs from the commonly recognized use of folklore in literature as product, situation, or medium. These texts are thus extremely useful in a folklore and literature class.

Teaching Literature through Film:
An Interdisciplinary Approach to *Surfacing* and *The Handmaid's Tale*

Mary K. Kirtz

As a professor at an open admissions university, I encounter an extremely broad range of student abilities and preparedness in my class on contemporary Canadian literature. Few students have done more than write plot summaries or subjective book reviews before entering my classroom. Margaret Atwood is a particularly difficult author for these students not only to accept, because of her strong views about the United States and women, but even to understand, because of the formal, imagistic, and thematic complexity of her novels. At the same time, these students, like most young people, are very much at ease with visual media, especially films.

One of the major tendencies in current interdisciplinary approaches, like culture studies, is to erase the boundaries between different media; since everything is perceived as a signifier of deeper cultural patterns, such a probing beneath variations in technique helps to identify deeper issues that underlie the presentation of these patterns in different media. Paradoxically, then, such an interdisciplinary view gives us a common ground on which to explore differences between the media, especially in their creation of meaning. By returning to a consideration of how each medium shapes these fundamental issues, we reinvoke the boundaries. Working through one medium to examine another (a kind of "intermediality," if you will) puts both into sharper perspective. I therefore ask questions that pit film and novel versions of a story more specifically against one another.

Does it make a difference if a statement made by one character in the novel is uttered by another in the film? If an action performed by one character is given to another to carry out? If the sequence of events is changed? If events are omitted from or added to the original story? How is the story changed by major structural shifts or omissions? Does the fact that the novelist and screenwriters are not of the same gender make a difference? And finally, what is the significance of these differences in terms of the original story's intentions? Has the message been substantially altered in the transfer of story from verbal to visual medium?

So that each student will have a firm sense of the novel before viewing the film versions, we begin our sessions in the traditional way, by reading and then discussing the novel in terms of its theme, plot, and character development. Before we watch the film, I ask the students simply to note the similarities and differences they see between the book and film versions. In addition to making this list, students write a personal response to both versions of the story before the next class. In that class, we start the discussion with the written responses; here I am primarily interested in getting all the students involved, so that the transition from subjective, specific responses to more objective, general conclusions will occur smoothly. Once the discussion is going, I ask students to focus on issues broader than students' original responses by referring to specific scenes in both novel and film. Using video equipment, I fast-forward to the particular scenes they point out. Invariably, these are the very ones that clearly indicate the differences between book and film presentations. Once we have reviewed these scenes in terms of specific questions raised during class discussion, we are able to examine, in both depth and detail, the implications of the answers.

Using this approach, I have found the movie versions of *Surfacing* (1979) and *The Handmaid's Tale* (1989) to be useful vehicles for helping my students get inside Atwood's texts. As accurate visual representations of the novels' plots and formal values, both films must be considered failures. Yet it is precisely their failure—the gap created by the differing aims of film and text—that foregrounds the values and structures of Atwood's works for my students more readily than does reading and discussing the novels alone. In fact, the greater the difference between the novel and the film, the easier it is for the students to focus on the distinctive features of the literary work. By considering how the film versions have changed, manipulated, omitted, or de-emphasized specific themes, characters, and plot elements, the students are better able to understand how the corresponding elements in the novels contribute to the wholeness of Atwood's vision.

Since we begin our study of the novel in terms of theme, plot, and character development and typically pursue the comparison between novel and film in these same terms, I will use these three elements to structure the rest of my discussion.

The major theme of the novel *Surfacing* is the unnamed protagonist's coming to terms with the fact of her abortion; while other issues arise, this is the central thematic thread running throughout the novel. She keeps her past a secret from her present friends by pretending to have been married, to have had a child, and to have been divorced. The narrator's repressed memories surface in the images of frogs in jars and in her fabricated recollections of her mother rescuing her brother from a near-fatal drowning. She finally acknowledges the truth when she discovers her father's dead body in the lake—a moment of epiphany that is one of the most powerful passages in the novel. The binary opposition set up between killers and victims, an opposition reinforced by an extensive series of images (descriptions of hunters and their dead prey, recollections of Nazi atrocities, the comparison of United States values spreading over Canada to a death-dealing virus), finally coalesces in her admission that she felt like a killer in acquiescing to the abortion.

The protagonist hides from her friends (who leave when they cannot find her) in order to go through a reparation ritual. Once she comes to terms with her abortion, she is prepared to rejoin the outside world; the book ends as Joe is calling for her, but she is not certain whether she will return to him.

In the film, by contrast, the major theme is refracted through a patriarchal prism. Rather than address the complexities surrounding the issue of abortion, the film emphasizes the protagonist's coming to terms with her "father fixation." Joe suggests that Kate (the name given to the protagonist) is afraid to see her father, and so they go to the island to "deal with this problem." Joe reassures her that "we'll go up. It's the only way you'll ever feel right about it. . . . It's gonna be all right. *I'm* gonna be there." The issue of abortion, in fact, is eliminated in the first ten minutes of the film when Joe says to the protagonist, "We did agree on a couple of facts. *You* weren't careful. *You* got pregnant. *You* got an abortion. I mean, it's all right in *my* mind. Why go back over that again and again?" Furthermore, making Joe, rather than her art professor, the one who impregnates Kate eliminates the older man–younger woman dynamic, another aspect of the novel's gender-as-power theme. Also underscoring this movie's patriarchal bias is Kate's recollection of almost drowning and being saved by her *father*. Mother and brother are never mentioned.

The film's final scenes preserve and reinforce its patriarchal perspective. In the novel, closing the cottage and burning its contents are significant gestures toward healing; in the film, after finding her father's body, Kate simply closes up the cottage, sends her father's drawings of petroglyphs to another researcher, and, in a voice-over, writes a letter to Joe: "He's dead, Joe. I said good-bye to him. I'm on my own now. I can manage with my hopes, my failures. Why should I be filled with death? In mourning? Everything is alive. Everything is waiting to become alive." These last two sentences, taken directly from the novel, underscore the travesty of the transposition—in the novel, the words come after the protagonist's journey into the depths of her psyche is completed. Here, she's just cleaning up, preparing for departure.

Plot divergences show equally telling differences between the novel and the film. In the novel, the comparison of the spread of United States culture to a virus is central to Atwood's concept of the virtually unacknowledged disappearance of Canadian identity, and the confusion surrounding the national identity of the hunters is a significant dramatization of this dilemma. When the protagonist and her friends run into the hunters in the wilderness, she assumes they are Americans and condemns them for killing animals wantonly, a habit she attributes to United States culture. During a friendly exchange, however, they are revealed to be Canadians; the discovery becomes a vehicle for emphasizing that we are all complicit in the human capacity for evil.

In the film, the episode becomes a scene that could have been an outtake from the movie version of James Dickey's *Deliverance*. The hunters, whose nationality is no longer an issue, become menacing marauders, threatening the women and using David, one of the friends, for target practice. This provides yet another opportunity for Joe to play the hero rather than an opportunity to dramatize the problematic of Canadian identity.

Character emphasis provides perhaps the most divergent and egregious gap between book and film. In the novel, the nameless protagonist is the principal character in a first person narrative. Joe, David, and Anna are seen through her eyes and serve only as foils to the protagonist's growing awareness of the deep wound in her psyche caused by her denial of the abortion. Portrayed as inept city folk unused to roughing it in the bush, David and Anna are a manipulative, warring married couple, and Joe is both inarticulate and passive. While the characterization of David and Anna in the film remains fairly faithful to their portrayal in the novel, Joe has risen considerably in stature. He is more than equal to the protagonist in importance.

As I have noted, Joe, and not the narrator (as in the novel), raises and dismisses the abortion issue. He is as involved as Kate is in outdoor activities, shooting rapids, gathering firewood, and climbing cliffsides. *He* saves the group from the hunters and rescues Kate from a rape attempt by David (in the novel, the protagonist is able, without anyone's help, to dismiss David's inept invitation to have sex). *He*, not she, finds the petroglyphs that her father had been drawing. Upon discovering them on a steep rock face, he falls and breaks his arm, thereby increasing his heroic stature. He leaves the island to get his arm fixed and promises to return for her, a far cry from his frustrated departure and tentative return in the novel.

This dramatic shift in focus from a woman's perspective to a man's is, in fact, one of the first things my students notice about character development in the film. What was a novel about a woman's problem has suddenly turned into a movie about a man's heroic posturing—Joe (played by the handsome Joseph Bottoms), having shot the rapids, rescued David from the nefarious hunters straight out of *Deliverance*, saved Kate's honor from the lecherous David, found the glyphs, and broken his arm, *still* returns to bring Kate back to the mainland. As they leave, Joe offers his good arm to the docile Kate, a gesture implying that she has transferred her dependence on Daddy to this sensitive, New Age guy. Focusing on the differences in the portrayal of Joe between the film and the novel is the simplest way to open up the discussion about the conflict between feminist and patriarchal values.

Pointing out the *Deliverance* additions in the film helps illuminate not only the purpose of Atwood's inclusion of an anti–United States theme in her novel but also the validity of her position in the light of the film's blatant dismissal of the question of Canada–United States relations. My students are often quite hostile to the anti–United States stance of the novel *until* they see how readily it is dismissed in the film—then Atwood's concerns about the disappearance of Canada as a distinct nation begin to make sense.

There are several minor differences between the novel and film versions of *The Handmaid's Tale*: the movie Handmaid's uniform allows her to see and, more important, to be seen. It also allows her to move more freely than the all-encasing nunlike habit described by Atwood. In addition, the long stretches of time the Handmaid spends in her room and the lack of communication between the various women of the household are eliminated, making Kate a much more active participant in the household and in Mayday activities than is her novelistic counterpart. Both changes suggest that the situation for women is not nearly as hopeless as it seems in the novel. These shifts are subtle, and students seldom notice them. There are, however, three significant changes between novel and film that virtually no one misses.

First, the film straightens the convoluted time sequence of the novel's narrative into linear time, opening with the capture of the Handmaid (interestingly enough, like the protagonist of the film version of *Surfacing*, also called Kate—changed to Offred in Gilead) and ending with her clearly successful escape from the Commander's household. We thus have a typical closed narrative, with an easily discernible beginning, middle, and end, a neatness that eliminates the reader's unease at the uncertainty and arbitrariness of life and death in the novelistic world where people simply disappear and remain unaccounted for.

The second major difference is that, in the film, Kate's husband, Luke, is clearly dead, killed in the opening sequence by the border guards, and she is therefore able to mourn him and free herself from the uncertainty that clouds every waking moment of the novel's Handmaid. In addition, the finality of his death makes her affair with Nick no longer problematic—the poignancy with which her guilt is treated in the novel is gone. Here she is just another damsel in distress lucky enough to find a hero to rescue her at the end.

The third difference is the dramatic divergence in the film from the novel's ambiguous conclusion. The "Historical Notes" section, which serves as an epilogue to the novel, is the key to understanding Atwood's condemnation of the patriarchal dominance that continues to devalue women, even into the kinder, gentler twenty-second century, when the symposium takes place. The historian uses the Handmaid's tapes, not to discover her identity but to focus on the identity of yet another great man, and he even chastises the Handmaid for not leaving the right kind of record—some vouchers, some letters. In short, anything from the man's office would have been preferable to the woman's story she actually leaves. Once again, a woman is rendered invisible and worthless within her own history.

No such epilogue exists in the movie. In fact, the Handmaid is given powers in the film that undermine the novel's message that the Gileadean regime both represses and suppresses women. In the novel, the Handmaid is hustled off to an unknown fate and Nick's role in her rescue is left unclear; since the tapes telling her story have survived, we assume that she also survived, at least for a time. Anything more about her life we cannot know, especially since even the historian is uninterested in pursuing this line of inquiry.

The film dismisses all such ambiguity. Furthermore, the film makes Kate much more heroic than the novel's Handmaid. In the novel, when Ofglen asks the Handmaid to help Mayday, urging her to look through the Commander's desk and telling her the underground group could get her a key, the Handmaid fearfully declines. The novel's insistence on women's impotence is severely undermined in the film when Kate is given not only the means and the opportunity, but also the will, to assassinate the Commander. At the same time, her apparent autonomy is compromised by the inflation of Nick's role. It is suggested that her involvement in the Mayday movement is largely due to his influence and even her decisive blow for freedom is traced back to her growing love for her heroic rescuer.

On the one hand, then, the film trivializes the gravity of this society's repression of women by having Kate kill the Commander. On the other hand, the film's conclusion suggests a complete capitulation to Hollywood's insistence on a happy ending, an ending that further undercuts the autonomy it apparently awards Kate. Our last view of her is at the door of a trailer somewhere in the mountains, happily pregnant and waiting for her lover. There is something terribly ironic about the fact that, having been rescued from being just another baby-making machine for the regime, her fulfillment is portrayed in those very terms.

Once again, as we question these differences, my students become aware of the change in message that accompanies the changes in plot, narrative structure, and character emphasis. Once again, they realize the power of the patriarchy, as a woman's story becomes only one part of a male-dominated resistance movement. Ironically, the insensitive treatment and outright omission of Atwood's main issues in these films does much more to awaken my students to these problems than reading the novels ever does. Reinvoking the boundaries between the media by pointing out the discrepancies between text and film allows my students to develop the larger cultural context of the questions with which Atwood is grappling. Working *through* the films, then, gives them an avenue back to the novels that reading the novels alone seldom affords.

The Journals of Susanna Moodie as Life Writing

Marlene Kadar

> These poems were generated by a dream. I dreamt I
> was watching an opera I had written about Susanna
> Moodie. I was alone in the theatre; on the empty
> white stage, a single figure was singing.
>   Although I had heard of Susanna Moodie I had
> never read her two books about Canada, *Roughing It
> in the Bush* and *Life in the Clearings*. When I did
> read them I was disappointed. The prose was
> discursive and ornamental and the books had little
> shape: they were collections of disconnected
> anecdotes. The only thing that held them together was
> the personality of Mrs. Moodie, and what struck me
> most about this personality was the way in which it
> reflects many of the obsessions still with us.
>   —"Afterword," *The Journals of Susanna Moodie*

Margaret Atwood published *The Journals of Susanna Moodie* in 1970.[1] To make sure the reader didn't expect to read the journal entries of the "real" English Canadian frontierswoman, Susanna Moodie, Atwood includes the notation "Poems by Margaret Atwood" on the cover of her book—a cover she herself designed for the Oxford University Press publication. Before we even begin reading the poems, then, we are made aware of genre: a journal and a poem are not equivalent. Atwood herself recognized the possible equivalencies. A journal is not a poem; it is an intimate form of life writing, but it may be constructed as a poem. Or, more likely, a poem may be constructed "as if" it were an entry in a journal or, at least, as if it could be read as that entry in a journal. Therefore, a poem may be read as a personal document that has not been highly stylized in order to satisfy the intellectually superior. A poem may be read as a personal document that is a day-to-day record of the events and feelings in a person's life, usually written for the writer's own pleasure and edification. In other words, just the idea of possible equivalencies between a poem and a journal entry can cause us to wonder about the expectations we have of a genre in a way that stimulates ironic readings. My assumption about life writing in particular is that it constitutes a more inclusive and democratic genre. Because life writing implies the personal, the private, the idea of a self—as problematic as such a totalizing term is (Mohanty 184–86; Smith 3–23)—not only professional critics have access to its world and its depth. In life writing, the author does not want to pretend that he or she is absent from the text, and such apparent lack of pretention welcomes the student of literature as a person who is able to read and whose life experience is valued (Kadar 12) and implicated "in the network of other selves" (Worth 26). This approach is significant, especially now that Canadian universities have responded to multiculturalism by opening their doors to "minority" students and by searching for suitable new pedagogies.

In the case of *The Journals of Susanna Moodie*, for example, diverse students twig immediately to the question of genre. First, they know that Susanna Moodie is a historical figure and that she looks like the woman in the sideways sepia cameo on the cover. Students therefore anticipate a narrative of fact of some kind. Second, they read the word *Journals* atop this slim volume, and they know that these must be very short journals. Third, they read that the book is in fact a collection of poems, and immediately want to know: How could this be? In effect, the student is "tricked" into reading poetry. In other words, as a series of poems (or entries), the book has a narrative component, and as poems that pretend to be "real" personal documents, it is historical and therefore knowable. At least this is the assumption we have made about historical documents in relation to the purely aesthetic, an assumption Atwood's narrator interrogates by stimulating an ironic reading of knowledge itself.

It is possible that all reading begins with a question—a version of "What is behind this title?"—but in this case the question has been carefully constructed before we encounter the journals themselves. The cover of the book may represent the dream vision Atwood refers to in the "Afterword," a vision that had set the "white stage" that was also already "empty." Like the disappointed journal keeper, students talk about themselves as sometimes disillusioned, as they too live the lives of relatively "new" Canadians or of the children of immigrants for whom the buzz word still is "survival." This enjoyment is heightened when students hear the poems being read by Mia Anderson; the perfect voice is accented in a British way; it does not represent all by any means. What, then, does the British voice mean—in a land of many mother tongues and two official languages—and to the narrator's Mrs. Moodie, a subject of the kingdom of England? It is in relation to country and homeland that Atwood's *Survival* assists in reading the *Journals* as life writing.

One of the central assumptions of the near-ignored criticism-manifesto, *Survival: A Thematic Guide to Canadian Literature* (we must remember that the book was published in 1972), still intrigues—that is, it is impossible for Canadian writing to forget that Canada is a colony and that its surviving "selves," therefore, are inscribed with the symbols of colonization. Susanna Moodie is both colonizer (British) and metaphorically colonized (by the foreign wilderness). Belleville, for example, "is still no place for an english gentleman" ("Thoughts from Underground" 55). Even if Canada is chosen as home, there are many parts in which immigrants still "move in fear" as "exiles and invaders" ("Afterword" 62). A "violent duality" hints at the ontological level of the *Journals*. All persons must negotiate the painful chasm between feeling at home and feeling alienated from it, both geographically, as immigrants, and ontologically, as suffering beings, and therefore not free. Atwood poetically constructs geographical and ontological dislocation through this violent duality in Moodie's selves. Moreover, I would argue that this violent duality opens the way for someone akin to Judith Fetterley's resisting reader, a reader who feels not yet at home in the Canadian wilderness—indeed, in any geographical or metaphoric wilderness—and does not want to be forced into identification with the historical Moodie. A resisting reading coexists with Shirley Neuman's idea that life writing is "produced by the conjunction of, as well as the gaps between, the 'selves' inscribed by the conventions of different genres" (333). In the *Journals* there is both a "conjunction" between the "real" Susanna Moodie, the one portrayed in a strictly autobiographical sense in *Roughing It in the Bush*, and the "more real" Susanna Moodie, as underwritten by Atwood in the *Journals*.

Students are eager to talk about the gaps between selves, and the contradictions inherent in the two genres—autobiographical journals and poetry—and in what the poet calls "the inescapable doubleness of [Moodie's] own vision" ("Afterword" 63), a doubleness that she comes to accept by the time her journals are ended. Students want to answer the following questions: Why does Atwood call the book of poems "journals"? Why are the three different journals dated; is chronology important? What is the meaning of the "Afterword," in which the narrator is the poet and she unpretentiously offers assistance in reading the journals? Atwood gives us a preliminary answer to these questions in the untitled, "autobiographical," prefatory poem:

I take this picture of myself
and with my sewing scissors
cut out the face.

Now it is more accurate:

where my eyes were,
every-
thing appears   (7)

Who is the "I," we all ask? The narrator pretends to be Moodie. She says that cutting out "the" face with "sewing scissors" makes the "picture of myself" more accurate—and replaces the bodily "eyes" with vision. In other words, the narrator assumes the identity of the historical person, Susanna Moodie, whose body tells the physical fact of her trials as a "new Canadian" who "hated" the land that she must make her own. Moodie illustrates this attitude through the epigraph to her sister Agnes Strickland in *Roughing It in the Bush*: "I sketch from Nature, and the picture's true; / Whate'er the subject, whether grave or gay, / Painful experience in a distant land / Made it mine own" (McClelland, v).

Moodie's confession is not substantial enough for Atwood. The narrator of the *Journals* must rewrite Moodie, filling in the gaps of her "discursive" and "ornamental" autobiography ("Afterword" 62) with feminist hindsight (resistance) and interpretation (the "other" voice) (Hutcheon, *Canadian Postmodern* 156). In spite of threat, as the "Afterword" proclaims, "[Moodie] refuses to be ploughed under completely." Not only is her refusal an engaging political act (otherwise the "journals" would not exist), but her literary self is transhistorical; she lives now, beyond her death. She could be any "old woman on a Toronto bus who reveals the city as an unexplored, threatening wilderness" (64), including an urban wilderness.

As Atwood further explains in *Survival*, the historical Susanna Moodie is offended by nature, and included in "nature" are other immigrants. In this crude, ethnocentric identification of nature with immigrant is another poetic opportunity for anagogic doubleness and paradox. From "Thoughts from Underground" the journal keeper writes: "I said I loved it / and my mind saw double." In "Alternate Thoughts from Underground" the narrator admits "I feel / scorn but also pity." It is at this point that the *Journals* can be read alongside *Survival* for further "autobiographical" context. Atwood says:

Again and again we find [Moodie] gazing at the sublime natural goings-on in the misty distance—sunsets, mountains, spectacular views—only to be brought up short by disagreeable things in her immediate foreground, such as bugs, swamps, tree roots and other immigrants.
(*Survival* 51)

The contradictions between foreground and background, between the sublime and the "disagreeable," fulfill one of the gaps that Neuman contends produces life writing. Journals pass on and record messages and pleasures, those "thoughts from underground" that the outside world denies. Journal keepers sense that they are forgetting or hiding something or that, like many female protagonists, they are not supposed to feel whatever it is they do feel. Thus women reclaim the journal. Even though Atwood works within the dominant ideology, readers are cognizant of the mediations of language, of "the Double Voice" (the title of the final poem in journal 2). What is remembered is set against what is forgotten, and the ironies (of power and voice) are feminist and thus political in their implications: they resist.

In *Survival*, Atwood encodes Moodie's contradictions by connecting them with other "survival" narratives. She explains that Moodie feels both "faith in the Divine Mother [nature]" and "a feeling of hopeless imprisonment" (51). She also implies that Moodie's experience of the contradiction is simultaneous. Students understand this because it is the way they experience their own contradictions. It is the privilege of poetry to reenact contradiction with few words, thereby exaggerating the feeling of simultaneity. Having practiced journal writing in the classroom laboratory, students understand firsthand how they feel themselves doubled and many-voiced, all at the same time; in other words, how they resist exclusion from Moodie's world.

We are authorized now to say that simultaneity is, to steal Adrienne Rich's phrase, "of woman born." In no way do I want to argue that "only" women experience "life" this way. But I do want to remember that—with the psychoanalytic feminists, such as Nancy Chodorow, and with the resistance-postmodern theorists of subjectivity and difference, such as Paul Smith, Peter McLaren, and Chandra Mohanty—simultaneity is associated with women's "relatedness" and is often (therefore) undervalued socially. But the life genres in general make it easy for the poet to represent the simultaneity of experience as valued, and therefore these genres empower women narrators. They assume a certain "inability" to narrate distance, feigned or otherwise. Indeed, without intimacy, feeling, comfort, the reader cannot "feel" the wisdom in the words, cannot really feel the poignancy of, in the case of the *Journals*, a female narrator's estrangement from the authorized discourse. Frank Davey is right when he declares that "in Atwood's texts [there is] a major feminist ideological critique of western culture that, while incorporating Ontario Loyalist and pastoral mythologies, overshadow[s] these in extent and power" (*Reading* 66). What a multiethnic classroom can add to Davey's comment is another critique: "a place where marginalized groups ['emergent ethnicities'] can speak from" (McLaren 128).

My own view of the *Journals* is that Atwood wants us to feel wisdom; she believes that to do so is our collective right, and as much as she wants to represent the life of a historical figure (i.e., "from a distance"), she also wants to contextualize her own life in 1970. However, we can only know that Atwood's narrator perceives some captivating dissonance between the poem and the journal, between a lyric (with images) and real history (a master-narrative with dates), between nineteenth-century Upper Canada and contemporary gendered, racist, ethnocentric, and suffering society. As the narrator says in "Further Arrivals," from journal 1: "I refuse to look in a mirror." As if looking in a mirror would not help, yes, but also because "refusing" is Moodie's trope. The narrator continues: "Whether the wilderness is / real or not / depends on who lives there" (13). It is Atwood's revision of Susanna Moodie's life story that engages us. The narrator problematizes the refusing, and therefore the gap between selves. As journal 2 begins, the foreigners, "the immigrants" Moodie sometimes deplored, become an aspect of her shifting self: "I wish I could forget them / and so forget myself" ("The Immigrants" 33). The desire to forget this shifting self constructs a narrative that collides with the more realistic autobiographical narrative Moodie herself has constructed in *Roughing It in the Bush*. The "journals" then represent the life Atwood imagines Moodie forgot to write, the one that is not public.

When students keep a journal of their own, they understand how one "real" self is reserved for public consumption; and another, no less real but less fixed, is written in a genre in which the author's expectation has always been that no one else will read it. As mentioned earlier, the experiment of assuming diverse personae assists students in unraveling the exciting contradictions between our expectations of a genre and what actually transpires in the course of its delivery. Students learn that these contradictions may be played out in a multivoiced narrative that prods them to inhabit their own contradictory and "different" subject locations themselves and to take stock of differences in a responsible, collective fashion. Thus students soon realize that their most personal entries are also cover-ups, frame-ups (Culler ix), and as such are constructed by an inconsistent, shifting, and fallible writing "self." Since Foucault, moreover, the self is acknowledged as a social construct quite apart from the historical person on whom that self is based. Differences in self-representation raise questions about how assumptions about language, gender, subjectivity, and ethnicity shape the discourse of the journal, differences that emerge when students are asked to assume Moodie's persona, and then Atwood's. We realize, too, that the persona is identified as much by its prejudices as by the material with which it is framed.

Finally, it seems that students are captivated by five complications, some of them ironies, in *The Journals of Susanna Moodie*. First, Atwood's *Journals*, meant for public consumption, also exploit the conventions of the journal genre in reproducing private, intimate, even secret thoughts and feelings. Second, the *Journals'* poem structure complicates our expectations that journals are necessarily a prose genre. Third, because these verse journals are not written by the person after which they are named, they present conflicting personal narratives and further intrigue the readers. As Atwood says in the quotation that opens this article, Moodie's books "had little shape." Fourth, the "subject" is a historical figure, remembered as a woman who confronted Canadian "nature" and survived; but clearly, at least according to Atwood,

Moodie left many silences in her own story of herself. These silences gave Atwood an opportunity to fill in the gap, to foreground and "shape" what she called "the personality of Mrs. Moodie," a personality that "reflects many of the obsessions still with us." Fifth, the historical figure is an anglophone immigrant whose prejudices inform the narrator's contradictory definition of "Canadian," of "wilderness," and, finally, of "city." As Frank Davey notes in *Margaret Atwood: A Feminist Poetics*, Susanna Moodie is a privileged, white, British-born immigrant, whose interests represent the dominant culture and discourse and, therefore, reproduce inequalities. But as Davey also recognizes, these interests are displaced in the *Journals* by another identity—gender (*Reading* 65–70). I would add to that formulation the more ambiguous identity of "home." We must ask: Whose home (country, colony, language, race) is this? Is it the one I understand is mine?

Therefore, like Moodie's "refusing," the most complicated reading of the *Journals* is also the most resisting. As Chandra Talpade Mohanty has explained, "knowledge, the very act of knowing, is related to the power of self-definition" (184). The only way many students (and some teachers) can "know" this "home" is by resisting it with their own self-definitions—unfixed as they may be, personal and culturally specific. Stimulating a traditional reading of Atwood's already politicized reading of Moodie as empowered (she "has become the spirit of the land she once hated" ["Afterword" 64]), as well as a further resistance to both, is a pedagogic challenge; it may even be a pedagogic responsibility. As Mohanty, Worth, and McLaren illustrate in their attempts to theorize multiculturalism, one way to lay claim to alternative histories is to uncover and reclaim subjugated knowledges. Mohanty elaborates, however, that laying claim means "taken the question of experience seriously" (185). Atwood has taken Moodie's experiences seriously. She concludes:

> [Moodie] claims to be an ardent Canadian patriot while all the time she is standing back from the country and criticizing it as though she were a detached observer, a stranger. Perhaps that is the way we still live. We are all immigrants to this place even if we were born here: the country is too big for anyone to inhabit completely, and in the parts unknown to us we move in fear, exiles and invaders. This country is something that must be chosen—it is so easy to leave—and if we do choose it we are still choosing a violent duality.
>
> ("Afterword" 62)

What will the student choose? It is in the Atwood classroom that student experiences, too, can be taken this seriously.

NOTE

[1] The epigraph of this essay is on page 62 of the *Journals*.

Atwood's *You Are Happy*: Power Politics, Gender Roles, and the Transformation of Myth

Helane Levine-Keating

Many undergraduate students are used to studying anthologized poems by a smorgasbord of poets, rather than a whole volume of poetry by an individual poet. Despite its complex, four-sectioned, multipersonaed structure, Margaret Atwood's *You Are Happy* (1974) is a volume of poetry that works successfully in diverse classes. Although it is currently out of print in North America, it is available almost in its entirety in both the United States and Canadian editions of Atwood's *Selected Poems, 1965–1975*. An abundant use of imagery, irony, personae, and allusion and short, accessible poems make it an excellent teaching vehicle in an introduction to poetry or introduction to literature class, and I have used it in advanced poetry and contemporary poetry classes as well as comparative literature and myth and literature classes, to demonstrate the thematic and imagistic integrity of the poetic sequence, the imagistic patterns of the tragic and comic vision, archetypal patterns in poetry, and the transformation of myth as a means of making public what is personal. Because *You Are Happy* portrays the struggle of a woman to escape her own victimization and enter into a trusting and liberated relationship with a man—a relation predicated on mutual vulnerability, in which the participants are, in Atwood's terms, no longer at war but "fellow traveller[s]" on the same "journey"—I have taught it in my British and American women poets course, and it lends itself to both women in literature classes and women's studies classes. Gender and power politics structure the four sections of the book as these sections trace the stages of this quest. What is also striking about these poems is not simply the movement from destructive anger to wholeness but also the use of the recurring images in a landscape that changes from "tragic" to "comic" in its depiction, suggesting the evolution of the female quest for fulfillment on many levels.

In the first section, the voice of the unidentified female speaker is angry and humiliated, and her attempts at "speech"—really dialogue—have failed. The opening poem, "Newsreel: Man and Firing Squad," establishes the landscape for this especially bitter section with its opening words: "A botched job." A man whose blindfold slips, enabling him to watch his own destruction as a firing squad shoots him, becomes a metaphor for two people watching as their relationship self-destructs. In this landscape neither person takes responsibility for this destruction: "We depart, we say good-bye / Yet each of us remains in the same place, / staked out and waiting" (*Selected Poems, 1965–1975*, Houghton, 179). Since neither one will budge, the "ground between" is blamed for moving them away from each other, preventing connection.

Other barriers preventing fulfillment are the difficulty in communicating verbally and the inability to see each other as whole, positive people. "Useless," the second poem in this section, focuses on words these two never said, "attempts at speech" (*You Are Happy* 10); in the poem "November," with its grim landscape in which "the sheep hangs upside down from the rope," the speaker complains: "Mournful November / this is the image / you invent for me" (*Selected Poems* 180). Bleak and despairing landscapes further characterize the poems "Digging," "Tricks with Mirrors," and "You Are Happy" and foreshadow themes and imagery of subsequent sections. As Sherrill Grace has written, "The poems [of *You Are Happy*] exist sequentially, but in order to understand them we can complement a linear reading with a reflexive one, working back and forth over the poems in terms of the images" (*Violent Duality* 65). In "Digging," for example, the speaker, armed with a shovel, encounters a tiny rodent pelvis while she digs in the barnyard. Her rancor forces her to perceive the body part as a potential amulet to be used to protect her from love. This bone, what Atwood calls "the strict dogma of teeth," suggests the *vagina dentata* motif and perhaps, by extension, the necklace of skulls worn by Kali, the dark Hindu goddess of creation and destruction, for "the destructive side of the Feminine, the destructive and deathly womb, appears most frequently in the archetypal form of a mouth bristling with teeth" (Neumann 168). As long as the speaker wants both to destroy and to remain a victim simultaneously, she will represent the "Terrible Mother," an archetype conveying male fear of women's maternal and sexual power.

In "Tricks with Mirrors," the speaker portrays herself as a mirror of her lover, suggesting that his hardness and coldness are reflected in her, that ultimately they are alike. In the second part of the poem, the speaker issues a warning: while the lover's body is "flawless," "there is more to a mirror" than his reflection—there are the frame and the nails (*Selected Poems* 184). Her anger at his self-absorption makes her want to crucify him or scratch him, as the nails on the mirror's back suggest; although in the third part she is proud of her craftiness as a mirror giving him back himself as he really is, her anger at his inability to see her surfaces in the fourth part, with its image of her "trapped" behind a door. The irony of the final words of the fifth part—"Perhaps I am not a mirror. / Perhaps I am a pool."—suggests he is drowning in her lack of ego boundaries and she can only accept without a choice what falls into her (186).

"You Are Happy," the final poem of this section and the most chilling in its landscape and mood, opens with the couple walking by the water in a winter fierce in its brutality. Only the man to whom the speaker directs her words is actually happy in this cold. He seems to enjoy the isolation just as he enjoys "the images / hitting into [his] eyes / like needles, crystals" (187). Images of "wind shoving," "erosion," and "gravel rasping" convey that nothing about the landscape is positive or even neutral. Like the decapitated deer carcass, the speaker clearly experiences herself as a victim—of intense cold, of her lover, of the destructiveness implicit in many male-female relationships.

A diverse catalog of personae are the speakers in the second section, "Songs of the Transformed," a series of poems dependent on imagery, metaphor, irony, and allusion. Here both men and women have been transformed—perhaps by Circe—into the animals their "real lives" suggest: pigs, bulls, rats, worms, and so on, yet the two most striking persona poems in this section are not "animal songs" but "Siren Song" and "Corpse Song." "Siren Song," alluding both to Greek mythology and Homer's *Odyssey*, foreshadows the arid, dangerous landscape of the temptress Circe's island. Just as the poems of the first section portray a woman and a man trapped in their roles, unable to move beyond learned parts, this female siren relentlessly traps men, preying on their vulnerability. Ironically, the poem traps the reader in much the same way sirens ostensibly trapped lonely sailors. When the siren cries "Help me! / Only you, only you can, / you are unique" (*Selected Poems* 196), she is "playing upon the egocentric sense of self-importance that we all individually feel" (Rosenberg, *Margaret Atwood* 76), enticing us by promising to tell us (or her victim) "the secret" of her magic if we (or the victim) will help get her out of her "bird suit"—the costume she's sick of wearing. In the final lines of this poem, however, her true cynicism emerges, for these words are, in fact, the siren song itself, as the speaker adds, "Alas / it is a boring song / but it works every time" (*Selected Poems* 196), and "the poem becomes a paradigm for our inability to break free of the patterns that control and deaden our existence" (Rosenberg, *Margaret Atwood* 76). Similarly, "Corpse Song" envisions a dead or deadened person trapped in his or her resentment: "I bring you something / you do not want: / news of the country / I am trapped in" (*Selected Poems* 199).

In the third section, the speaker of "Circe/Mud Poems" is Circe herself, the goddess/temptress, and the series reflects her perspective. This sequence works best when students are familiar with the complete *Odyssey* or at least the Circe chapter; if they are not, I give them a handout of the chapter and a plot synopsis. The twenty-four-poem cycle suggests the repetitive cycle of the earth's daily rotation, alluding to Circe's position as daughter of Helios, the sun, as well as conveying the circular nature of both her own name and the palindromic name of her island, Aiaia. In Atwood's version, a subjective, bitter, bored Circe resents the power of Odysseus and slowly becomes aware she is a victim—not merely Homer's crafty sorceress—through Odysseus's sojourn on her island. The series functions as the transition from the first part of *You Are Happy* to the fourth part, from angry female victim beginning to recognize both her power and the sources of her victimization to a "whole" human being who perceives life's options. Although the first poem—untitled, as are all twenty-four—begins with the arrival of Odysseus and his "power impinging," by the twenty-fourth poem Circe realizes that a new, fertile landscape that both she and Odysseus have never before visited might be possible.

In the first six poems, the uninviting landscape, with its "blunted trunks," "charred branches," "seared rocks," and "worn down" grass and roots (201, 204), recalls the equally grim landscape of the volume's first section. Like the landscape, language, too, is bereft of life as Circe spends her days collecting the "few muted syllables left / over" (204). Unable to see herself as a victim because she is in what Atwood calls victim *"Position One: To deny the fact you are a victim" (Survival* 36)—she disclaims any responsibility for Odysseus's arrival: "I made no choice / I decided nothing / One day you simply appeared" *(Selected Poems* 205). As long as Odysseus—the archetypal hero—can be blamed for everything, Circe has no cause to look within herself or blame her own magic.

By the seventh poem, a new theme is introduced: the awareness of subjectivity. Without this awareness, there is no way to move ahead in the quest for mutuality. After describing the ennui of her island, she tells the apostrophized Odysseus that "travel brochures . . . do this better" and "all advertisements are slanted, including this / one" (207). In the eighth poem, Circe's subjective fear of being hurt surfaces, a subjectivity entirely absent from Homer's equally slanted version, and by the ninth poem, submission, giving, and vulnerability emerge as Circe's reserve softens. While the eleventh poem returns to the brutal terms of "Tricks with Mirrors," as Circe says "Face of steel. / Look at me and see your reflection" (210), in the twelfth poem Circe moves from Basic Victim Position One to Basic Victim Position Two: *"To acknowledge the fact that you are a victim, but to explain this as an act of Fate, the Will of God, the dictates of Biology (in the case of women, for instance), the necessity decreed by History, or Economics, or the Unconscious, or any other large general powerful idea" (Survival* 37). Circe blames "the fist, withered and strung / on a chain around [her] neck" for the command to transform Odysseus into an animal and refers to "the worn moon rituals." Even her magic has become barren, like her island and the language men and women speak. Yet when Circe says at the end of the poem, "You unbuckle the fingers of the fist / you order me to trust you" *(Selected Poems* 211), she is still blaming some power greater than she for her own actions, just as Odysseus is still brazenly believing that his force and manhood can engender trust. By the fifteenth poem, however, Odysseus has obviously become Circe's lover, and, despite her critical eye, admiration has begun to color her description of him. This "flawed," imperfect Odysseus—unlike the cold and "flawless" man of "Tricks with Mirrors"—is the survivor Circe longs for back in the second Circe/Mud poem. Yet the poem's last two lines, "This is not what I want / but I want this also" (213), suggest her ambivalence.

The powerful sixteenth poem, a prose poem, tells the story of the "mud woman" and suggests the meaning of the second half of the section's title:

"Mud Poems." This mud woman is both a male creation and a male projection of desire, for this woman possesses neither head nor hands nor feet, instruments of independence and autonomy. Instead, she is breasts, belly, womb, all-embracing, nonthreatening, mute. With the mud woman for lover, the traveler need not be threatened by the fact that "a woman's ability to perform sexually is limitless compared to his own" (Hays 290) or that another, more potent or pleasing man might be preferred over him. The paradox, of course, is that the mud woman in her simplicity is also a temptation for Circe: "Is / this what I would like to be? It would be so simple" (*Selected Poems* 214). As Atwood illustrates, women continue to be conflicted by the temptation to be male-defined or male-identified, in lieu of the harder work required by self-definition and individuation.

In the eighteenth poem, in which the amulet image of "Digging" reappears, Circe admits to her fear of the "queen of two dimensions" who "wears a necklace of small teeth" and, knowing "the ritual," gets "results" (216). Here she alludes to Hecate, the crone, who—when angry—"can close the wombs of living creatures, and all life stands still" (Neumann 170). Able to condemn Circe to a barren existence, Hecate is also the one who encourages Circe not to "accept, accept, accept"—like the "pool" of "Tricks with Mirrors" or the "mud woman"—but to say instead, "I don't have to take / anything you throw into me" (216). Although the only way for her not to "accept" is to close herself over, this is still a progression from Basic Victim Position Two to Basic Victim Position Three, where "You can make real decisions about how much of your position can be changed and how much can't (you can't make it stop snowing; you can stop blaming the snow for everything that's wrong)" (*Survival* 38).

The nineteenth through twenty-third poems all occur during a period of time from the middle to the end of Odysseus's sojourn. By now they have established a relationship that extends far beyond the initial power struggle: thus, he has come to trust Circe and is "no longer cautious" (*Selected Poems* 217), and she has come to care for him to the extent that she is capable of jealousy on his account. Since Circe knows how the future will spin out (at the hands of the Fates), she knows with certainty that Odysseus will eventually sail home to Penelope, his wife. Unexpectedly, however, the landscape in poem 22 shifts to winter, for winter suggests the year's end—the length of Odysseus's sojourn on Aiaia as well as Circe's own coldness as she closes him off, preparing herself for his departure. Since winter is the dissolution phase, the phase of darkness in the seasonal cycle of the year, as well as in the organic cycle of human life, myths of the triumph of these powers as well as the defeat of the hero abound (Frye, *Fables* 16), and in the twenty-third poem Circe focuses on her own darkness after Odysseus departs. Frightened that once Odysseus leaves, her magic will also disappear, she can't imagine how she will be able to return to the boring, repetitious, unenlightened existence she lived before his arrival. When Homer's objective temptress is transformed into a subjective human being, she, too, has a future.

The first half of the twenty-fourth poem describes life on the island as if it were a motion picture one could replay and replay, running the film backward or forward at will. Nothing is new, for there is a set pattern to follow. Yet in a striking revelation, Circe says, "There are two islands / at least," and "they do not exclude each other." Furthermore, on the first island, she is "right." Just as "all advertisements are slanted," this first island is Circe's "correct" version of what has transpired. Like the circular twenty-four poems of the series or hours in a day, it all begins again "without looking, the animals / the blackened trees, the arrivals / the bodies, words" (*Selected Poems* 222), and there is nothing to free them from this timeless loop, always ending with his departure. The second half of the poem, by contrast, flirts with the possibility of Basic Victim Position Four, "a position not for victims but for those who have never been victims at all, or for ex-victims. . . . In Position Four, creative activity of all kinds becomes possible. . . . Victor/Victim games are obsolete. You don't even have to concentrate on rejecting the role of Victim, because the role is no longer a temptation for you" (*Survival* 38–39). This is a position—or in the poem, a landscape—the speaker has not yet experienced "because it has never happened" (*Selected Poems* 222).

The landscape of these last six stanzas is entirely new: the speaker and her lover walk together, but there is no feeling of isolation. The warm and autumnal yellow, gray, and orange replace the stark red and white of earlier poems and the "low pink sun" of "You Are Happy." The orange of the apples is "astonishing," and instead of the "crystals" and "needles" that "hit into the eyes" in "You Are Happy," even the cold is softened, benign. The lone bird "running across the glaring / road" of "You Are Happy" multiplies into four birds that disappear with no qualifications; the water that "turns / a long way down over the raw stone, / ice crust[ing] around it," is transformed into "a stream, not frozen yet"; the violent images of "In the ditch a deer / carcass, no head" become the peaceful image of "in the mud / beside it the track of a deer" (223). Ostensibly, then, by moving out of a victim position, one no longer sees winter as antagonistic, synonymous with oppressor, for "Only the general comic or tragic context . . . determines the interpretation of any symbol: this is obvious with relatively neutral archetypes like the island, which may be Prospero's island or Circe's" (Frye, *Fables* 20).

In the fourth and final section of *You Are Happy*, a shared, loving relationship with a partner begins to be lived, and everything is possible. The speaker takes responsibility for herself for the first time, and in "Is / Not," the second poem of the series, she proclaims, "you are not my doctor / you are not my cure, / nobody has that / power, you are merely a fellow / traveller" (*Selected Poems* 224). Instead of the angry, grudging tone of the earlier poems, a new, optimistic perspective has begun to surface. In "Four

Auguries," an owl "With its hooded predator's / eyes" blesses the speaker and her lover (231), and in "Head against White," a poem recalling Circe's description of Odysseus in the twelfth poem, the speaker actually experiences transcendence and mutuality through her own love: "oval / dent in the skull / my fingers return to mention with touch, cherish / as though the wound is my own" (232). But instead of Circe's somewhat resentful admiration of Odysseus's "marred" body, this speaker experiences her lover—flawed as he is—as both self and other.

Movement toward fulfillment of the speaker's quest quickens with the last three poems of the series and volume. The ambivalence of the earlier poems, followed by the inability "to say how much I want you" of "Four Evasions" (*You Are Happy* 77), has finally been transformed to a cautious but clear "yes" in "There Is Only One of Everything." As the speaker watches her lover dancing by himself in the kitchen, spoon in one hand and hair sticking up, she is at last able to articulate her feelings: "I can even say it, / though only once and it won't / last: I want this. I want / this" *Selected Poems* (236). Likewise, "Late August" directly transforms the death-polluted landscape of the first three sections into a landscape characterized by consummation.

The concluding poem of both series and volume, "Book of Ancestors," sets in relief much of "Circe/Mud Poems." Here "the demands of the gods" are a metaphor for the age-old patterns of societal behavior, which must be overcome if love is to exist. In the second part of the poem, the speaker destroys shackles and myths, allowing no distortions to mutilate this new landscape. And in the final part of the poem, the female quest for wholeness, individuation, and transcendence of history's limitations is completed. Both speaker and lover undergo transformation to achieve their goal of openness and wholeness. Not only must he cease to be the powerful and overwhelming hero who she tends to forget is really a mortal, but she must cease to be crafty Circe, the evil/wise sorceress, for this role locks her in a primordial, unliberated state. Just as Homer's Odysseus must descend to the underworld and consult with the hermaphroditic Tiresias as a necessary part of his journey home, so must Atwood's persona, the contemporary woman, plumb the depths of her own being to expand her consciousness, reject victimization, and arrive at the world of fulfilled desires (Levine-Keating 109–10).

While the tragic vision "sees the quest only in the form of its ordained cycle" (Frye, *Fables* 19), the world of fulfilled desires is analogous to the comic vision, another form that the quest can take. "Circe/Mud Poems," with such lines as "the events run themselves through / almost without us," represents the tragic vision of the quest. Circe, her animals, and her landscape correspond to aspects of the tragic vision characterized by the presence of the witch or harlot, "beasts and birds of prey," "rocks and ruins," and "a sinister forest . . . or a heath or wilderness, or a tree of death," reflecting Northrop Frye's theory that the quest myth can be seen as a pattern of imagery. In contrast, the final section belongs to the comic vision, in which the hero seeks fulfillment. The imagery of these poems corresponds to the predominant images of the comic world, a world of fulfillment marked by "symposium, communion, order, friendship and love," as well as "marriage or some equivalent consummation" (19). Instead of the frightening animals of the tragic vision, the comic vision is populated by domesticated or gentler animals; consequently, "the deer carcass" of "You Are Happy" is now the "track of a deer" that is alive in the last half of the final Circe poem. As "the whole comic series, especially the tree, can be conceived as luminous or fiery," it is fitting that "Eating Fire" envisions the lover as a tree, lit up from within. Finally, in the unformed world of the comic vision, there is traditionally a fourfold river (20), much as there are four birds and a stream on Circe's imagined "second island" and "Four Auguries" in the final section.

Thus in *You Are Happy*, Margaret Atwood's transformation of her contemporary Circe from the tragic vision to the comic vision clearly demonstrates a quest for fulfillment. By exploring the entire volume of poems, students will be better able to understand the images that define this quest and the inner emotional experience of this particular female struggle. Students are empowered by the speaker's transformation from victim to partner. That Atwood does not stop with the tragic vision of the female quest myth but moves into the comic vision signals a new dimension and a new female hero for the archetype of the quest.

Atwood's Female Quest-Romance:
A Psychoanalytic Approach to *Surfacing*

Shuli Barzilai

A father's absence sets and keeps the plot of *Surfacing* (1972) in motion. In a typical travel-romance manner, the protagonist leaves the city, ventures into infrequently traveled country, undergoes a series of trials, and after several valiant but failed attempts, finds the sought-for truth (about her father, about her self) and presumably returns to civilization, transformed in the crucible of her experience. The call to seek her father, a call leading to the daughter's quest for self-discovery or voyage in, comes from without: "Your father is gone, nobody cant find him" (Virago, 24; ch. 2). The mother, already dead several years before the father vanishes, appears only at the margins of the main story. Like many narratives about women's lives, *Surfacing* can be seen as predominantly, though not exclusively, constituted in relation to men: the present search for the father and the past affair with a married man.

Margaret Atwood's remarks about her next novel, *Lady Oracle* (1976), seem to reinforce this patrilineal orientation:

> There's a passage in Virgil's *Aeneid* which I found very useful, where Aeneas goes to the underworld to learn about his future. He's guided by the Sibyl and he learns what he has to from his dead father, and then he returns home. (Sandler 16)

The goal of this mythic journey is the lesson of the father, whereas the sibylic, or feminine, function is reduced to an intermediary, a go-between for men. *Surfacing* coincides with the traditional pattern, even though Atwood's voyager is a young woman. What role, then, does the mother play in the protagonist's quest? More broadly, in what ways does this narrative of descent and return diverge from the male quest-romance, if fundamental differences exist at all?

I teach *Surfacing* in an undergraduate seminar on voyages of self-discovery in the twentieth-century English novel, including such works as Joseph Conrad's *Heart of Darkness*, James Joyce's *A Portrait of the Artist as a Young Man*, Doris Lessing's *The Summer before the Dark*, Patrick White's *A Fringe of Leaves*, and Virginia Woolf's *The Voyage Out* or *To the Lighthouse*. The direction our classroom explorations take—and I clarify this approach from the first meeting—is informed by psychoanalytic criticism and feminist theory. To demonstrate the types of response a psychoanalytic approach can provide, as well as the ways its presuppositions reflect certain sociocultural beliefs, I ask students to prepare excerpts from Sigmund

Freud's essay "Femininity." Freud elaborates a theory of libidinal normalization that suggests one possible reading of the mother's role. After summarizing the main points of his argument, we examine its relevance to *Surfacing*.

In young boys, Freud writes, anxiety about castration (the "castration complex") occurs after they learn from seeing the female genitals that "the organ which they value so highly need not necessarily accompany the body." The parallel discovery in a young girl—"the sight of the genitals of the other sex"—teaches her that she is already castrated: "Her self-love is mortified by the comparison with the boy's far superior equipment." Hence the daughter proceeds to blame and reject the woman who put her at such a disadvantage. Freud relates how surprised he was to find that "girls hold their mothers responsible for their lack of a penis" (124, 125, 126). Compensation for this "lack" is sought when the girl turns to her father for the gift her mother failed to bestow. The wish for the missing organ is replaced by a wish for a baby—initially from the father himself and, especially, for a baby boy.

These by-now-familiar and deconstructed arguments can nevertheless account for a sequence of episodes in *Surfacing*. (For advanced students interested in a critique of Freud's theories of female sexuality, I recommend Luce Irigaray's "The Blind Spot of an Old Dream of Symmetry.") The narrator presents herself as distant and estranged from her mother. She visits her dying mother in the hospital after several years of absence from home: " 'I'm not going to your funeral,' I said. I had to lean close to her, the hearing in one of her ears was gone. I wanted her to understand in advance, and approve" (22; ch. 2). From a Freudian perspective, the daughter's need to have her mother understand and even approve may be read as a disguise, or masking—and the narrator is a cover artist, literally—of a deferred wish for reprisal. The genital deficiency first apprehended in childhood has been intensified through the adult daughter's unwanted abortion. Retribution finds its exact and last-minute expression in the announcement "I'm not going to your funeral." An absence will be paid for by an absence. The frustrated wish for a symbolic equivalent (a baby) from her surrogate father (an older married lover) could also explain her increasing alienation from reality, an alienation culminating in a psychotic episode.

The difficulty with this psychoanalytic reading, I propose, begins with an ambiguity concerning the male organ. There is a slippage in Freud's formulations between literal and symbolic domains. At times, Freud refers to an actual organ; but, in such phrases as "the boy's far superior equipment," the societal valuation of masculinity takes over. In yet other instances, the two domains are indistinguishable: "as a result of the discovery of women's lack of a penis they [women] are debased in value for girls just as they are for boys" (see "Femininity" 125–27). This blurring allows the equation of a symbol of creativity and potency (as constructed by patriarchal thinking) with male genitalia. And thus an anatomical difference translates into an irreversible deficiency for woman: the symbolic is perceived as literal, the cultural endowments of man as natural.

At this point, I introduce a second term into the discussion of sexual differences. Jacques Lacan, a revisionary reader of Freud's writings, proposes that the signifier "phallus" be used to designate the symbolic function and "penis" retained for the literal. As Lacan defines the concept of the phallus, "It is even less the organ, penis or clitoris, that it symbolizes" (285). In other words, the phallus is not itself a body part. Rather, it acquires the potential for symbolizing the presence as well as the absence of a desired object. It is no more the property (or lack) of man than of woman. If we bear this distinction in mind, we can counter Freud's assertion of a biological disadvantage by another claim: little girls are not always already castrated. One is not born but becomes a female without a phallus.

From the symbolic dimension just delineated, I now suggest, Atwood's protagonist is doubly deprived before her journey begins. At an unspecified point in the past, she allowed herself to be cut off from two crucial sources of self-empowerment and creativity. These experiences of symbolic castration are specifically related to her gendered identity. First, she capitulated to her lover's persuasion that she compromise her artistic vocation: "I do posters, covers, a little advertising and magazine work. . . . he said I should study something I'd be able to use because there have never been any important woman artists" (52; ch. 6). Her lover-teacher untaught her. He exploited what Sandra Gilbert and Susan Gubar identify as woman's anxiety of authorship: "a radical fear that she cannot create" (*Madwoman* 49). Second, in further compliance with her lover's wishes, she severed another vital part. The abandoned creation of her child followed (and perhaps was facilitated by) the renunciation of her art. She installed his portrait of her as a nonartist and a nonmother within herself.

Images of dismemberment, of sundered connections, of castration symptomatically recur in her narrative. We look at passages such as these: "it [the baby] was taken away from me, exported, deported. A section of my own life, sliced off from me" (48; ch. 5); and "I'd allowed myself to be cut in two. Woman sawn apart in a wooden crate. . . . I was nothing but a head, or . . . a severed thumb" (108; ch. 12). Similarly, her childhood recollection of the one-handed woman known as "Madame" may be read as a self-fulfilling prophecy for the little girl and an analogue for the adult narrator: "I wanted to know how the hand had come off (perhaps she had taken it off herself) . . . and especially whether my own hand could ever come off like that; but I never asked, I must have been afraid of the answers" (27; ch. 3). In the parenthetical speculation, which amplifies a seemingly fantastic way of becoming crippled, she implicates the woman in the loss of her own hand. Madame of the missing hand represents the amputation to which the protagonist acceded by failing to resist the male "muse" who negated her creative endeavors. As her journey to the interior begins, she is bereft of an artist's hand, often mute or inarticulate ("I was . . . translating badly, a dialect problem" [76; ch. 9]), cut off from her past through partial amnesia and estranged from self and surroundings.

I return to the question of the mother: What influence does she have on the daughter's quest? If that quest entails self-recovery after near annihilation, how can the dead mother impede, help, or have any effect at all? As we have seen, Freud contends that mothers generally represent a source of disappointment for their daughters; the little girl therefore turns to the paternal possessor of the "longed-for" penis. Yet a few comments Freud makes about the preoedipal mother-daughter relationship allow a different reading of what the protagonist lost with her abortion. After completing his narrative of the girl's repudiation of maternal agency in favor of the powerful father, Freud briefly presents this prestory:

> It has not escaped us that the girl has wished for a baby earlier . . . that, of course, was the meaning of her playing with dolls. But that play was not in fact an expression of her femininity; it served as an identification with her mother with the intention of substituting activity for passivity. *She* was playing the part of her mother and the doll was herself.

Two points require elaboration here. According to Freud, identification with the mother is not compatible with a fully evolved femininity; moreover, passivity needs to be reinstated at a later stage for womanliness to receive its mature "expression"—namely, penis envy and the concomitant wish for a baby. Freud nonetheless acknowledges that, in "substituting activity for passivity," the little girl who plays with dolls experiences the pleasures of self-mastery and control, as well as identification with her mother. In her childhood games, "she could do with the baby everything that her mother used to do with her" ("Femininity" 128).

This psychoanalytic account implies that, at a very early phase of female self-formation, a chain of identifications is established: mother-daughter-baby. Even if what Freud calls "the wish for a penis" alters this chain, there are no grounds to presume the baby doll completely ceases to represent both the subject and the tie with her mother ("Femininity" 128). As Freud observes elsewhere, nothing is less easily surrendered than "a pleasure . . . once experienced"—and he himself identifies the pleasurable mastery that infuses the preoedipal, mother-connected girl's activities ("Creative Writers" 145).

Because the narrator of *Surfacing* lives in a state of disavowal (denial) in which the actual past is veiled, it is difficult to reconstruct the mother-daughter bond before the events that led to her leaving home. Nevertheless, her unwanted abortion apparently triggered a break in the chain of primary identifications. For while the ostensible purpose of her journey remains the call to find the father, the need to reestablish connection with the mother also becomes compelling for her. Traditional mythic roles thus are reversed: Persephone sets out in search of the lost Demeter, as if the mother had been carried away instead of the daughter. (I recommend Sherrill Grace's essay "In Search of Demeter" and Marianne Hirsch's "Prelude" to *The Mother/Daughter Plot* as background reading.) Viewed from another perspective, "nine years" (34; ch. 4) or more before her present quest, the protagonist was swept off her feet by a lover; yet issues of choice and responsibility entered into her story as they do not in the myth. She belatedly acknowledges, "I could have said no but I didn't" (145; ch. 17). In the disavowed past, after agreeing to the abortion but deferring her complicity and guilt—"they had planted death in me like a [pomegranate?] seed" (144; ch. 17)—she felt compelled to depart from home.

We now retrace the narrator's return home, stressing the search for her mother. Class discussion focuses on numerous objects, words, and gestures signaling this unavowed but crucial quest. For example, while still on the road, the protagonist remembers the Lifesavers her mother handed out whenever she and her brother felt carsick. Shortly after, "seeing the old road billowing along at a distance . . . makes me reach into my bag for the Lifesavers I brought" (14; ch. 1). Since almost any candy might do, I ask, why are Lifesavers particularly appropriate? The brand name gradually becomes emblematic of an asymmetry between mother and daughter. The narrator mentions two childhood scenarios in which her mother figures as a literal lifesaver. In one instance, she saved the brother from drowning: hauling him out of the lake, the mother "raised [him] from the dead" (74; ch. 8). In another, she shooed away an enormous bear that invaded their campsite, leaving the young daughter convinced her mother "knew a foolproof magic formula": "That was the picture I kept, my mother, seen from the back, arms upraised as though she was flying" (79; ch. 9). The association of flight with mythical, maternal prowess reappears at a turning point in her quest for connection.

The narrator also recalls, directly after she herself kills a fish, how her mother found even wasps worthy of protection: " 'Don't bother them and they won't bother you,' our mother would say when they lit on our plates." The memory of her mother's respect for life follows an allusion to the abortion: "I've killed something, made it [fish or fetus] dead" (65; ch. 7). All occasions do inform against the mother-haunted daughter. To keep live bait inside a can, she uses grocery paper and a rubber band. This action too evokes a memory. "My mother was a saver: rubber bands, string, safety pins, jam jars" (61–62). Jars, as the alert reader knows, often are associated with her unborn child. Thus the words "jars" and "a saver" are antinomies, implying a distance between the daughter as destroyer and the mother as preserver. Lifesavers, rubber bands, hand outstretched to birds (77, 93, 107; chs. 9, 11, 12), or recycling her mother's exact words (44, 65; chs. 5, 7): the narrator creates a field of transitional, mother-related symbols to help bridge the gulf between them. Whereas D. W. Winnicott uses the concept of transitional objects and phenomena to mark the child's first efforts to build a world independent of the mother (see 14–17), for Atwood's protagonist these symbols serve an opposite purpose. The ties necessary for her sense of continuity and identity have been rent. So the efforts to make amends through objects, tokens, messages may be read as progressive and not regressive; contra Freud, libidinal normalization consists in the daughter's reidentification with her mother. In other words, she can move forward only after going back.

This tendency culminates during the purgative period of her madness. She decides "tin cans and jars are forbidden"; only unprocessed food obtained from the mother earth may be consumed: "I eat the green peas out of their shells and the raw yellow beans, I scrape the carrots from the earth" (178; ch. 23). Like Marian in Atwood's *The Edible Woman* (1969), not eating represents a refusal of consumer society (which is, in Lacanian terms, the paternal symbolic order) and the food or words it would put in her mouth. In her madness, the protagonist in *Surfacing* reasons: "I will never teach it [her newly conceived baby] any words" (162; ch. 20). She simultaneously avoids enclosed spaces and moves outside of houses or, as she says, "against borders" (180; ch. 24). Her rejection of "normal" food, language, and borders (the symbolic) is accompanied by a revitalization of the preoedipal disposition linked to maternal agency (the semiotic). Its first sign is an apparition of her mother caring for the birds under her protection: "Then I see her. She is standing in front of the cabin, her hand stretched out. . . . She doesn't move, she is feeding them: one perches on her wrist, another on her shoulder" (182; ch. 24).

More than a mere guide to the underworld, the occulted mother also returns with an offering for her daughter. She presents a futurity to counterbalance the failed flights of the past: a vision of metamorphosis, a bird woman ready to soar. Suddenly she is no longer earthbound, motionless, or dead. "The jays" in the narrator's visionary experience "are there in the trees. . . . I squint up at them, trying to see her, trying to see which one she is" (182). The childhood memory of her mother's magic, "arms upraised as though she was flying," is now reaffirmed as an image of potential transcendence. "I go up to where she was," says the quester. In so doing, she reverses the narrative pattern of descent and resumes the bond with her mother. This movement marks the beginning of her rebirth into sanity, as she becomes endowed with new possibilities for self-exploration.

NOTE

The research on which this article is based was supported in part by a grant from the Israel Association for Canadian Studies.

A Writer for All Theories: Using Atwood's Works to Teach Critical Theory and Praxis

Theodore F. Sheckels, Jr.

An undergraduate literary criticism course should be empowering. This assumption leads me to the three defining characteristics of the course I have taught for more than a decade: first, it introduces students to many critical perspectives from which students are encouraged to develop their own repertoires; second, the course equally emphasizes theory and praxis; third, the course provides students with many successful experiences practicing varied critical approaches. For the course to be empowering, students must read some expositions of theory, and several good anthologies of contemporary criticism exist to meet this need; furthermore, students must read literary texts that lend themselves well to the approaches the course presents. Margaret Atwood offers the instructor of literary criticism to undergraduates so many texts that provide empowering experiences that one could conceivably use only her work in introducing students to contemporary critical praxis.

Since the 1970s, literary criticism has evolved at an accelerated clip. As a result, each time I teach the subject, I find myself deleting and adding perspectives. In the late 1970s, for example, Mikhail Bakhtin and the new historicism were not part of the course, and feminist criticism was briefly mentioned. Now, Bakhtin and the new historicism are treated at length, feminist criticism is stressed (so much so that the course counts toward the college's women's studies major), and some of the staples of 1978—for example, Northrop Frye and Jacques Derrida—are not emphasized as much. But let me freeze the ever-changing syllabus and assume, for the sake of my argument concerning Atwood's works, that the course introduces undergraduates to a dozen perspectives, ranging from traditional literary scholarship through reader-response and feminist criticisms to the new historicism and dialogism. Space limitations permit me only to sketch the outlines of this course and suggest the richness and complexity of class discussions. The reader, then, should view this essay as no more than an introduction to the course, just as the course itself is but an introduction to critical theory.

Among the many tasks traditional literary scholars embraced was the accumulation and study of sources and analogues. Undergraduates need to see how such a study can enrich their reading experiences. Atwood's *The Journals of Susanna Moodie* (1970), when placed next to excerpts from Moodie's *Roughing It in the Bush* (1852) and *Life in the Clearings* (1853), can reveal not only how Atwood "used" the historical material but also how she interpreted it from the perspective of a late-twentieth-century feminist, thereby giving the historical Moodie a voice she could not have had in 1852–53.

Atwood's *The Journals of Susanna Moodie* is, of course, an obvious example of an author's using a source. Less obvious is what Atwood arguably does with fairy-tale sources and analogues in three of her novels. Students can examine *Surfacing* (1972) along with the Grimms' "The Juniper Tree" and "Fitcher's Feathered Bird," much as Elizabeth Baer does ("Pilgrimage"); students can read *The Edible Woman* (1969) along with Grimm's "Little Red Cap" and the popular "gingerbread man" story, as T. D. MacLulich does ("Atwood's Adult"); or they can study *Lady Oracle* (1976) along with Hans Christian Andersen's "The Red Shoes" and "The Little Mermaid," as Emily Jensen does ("Atwood's *Lady Oracle*").

Although instructors could demonstrate the New Critics' emphasis on the special imagery-laden language of literature, as well as their delight in such traits as tension, by explicating any number of Atwood's lyric poems—for example, "The City Planners" from *The Circle Game* (1966) and "Late August" from *You Are Happy* (1974)—the more interesting text to examine may be *Surfacing*, with its deceptively tidy dialectic of natural and unnatural imagery. Class discussion of Atwood's implicit indictment of all forces violating nature might lead to a consideration of the morality of literature—a way of getting at Plato's *Republic* (and even Yvor Winters's *The Function of Criticism*) indirectly.

After studying the New Criticism, undergraduates should learn—in no particular order—about the numerous schools that developed in response to the Vanderbilt circle. Because Northrop Frye's discussion of the mythoi of Spring and Summer fits *Surfacing* well, students would probably find mythological criticism in general and Frye's monomythological approach in particular a logical next step. *Surfacing*, however, need not be the text of choice, for both *The Edible Woman* and *Bodily Harm* (1981) are good examples of works that "try" to be comedies or even romances, as Frye defines these genres in *Anatomy of Criticism*, but drift toward wintry irony. Although the two novels perhaps have different tones, they both approach irony in their insistent satire of the patriarchy and—more important, given Frye's emphasis on a work's structure—in their problematic endings. Students will have to wrestle with the symbolic significance of Marian McAlpin's devouring the female-shaped cake she baked and then offering some to Peter and Duncan (*Edible Woman*); in *Bodily Harm*, students may ponder the question of Rennie's fate—was she rescued or is she still a victim in a Third World prison? Do these novels, in other words, offer natural or magical redemption, or is the hope we may experience as false as that we feel for Lear and Cordelia before the old king enters carrying her corpse?

Students need to shift their attention from artifact to audience. This refocusing is initially accomplished by applying the neo-Aristotelian methods of rhetorical criticism, with its emphasis on a work's final effect and the choices an artist makes to achieve that effect, to a problematic text like *Life before Man* (1979). This novel has certainly been the one that Atwood's critics have had the most difficulty responding to. The novel puzzles critics. Why, for example, does Atwood choose to give us four major live characters (Elizabeth, Nate, Lesje, and William) but use only three as narrators? Why is William so marginalized? Why do the dates appended to the chapters become progressively farther apart? Does the speeding up signal a rush toward a kind of apocalypse? Does the reduced amount of reflection by the characters suggest a drift toward silence or numbness? Is the novel's dominant setting, the Royal Ontario Museum, incidental, or is it symbolic of the pending extinction or fossilization of human love? Are the numerous intertexts pessimistic or (as Carol Beran has argued, in "Intertexts") optimistic? How many puns are wrapped up in the title, or, put another way, does the title suggest a prospect (the life that is *ahead* for man) or a retrospect (the now-extinct life that existed before man's time that may prefigure man's fate)? Students can determine the novel's final effect on readers and then proceed backward, as Aristotle did, to find the answer to these and other puzzles with the assumed effect in mind.

Shifting the focus to the audience sets the stage for an exploration of reader-response criticism. My exemplar has always been Stanley Fish, and I find it pedagogically useful to talk about the early Fish of *Surprised by Sin* and *Self-Consuming Artifacts*, in which the emphasis is on the therapeutic game the author plays with the reader, and the later Fish of *Is There a Text in This Class?*, in which the emphasis is on the reader's creation of meaning. *Surfacing* and *Bodily Harm* are instructive texts for discussion because both "Fishes" apply but apply very differently. Students following Fish's early theory would explore the ways both novels seem to trap readers into misinterpretations—into assuming that all the nameless narrator's stories in *Surfacing* are true and maybe again into assuming that she is, in the end, redeemed; into assuming that rescue is imminent several times for Rennie in *Bodily Harm*. The discussion would consider such matters as unreliable narration in the first book and the generic expectations of a formula romance in the latter. Students applying Fish's later theory would, of course, respond more personally. My experience with these texts suggests that students in the United States will respond with hostility to *Surfacing*'s anti–United States rhetoric and with different attitudes toward the narrator's behavior at the novel's end. Men and women will respond quite differently to the sexual oppression depicted in *Bodily Harm*, particularly to the novel's treatment of breast cancer and Rennie's surgeon, Daniel. The men will resist seeing him as an oppressive figure unless they have read about unnecessary breast cancer surgery and sexist postmastectomy treatment *and* realize that what seems to be a consensual affair between Rennie and Daniel is not, because of the power he has acquired over her.

To introduce structuralism, I use an excerpt from Robert Scholes's *Semiotics and Interpretation* (1982) as a representative example of structuralist assumptions and goals. His distinction between *récit* (the narrated text) and *diegesis* (the events arranged in a reader- and culture-determined order), like Russian formalist Victor Shklovsky's distinction between story and plot, opens up texts for students. Applied to Atwood's *The Handmaid's Tale* (1985), this distinction leads students to explore the levels of intermediation that exist between Offred and readers. Students readily recognize the several ways in which the *diegesis* they create (they are compelled by the patriarchy to create) differs from a *récit* that may well be so marginalized that it is beyond recovery. For example, students see, first, the prominence of the "Night" chapters in the structure and, second, the gradual change in these chapters from reflection (with a woman privileged) to action (with men privileged and controlling) as a pernicious rendering of the *récit*. Further, the "Historical Notes" becomes for them, as for Michele Lacombe ("The Writing") and Arnold Davidson ("Future Tense"), not an appendix to be skipped but a source of much information about how and why Offred's *récit*—her story—has been lost.

Those "Historical Notes" can also profitably be deconstructed, for the language of the scholars gathered at the 2195 Nunavit meeting clearly represses meaning and oppresses the disempowered. This example of deconstructing is especially instructive for students, for it demonstrates how methods that some critics have called nihilistic have been appropriated for political ends by those who are not completely in agreement with Derrida et al. Another fruitful application of deconstructionism's more accessible methods would be to the words and plot structures that suggest that certain characters in *Bodily Harm* are heroes or would-be heroes. The words and especially the structures, for example, privilege Paul, and, as Elaine Hansen ("Fiction") suggests, the climax of the novel ought to occur when Paul restores Rennie's sense of her body's worth by making love to her. The *aporia* between these words and plot structures, and the meaning students gradually make as they read the rest of the novel and realize that sexual intercourse with Paul resolves little, causes students to return to the text and see what it has suppressed or, in many cases, only partially suppressed.

This treatment of deconstructionism suggests that, as a recent text has noted, "Over the last twenty years, deconstruction has certainly declined in importance . . . and it has . . . found itself absorbed and adopted by other approaches and not so much practiced on its own as it once was" (Guerin, Labor, et al. 258). This treatment further suggests that perhaps the approach that has absorbed deconstruction's methods the most profitably is feminist criticism. As one would expect, feminist criticism works well with numerous works by Atwood.

Feminist criticism is, of course, far from monolithic. Students should be led through its history and introduced to both feminist criticism that critiques the writing of the patriarchy and feminist criticism that is in line with French *écriture féminine* (and its Anglo-American modifications, or both). Furthermore, students need to know that there is tension within feminist criticism between those who wish to embrace the cause of the oppressed globally, including minority women in the United States (with a criticism rooted in many of the insights of feminism), and those feminist critics the first group views as "developing their ideas only in reference to white, upper-middle-class women who oftentimes practice feminism only in order to become part of the patriarchal power structure they criticize for excluding them" (Guerin, Labor, et al. 207). Atwood's works allow students to grasp this entire complex picture. In *Bodily Harm* and in *The Handmaid's Tale*, Atwood uses the conventions of patriarchal discourse but, of course, undermines them. By examining how Atwood as artist resists oppressive readings and structures, students learn how to become what Judith Fetterley has termed "resisting readers" of patriarchal literature and how to read what Elaine Showalter ("Feminist Criticism") has dubbed "double-voiced discourse," which uses and undermines patriarchal language and conventions.

In *Cat's Eye* (1988), Atwood approaches *écriture féminine* in the text's nonlinearity and in her use, as a structuring principle, of the connected experiences of Elaine Risley as girl, as adult, and as artist. With the text's structure in mind, students can then ask in what ways *Cat's Eye* is a woman writing as a woman. And although Atwood's approach to form is not as radical as, for example, that of her *québecois* sister Nicole Brossard, it is nonetheless distinctly female. The same could be said of Atwood's earlier *The Journals of Susanna Moodie*, especially as Diana M. A. Relke has read the collection ("Double Voice"). In *Bodily Harm*, Atwood may even, as Hansen has suggested, be critiquing facile "First World" feminism. The novel certainly raises some of the global issues that nonwhite, non–United States, and non-European feminists wish raised.

Some contemporary feminist criticism, most notably Julia Kristeva's, uses the psychoanalytic thought of Jacques Lacan as its base. In teaching Lacan to undergraduates, one must not repeat the mistakes that were made when Freud was in vogue: teaching Freud meticulously but naively, with the result that amateur Freudian psychoanalysts made bizarre observations about authors and their works. Undergraduates need a small dose of Lacan, a sense of how his ideas might provide a filter through which they can comprehend literary works more fully. Thus a discussion of the importance of self-identification, confrontation of the "other," and the various ways the unconscious "writes" itself in Lacan's theory could illuminate this very process in Atwood's *Lady Oracle*. Such a discussion would deepen one's understanding of Joan Foster's rebellious childhood and the various ways she, as an adult, creates alternative stories to replace the one "others" have scripted for her. Furthermore, a discussion of Lacan's notion of a prelanguage (and therefore prepatriarchal) existence illuminates many of Atwood's poems, such as "Progressive Insanities of a Pioneer" from *The Animals in That Country* (1968) or "Two-Headed Poems" and "You Begin" from *Two-Headed Poems* (1978).

Feminist criticism is certainly one of the dominant approaches in the

1990s; many would argue that new historicism, associated with Stephen Greenblatt, is another. Students could be profitably introduced to this approach through *The Edible Woman*. The novel reflects the early 1960s, and, although we may like to think of those years as the present, for our students they are history. To understand Atwood's novel, then, necessitates an immersion in the social history of those years—especially the social history of young women. The research that students would have to engage in would probably mix methodologies: they would look at books and articles on 1958–64; they would also look at artifacts that we (or others) might supply. *The Edible Woman*, insofar as it was Atwood's first published novel, would also allow students to consider the material circumstances a relative unknown would have faced in getting a novel published in the mid-to-late 1960s. This question would spin off related ones concerning, for example, the aspiring author's gender, the aspiring author's Canadian nationality, and the extent to which any young author can control such matters as cover art or promotional blurbs. (Early paperback editions of Atwood's novels are instructive—for example, the early Bantam *Bodily Harm* that looks like a Harlequin suitable for on-the-beach reading.)

In practicing Marxist criticism, students would also contextualize Atwood's work. For example, they might place *Bodily Harm* in a global context and discuss what the novel says about oppression in the developing world, as well as what the novel says about the developed world's responses. They might contextualize *Life before Man* by, perhaps, examining the novel's treatment of work. Such an examination would reveal that the meaningless work (at the museum, at law offices) valued by Western capitalist society is associated in the novel with the impending extinction of the human race. In reading *The Edible Woman*, they might consider what it has to say about consumer trends that emerged in the early 1960s and the way those trends affected not only how we consumed goods but how men related to women and women to men.

Finally, students need to know about Bakhtin. Atwood's fiction does not often seem dialogic or "carnivalesque," to use the two key terms in Bakhtin's approach. However, one work is illuminated in interesting ways by students' applying Bakhtin. That work is *Life before Man*, in which multiple voices seem to be wrestling with questions without the controlling mediation of an authorial consciousness. And just as carnivals, viewed sociologically, are ambiguously sad and happy, so are most readers' feelings at the end of Atwood's novel. In proceeding dialogically in *Life before Man*, Atwood is much more like her poet self, for we find the same unresolved dialogic quality in "The Circle Game" (1966) and "Two-Headed Poems," both of which can be examined by students using Bakhtinian ideas. (Jerome Rosenberg ["For of Such"] and Judith McCombs ["Politics"] offer useful discussions of the voices in these poems that can help student discussion along.)

Rarely, it seems to me, does one author's work lend itself to such a pluralism of critical approaches. Although I would not use only Atwood in teaching critical theory to undergraduates, I could. From having used many of the texts discussed in this essay in most of the ways I've outlined, I know the course would be a success. Atwood's work engages the minds and imaginations of undergraduates, but that is not the primary reason the course would be a success. The primary reason is that Atwood's novels and poems *work well* with the varied approaches and therefore provide students with the successful experiences that are truly empowering. And, again, that is what I believe those who teach literary theory and praxis to undergraduates should be doing—not involving students prematurely in esoteric critical wars but instead empowering them as readers of literature and other texts.

Cat's Eye as a Reenvisioned Portrait of the Artist: A Visual, Canadian Studies, and Feminist Approach

Judith McCombs

Margaret Atwood's compellingly real *Cat's Eye* portrait of a contrarily feminist-oriented Canadian artist is worth teaching in introductory and advanced courses in fiction, advanced fiction-writing workshops, specialized Canadian or North American or modern courses, or images of women or women's studies courses. My favorite *Cat's Eye* course, however, would be called Portraits of the Artist as Various Persons; it would be English-language fiction, organized somewhat unchronologically to compare and contrast gender, class, kind of art, society, and era. The portraits would be mostly of Canadian and women artists, and, except for the contrasting Arnow and Ondaatje, of precursors and models for *Cat's Eye*. "Various" would begin, of course, with James Joyce's *Portrait of the Artist as a Young Man*; followed by Alice Munro's *Lives of Girls and Women*; Virginia Woolf's *To the Lighthouse*; Harriette Arnow's *Dollmaker*; Doris Lessing's *Golden Notebook*; Sinclair Ross's *As for Me and My House*; Margaret Laurence's *Diviners*; Michael Ondaatje's *Coming through Slaughter*; Paul Hiebert's parodic yet empathic *Sarah Binks*; and, finally, *Cat's Eye*.

Teaching *Cat's Eye* as a reenvisioned, Canadian, and female portrait of the artist presents, in any course, a number of challenges and openings; as I have argued elsewhere, *Cat's Eye* plays, complexly and sometimes contrarily, with concepts of the artist and self, creativity and art, feminism and female archetypes ("Contrary Re-memberings"). James Joyce's germinal *Portrait of the Artist* (1916), which depicts an aspiring young Irish writer, reinforced the traditional image of the artist as male. Atwood opens up the tradition by portraying the artist as a visualizing and visionary middle-aged Canadian woman, the painter Elaine Risley, whose work is having its first retrospective.

Atwood in 1973 saw the human self as "a place in which things happen," a place changed by things happening in it (qtd. in Grace, *Violent Duality* 86). Elaborating this spatial, creative concept, Atwood in *Cat's Eye* (1988) portrays the painter-narrator's self as multilayered, with shifting, fluid, and buried layers, where things long lost to consciousness surface through "memory [that] is tremulous, like water breathed on" (Bantam, 417; ch. 69). Risley's opening, spatial image visualizes time as "a shape, something you could see, like a series of liquid transparencies, one laid on top of another. You don't look back along time but down through it, like water," to see what comes to the surface—this, or that, or nothing (3; ch. 1). Risley's multilayered image is a painter's three-dimensional visualization of the word *retrospective*, seen *down into* and *through*; her retrospective re-memberings of the time stored in her head thus become descents into layers of consciousness.

What also surfaces in this image is Risley's visionary thinking, which students should watch for. In *Cat's Eye* as in Atwood's other books, the text may be psychological realism, but the subtext carries layers of visionary and supernatural lore. Gazing into water is an ancient method of divination, and Risley uses it here to call up the ghost of her brother, Stephen, as he was in their shared childhood. Marbles are another ancient means of divination: when Risley and her dying mother retrieve Risley's childhood cat's-eye marble from the family steamer trunk, Risley looks into her long-lost talismanic marble and sees her "life entire" (420; ch. 69). What Risley sees are the long-buried childhood torments and envisioned rescue that have haunted her life below the levels of her conscious knowing. Seeing her "life entire" enables Risley to re-member its story in the novel and to paint the summing-up pictures of her retrospective—especially *Cat's Eye* and *Unified Field Theory* (430–31; ch. 71).

In the inner-city Detroit BFA art and design college where I taught, students could usually recognize Risley's specifically right-brain, visual perceptions. Some of the fine arts majors would have already used Betty Edwards's artist-oriented *Drawing on the Right Side of the Brain* (1979), which explains the right hemisphere as nonverbal, synthesizing, image-making, seeing in a deep and time-free way; and the left hemisphere as analytical, rational, verbal, symbol-using, time-counting, linear—and quick to dominate the slower right side. Because our society educates people for left-hemisphere work and mostly ignores or dismisses right-hemisphere thinking, nonarts students reading *Cat's Eye* would especially benefit from an introduction to Edwards's book (vi–vii, 25–43).

Elaine Risley's earliest memory in *Cat's Eye*, for example, is a portrait of a visual artist-to-be. Sometime before her eighth birthday she is traveling with her nomadic family, sitting with the luggage in the back seat, focusing on the shapes of her father's and mother's and brother's ears in front of her, and comparing these shapes with the shapes stored in her visual memory (22–23; ch. 4). Edwards would point out that ears seen from the back are shapes, not specifically named in our language, not known as ready-made symbols in the way that ears seen from the side are; Elaine is seeing these shapes from the right side of her brain. This scene is a visual version of Atwood's apparently autobiographical portrait, in "Unearthing Suite," of a young writer-to-be, traveling with her nomadic family and beginning to translate the world into words (*Bluebeard's Egg*, Fawcett, 310–11); another portrait-of-the-artist story, "The Sunrise," also in *Bluebeard's Egg*, prefigures *Cat's Eye*.

From childhood on, Risley's head is full of visual images, many seen so eidetically that decades later she can resee them, or paint them, rendering exactly their colors, shapes, shadows, likenesses. The illuminated, stained slides in her father's laboratory, and the stained-glass windows at the Protestant church the righteous Smeaths take Elaine to, imprint her visual imagination: years later, as a young art student, Risley teaches herself the painstaking technique of egg tempera so that she can create the kindred "luminous flatness" of early iconic pictures (346; ch. 58).

As a painter, Risley retains and re-creates the few art forms of her childhood: the iconic gas pumps, the illuminated windows and slides, the sequential frames and gradual, violent, and horrible transformations of comic books. Hidden mysteries and confusing or mysterious words trigger images in her head, which may combine and, under the pressure of intense fear, shame, or hatred, metamorphose into archetypal visual imagery. If students keep a set of file cards on each painting and the re-membered images behind it, they can trace some of these processes of Risley's visual creativity. In *White Gift*, for example, Mrs. Smeath's mysterious "bad heart" is combined and metamorphosed with images that include the turtle's cut-open heart and the Catholic Virgin Mary's pierced external red heart (61–62, 182, 194–97, 372; chs. 11, 32, 34, 62).

Further discussion can focus on crucial aspects of Risley's creative development. Her innate seeing, inherited ability to draw, and art education are all necessary to her becoming an artist. But does Risley's knowledge of her vocation (274; ch. 46) come as an ambition, a conscious, left-brain decision, or as a sudden illumination from the right brain? What emotions trigger Risley's first creative breakthrough, her first real paintings (356–58; ch. 60), when she "begin[s] to paint things that aren't there"? Does her right brain see what her left brain cannot consciously know? When were those images formed?

Should the victimizing Mrs. Smeath be seen as Risley's muse, as Earl Ingersoll ("Atwood's *Cat's Eye*" 22) argues? Are victimizer/victim Cordelia and the rescuing Virgin also muses? Atwood's *Survival* (1972) argued that Canadians should use rational, conscious strategies to stop being victims (36–39). Ten years later, in the last essay of *Second Words*, Atwood affirmed Blake's remark that "creative energies are more likely to emerge from the underworld than from the upper world of rational order" (417). If Risley had been able to resolve her victimhood consciously at the time, so that it was not repressed and buried in a psychic underworld, would she have become an important visual artist? Do the new retrospective paintings, and the final but yet unpainted vision of Cordelia, come out of energies different from those of Risley's first creative breakthrough?

Comparing Risley's intensely individual, iconic, surreal realism with the work of the two men artists in the novel—the older, romanticizing, European-oriented Josef and the younger, concept-discarding, New York–oriented Jon—suggests the general, but not invariable, pattern of male artists' peer and school orientation versus female artists' isolation and inner vision. Risley's independent vision and inner resistance to feminist interpretations recall Georgia O'Keeffe's maverick vision and outspoken rejection of Freudian and feminist interpretations in her 1976 retrospective book.

Risley's paintings can be set in a visual context by bringing in slides and books from some of the artists named in *Cat's Eye* and its prefatory list (vi) and from certain other comparable twentieth-century artists of both genders. Risley's *One Wing* triptych for her brother (429–30; ch. 71) may have been evoked by the plane crash paintings and constructions in *Joyce Wieland* (see esp. 55, 57, and color plate 42 [132]). Risley's cat-eyed *Nightshade* memories and painting (113–14, 357–58; chs. 20, 60) recall the cat-haunted undergrowth of Emily Carr's 1931 *Zunoqua of the Cat Village* (in Shadbolt 88–89, 205). Remedios Varo's scientifically detailed, surreal, iconic paintings, analyzed in Estella Lauter ("Remedios"), seem closely akin to Risley's work.

Compare also Alex Colville's meticulously detailed magic realism; his *Nude and Dummy* (1950) and self-portrait, *Target Pistol and Man* (1980), may resonate with Risley's *Half a Face* and *Cat's Eye* self-portrait (Burnett 71, 16; *Cat's Eye* 243, 430; chs. 41, 71). Edward Hopper's *Gas* (1940), a painting of a service station, reproduced in David Burnett (153), may prefigure the iconic gas pumps in *Picoseconds* (*Cat's Eye* 24, 427–28; chs. 4, 71). Andrew Wyeth's unusual childhood, haunted mysticism, and painstakingly realistic tempera seem very closely akin; compare the concealed personal traumas in Wyeth's *Winter 1946* (Corn 58–59) and Risley's *Falling Women* (*Cat's Eye* 286; ch. 47). For reproductions and analyses of Atwood's own visual art, see Sharon Wilson's "Sexual Politics" and *Margaret Atwood's Fairy-Tale Sexual Politics*.

In *Cat's Eye*, as in Munro's *Lives of Girls and Women* (1971), Laurence's retrospective *Diviners* (1974), and most of Atwood's earlier fictive portraits of the artist, the foregrounded realities are Canadian and female (McCombs, "Fictive Portraits"). Risley's harrowing childhood victimization by girls and women, and her Mrs. Smeath paintings, belong to a Southern Ontario Gothic where, as in Alice Munro and James Reaney, horror and grotesques lurk beneath ordinary surfaces. Risley's failed, traumatic, haunting quest for female friendship, and her revelation of the secret lives of girls and women, extend the genre of untold women's friendship stories that Virginia Woolf's germinal feminist *A Room of One's Own* (1929) called for, to include crucial girlhood ties and negative as well as positive female powers (86–88).

Students should note the regionalism, gender and class divisions, cultural mosaic, and layerings of the Canada foregrounded in *Cat's Eye*: the frugal, self-reliant, intellectual Maritime values of Elaine's parents; the urban consumerism and feminine standards of her Toronto girlfriends' families; the righteous, bigoted Puritanism of the lower-middle-class Smeaths and the more sophisticated cruelties of Cordelia's privileged family; the imperial British education given to Canadian schoolchildren, who are considered inferior to Britons; the older Scots and newer minority immigrants; the Vancouver resentment of easterners; the "world-class" glitz of 1980s Toronto.

Students should note especially how the upsurge of Canadian and feminist consciousness, which began in the late 1960s and early 1970s, helps to keep Risley going as a painter and to make her success possible: the government's junior artist grant and New York show; the Toronto and Vancouver women's groups and shows; the alternative women's gallery, Sub-versions; the "regular" galleries (402; ch. 66); the buyers that support a living Canadian woman painter.

Is Risley a feminist? a purely apolitical artist? an antifeminist? a feminist artist? Students will need to consider carefully Risley's layered, right- versus left-brain reactions, and compare her thoughts, speech, deeds, and art. And, as with Joyce's *Portrait*, students should watch for the novel's ironic exposures of its fallible, subjective artist.

Certainly Risley's feelings about women and feminism are mixed and, like her feelings about Toronto, profoundly traumatized by her childhood victimization by girls and women. On the one hand, Risley does come back to her dreaded Toronto for Sub-versions; on the other hand, like any ambitious artist, she would of course in her heart prefer a more prestigious Art Gallery of Ontario retrospective to one "at an alternative gallery run by a bunch of women" (16; ch. 3). In the interview Risley contrarily and superstitiously resists being pigeonholed as a feminist or as a woman painter and gives "unhelpful" and "dubious" answers to questions that hit home (94–95; ch. 16). Nonetheless, Risley has lived up to feminist ideals: she has struggled to become, in Simone de Beauvoir's terms, a creating Subject, not a dependent Other (*Second Sex* xvi–xvii).

Although Risley's contrariness and her traumatizing story have disturbed some readers (see Greene, Rev.), the novel clearly shows that Risley's life, career, and art have been profoundly shaped by feminism. Before she joins the Toronto consciousness-raising group of women artists, Risley has lost confidence in herself and her art and is passively sulking as her marriage goes sour. The women's revelations make her "feel more powerful" in some ways, but also "nervous," as if her female peers are judging her, as happened in the childhood scapegoating she could not consciously remember. "Sisterhood is a difficult concept for me," Risley tells herself (365; ch. 61). But, though she resents the women's implied criticism of nuclear families, she begins to stand up for herself at home and to paint again, despite her husband's complaints.

Most of Risley's paintings re-create her experience among girls and women; many paintings re-create specific feminist concepts or, though Risley seldom says so, reclaim female archetypes (McCombs, "Contrary Re-memberings"), as feminists have urged that women do. Risley's anxiety-suffused *Wringer* and *Toaster* reimage her girlhood traumas; so does *Falling Women*, despite Risley's screening, left-brain explanation of its surface, heterosexual symbolism (357, 286; chs. 60, 47). Her retrospective *Cat's Eye* self-portrait, with Risley's falsely belittling girlfriends reflected in a pier (peer) glass behind her head, is an all-female version of Woolf's statement about woman serving as man's falsely enlarging mirror (*Room* 35–36). Risley's paintings of the bad-hearted Mrs. Smeath reveal, as the Smith-Teeth name suggests, devouring Teeth Mother and Kali Ma archetypes (Walker 488–94).

Risley consciously intends her early painting of the Virgin Mary as a fierce, lioness-headed mother to be a new, female iconography, one "more accurate about motherhood than the old bloodless milk-and-water Virgins of art history"; she also paints the Virgin as a tired, grocery-laden Everywoman, or Everymother. That these two Virgin paintings come immediately after Risley's "sisterhood is a difficult concept" protest (365; ch. 61) is characteristic of her surface resistance and deeper feminist orientation—a dynamic that prevents Risley from becoming a one-dimensional feminist hero. That Risley envisions and seeks a female savior adds another dimension: her Virgin of Lost Things, painted in the retrospective *Unified Field Theory*, is a merciful female creator who goes back to pre-Christian archetypes of the Great Goddess (*Cat's Eye* 202–06, 211–13; chs. 35, 36, 37; Walker 602–13).

Of all Atwood's books, *Cat's Eye* goes most deeply into her time and art. By looking *down* and *through* Risley's retrospective, this essay argues, we can see how profoundly the sometimes overlooked Canadian, female, and feminist elements shape her bildungsroman. And by drawing on visual sources, we can see more clearly Risley's creative development and vividly rendered paintings.

Negotiating *Wilderness Tips*

Arnold E. Davidson

The conjunction of "wilderness" and "tips" in the volume's title (and the title story) provides an early clue as to how teachers and students might navigate the narrations that, individually and collectively, constitute *Wilderness Tips*. For the two words would seem to be at obvious cross-purposes. Tips are precisely what you do not expect in the wilderness. What someone has already explored, leaving helpful suggestions as to how others might do so as well, is no longer wilderness. It is mapped territory, known and knowable. In short, if every text contains, as some critics have argued, the grounds for its own deconstruction, Atwood's title particularly does so. The title *Wilderness Tips* can hardly be taken at face value, nor, for that matter and after their juxtaposition, can the terms *wilderness* or *tips*.

Wilderness Tips, moreover, is named for the story "Wilderness Tips" that is itself named for another, earlier book featured in the story and one that also fails to ground the title in either a believable wilderness or serviceable tips. Admittedly, this turn-of-the-nineteenth-century *Wilderness Tips* sets forth some "Happy Homemakers"–style advice (McClelland, 207) on "how to build shelters, make clothing from skins, [and] find edible plants" in the forest. But it also advocates a Sir Robert Baden-Powell-ish Boy Scout going native, provided the natives emulated are "brave, faithful, clean, reverent, hospitable, and honourable." Yet going native—that is, wearing "a tea towel tucked into the front of his bathing suit for a loincloth" and war-painted "with red paint swiped from [his sister's] paintbox" (213)—brings, in the story, a book-inspired Boy Scout "Indian" to come close to killing the same sister when, pretending she is Custer, he sneaks up on her with his newly made stone axe. The near killing, however, derives not from pretense but from the failure of pretense. As he "rais[ed] the axe" to see "the convincing silhouette his shadow made," the axe head "fell off, onto his bare foot." She turned around at his cry of pain, "guessed in an instant what he was doing, and laughed herself silly. That was when he'd almost killed her. The other thing, the stone axe, had just been a game" (214).

That game in the text is part of the text's game. A tea-towel Indian is prompted—almost!—to savagery because his tea towel is derided, all of which happens at Wacousta Lodge, a place named for another book, *Wacousta*, that also famously confused the ostensible boundary between civilization and savagery. Indeed, in Major John Richardson's 1832 novel, Wacousta, the savage Indian leader feared by the white settler, turns out to be just another paleface in dubious disguise. So Atwood's deconstruction of "civilization" defined in terms of a countering "savagery" is anticipated by Richardson's, and two deconstructions hardly make a "construction" that reestablishes the original distinction. Far from it. Richardson's text can well be seen as the first and paradigmatic example of a Canadian propensity to cast its "raw" and its "cooked" as, in Peter Dale Scott's evocative phrasing, "the raw and the Fryed" (6), a distinctly less polarized dichotomy. Atwood carries that process one step further to give us what might be termed the fried and the Fryed. Being at home in the wild as well as acting wild in the home are both mundanized and mythologized.

Thus, in the title story itself, the boy who played Indian is comically misnamed Roland. *The Song of Roland* is not *The Song of Hiawatha*. Grown to adulthood, Roland, throughout most of the story, chops wood, not enemies. But more effective and with a more effective axe, he is still missing his real target when, with every blow, he imagines himself splitting his brother-in-law's head in two. That brother-in-law, George, misnamed too, is the dragon of the piece, not the hero, and the story concludes with him married to one of Roland's three sisters, conducting a long affair (which predates the marriage) with another, and commencing a sexual relationship with the third. That last wanton (wilderness) act, betraying the marriage and betraying the husband's earlier promise to himself that "he will perform no violations" (199) at Wacousta Lodge, is discovered in terms impossibly, ironically homey. The wife hears rustling and heavy breathing from the boathouse: "It can't be Prue [the sister whose long affair with George she has known about from the start]; Prue is up on the veranda. It sounds like her mother, like her mother opening birthday presents—that soft crescendo of surprise and almost pained wonder. Oh. Oh. *Oh*" (220). Roland's domesticity—chopping wood for the fires—also enacts his desire to kill his brother-in-law. George's final betrayal of his wife's family—the assignation in the boathouse—is described in terms that recall intimate ceremonies celebrating the cohesiveness of that family. Just what cancels out what with these juxtapositions?

"Oh," of course, is also homophonically suggestive of 0 as zero, as nothing, which is to say that three "Ohs" (sex in the boathouse—one form of wilderness) constitute an amply empty center (another form of wilderness) on which the tale turns toward desolation and a perhaps impending death (still another form) in the family as an alternative—or even corrective—to imagined survival in the imagined wild. The discovery of yet another infidelity sends the wife toward what might be a self-inflicted drowning as she swims out into the lake and to a vision of everything "finished . . . over . . . dead!" But this is not conclusive either. "With only her head above water," she notes, in the last words of the story, that "nothing has happened, really, that hasn't happened before." So "she could swim out further, let go, and sink" (221). Or she could swim back to the same old life with George. Or perhaps to a baptized or reborn new beginning (birthdays again) of a different life, presumably without George. Wilderness lake, wilderness cottage, and the intermediary boathouse—each is a signpost sending the ending and the story in a different direction.

An only ostensibly "trackless wilderness" (111) is oddly deployed in another story in *Wilderness Tips*, "Death by Landscape." This wilderness exists first, dubiously, as the asserted setting for an extended canoe trip to be taken by the oldest girls at a northern lakeshore summer camp. Entering that not so wild world, they are going where many have gone before. Yet they still manage a venture into a different wilderness, a phenomenological and narrative one rather than a land and lake one. At a regularly frequented, officially designated campsite, two of the girls take the trail to the nearby cliff that gives the place its name, where one of them completely and mysteriously vanishes. There is no explanation for this action, yet hints abound, starting even with the names. At Lookout Point on Lake Prospect, Lucy (light) vanishes from sight. Already the narrative seems to have overencoded a parable on the problematics of perception.

"It would be quite a dive off here" (122), Lucy herself had teased Lois, her vertiginous companion, to whom she had also earlier confided that "it would be nice not to go back" to her broken family in Chicago (121). "Sometimes we get really mad and we don't even know it. Sometimes we might do a thing without meaning to," the camp owner accuses Lois, and reads in her "I didn't" denial ample proof that she did: " 'Didn't what?' says Cappie softly, 'Didn't what, Lois?' " (126). That contradictory mundane (early adolescent angst in the form of a suicidal leap or a fatal shove) is itself contradicted by contradictory hints of the mythological. Just before the disappearance, "a hoarse single note" of a raven sounds, and Raven was a traditional native trickster. Then another cry is heard: "not a shout of fear. Not a scream. More like a cry of surprise, cut off too soon. Short, like a dog's bark." Or perhaps a coyote's bark, which brings in another native trickster figure. Still another possibility is also suggested in the story—the cry of the girl turning into a tree, one bark being cut off by another, which gives us a different mythology entirely—Old World instead of New World. And even the problematic cry is still more problematic in that it is a re-presented cry, not the original one, which is "obliterated" by being "gone over and over" afterward (123).

So Lois can deny the unfair charge of murder with the compulsively reiterated retrospective account of what happened as she "knows it" but know, too, that "she no longer believes" that account because "it has become a story" (126). The consequence of this contradiction is that "for the rest of her life . . . she felt she had been tried and sentenced . . . for something that was not her fault" (127). Metafictionally sentenced both by and in the story, Lois looks for another avenue of escape and finds it, in a sense, by relocating Lucy in another medium. She collects paintings of "the same landscape they paddled through, that distant summer" and in the "tangle," the "receding maze," the "foreground that goes back and back, endlessly, involving you in its twists and turns of tree and branch and rock," she posits Lucy "behind the tree that cannot be seen because" it is always the "one . . . further on," deeper in the maze of the landscape and painting (128–29).

The infinite regress of this final solution to the mystery of Lucy's disappearance is not the least of its problems. The delineating of a maze does not preclude being lost within it. Lucy's vanishing, for example, is itself a version of Tom Thomson's death on a canoe trip through that same wilderness he painted. Neither does a prose rendering of the paintings translate the story into another medium, and it concludes—"this is where Lucy is. She is in Lois's apartment, in the holes that open inwards on the wall, not like windows but like doors" (129)—still very much in the realm of narration. So Lois, looking into the paintings, is mirrored by Lucy looking out—looking out, indeed, from Lookout Point—and, in that mirror play, presence and absence, life and death, lakeshore camp and waterfront condominium all become wavering fictional reflections of one another.

"Wilderness Tips" and "Death by Landscape" particularly problematize "wilderness," and "Hairball" (another story in the collection) performs much the same function with respect to "tips." The protagonist of this story, Kat, is a lifestyles writer and editor who thinks she knows just how empty the fashion tips she regularly dispenses really are: "What you had to make them believe was that you knew something they didn't know yet. What you also had to make them believe was that they too could know this thing, this thing that would give them eminence and power and sexual allure . . . but for a price. The price of the magazine." But "it was all photography . . . all iconography . . . all in the choosing eye"—in short, all contrived surface and a surface contrived to deceive. Neither does Kat's seemingly successful career of providing shoddy advice particularly serve her, for she "herself could not afford many of the things she contextualized so well" (45).

Kat's own hard surface of stylized success is controverted by an ovarian cyst with a rather different surface of its own. What the doctor removes is a tangle of "long strands of [red hair] wound round and round . . . like a ball of wet wool gone berserk" and containing "fragments of bone," a "scattering of nails," and "five perfectly formed teeth" (42). Kat names the cyst Hairball and at first puts it, in a jar of formaldehyde, on her mantel, which, for her lover at the time, is definitely going too far. She soon goes further. Gerald, the lover who hired her to revitalize a Canadian fashion magazine and then hindered her efforts (even then she was going too far), fires her as she is recovering from her operation and even assumes her position himself, also assuming that they can continue their liaison. Invited to a cocktail party at his home, presumably to celebrate his new position, she sends Hairball in her place.

Drained and dried, powdered (with cocoa), party-dressed in pink tissue paper, and boxed up as the best chocolate truffles in Toronto, Hairball goes to the party as a parodic version of Kat's and her lover's striving after similar surface effect. Hairball goes, too, to achieve Kat's appropriate revenge: "There will be distress, there will be questions . . . everything will go way too far" (56). Furthermore, Hairball is both "thwarted child" and "undeveloped twin" (54). In the one capacity, the father is being given custody of the flawed product of a flawed relationship; in the other, he is being allowed an alternative to it. Perhaps you might prefer my sister, Kat, in effect, says. She is a wild woman as well—witness all that tangled hair—but a much more restrainable and containable one. Put her on the shelf and she will stay there.

Effective as the revenge is, however, there is a way in which it doesn't work, and appropriately so. The protagonist does not get her job back, or her lover either. Furthermore, she wants him back in his original "stable, unfashionable, previous, tight-assed" form, not the "smooth as lacquer" product "she's made in her own image" (52) and according to her advice. She is no happier with her own polished image. But neither has she, especially with the revenge, acted to alter it. The revenge, moreover, follows still other advice. As she cried over Hairball, feeling sorry for it and for herself, it responded, "without words," to tell her "everything she's never wanted to hear about herself. This is new knowledge, dark and precious and necessary. It cuts." It cuts, like the operation, but it does not cure. The economy of tips is consistent to the end. If Kat's revenge is the product of Hairball's wordless advice, all it accomplishes is the loss of her "ugly" child that "only a mother could love" (54). She ends up bereft of job, Gerald, and Hairball.

Distinctions—between civilization and wilderness, between tips as saving counsel and tips as disastrous slips, between the past with all its certainties and the present with all its doubts—are undone in the stories. And so are the distinctions between story and story. The miswriting and misreading of romance in "True Trash," the first story, reappears as the miswriting and misreading of news (especially when it is turned into toilet paper) in the last story, "Hack Wednesday," and to much the same end, a shoring of prose against the ruins of time. Or the affair displayed in "Hairball," the second story, like the one discovered in "Wilderness Tips," the second to the last, implicates all parties in each interrelationship. Even the different final states of the different female protagonists—the mistress in "Hairball," "light and peaceful and filled with charity" (56); the wife in "Wilderness Tips" on the verge of return, rebirth, or suicide—are each strangely grounded in a figurative return to childhood. Similarly, the dead woman poet in "Isis in Darkness," the third story, is paired with the murdered woman lawyer in "Weight," the third from the last, just as a dead man excavated in "The Bog Man," the fourth story, is excavated again in "The Age of Lead," the fourth from the last. And at the center, in "Death by Landscape" and "Uncles," the fifth and sixth of the ten stories, a dead friend and a dead father preside over other possibilities of what a female protagonist's life might have been or might be.

That presiding, moreover, suggests the logic of the pairings just examined, the way story is countered by similar yet different story in the overall design of the volume, a feature of the individual stories, too, in that they all pointedly suggest other possible versions of themselves. For example, Donnie, in "True Trash," might have found out that he fathered Ronette's illegitimate baby; or Lucy, in "Death by Landscape," might not have gone missing; or Marcia, in "Hack Wednesday," could have commenced the affair she only half contemplates—all of which is to say that each narrative is haunted by others paradoxically evoked by their emphasized absence. Just as the title of *Wilderness Tips* self-deconstructs, the tales, individually and collectively, set forth countering versions of the narratives they purport to relate and so constitute an apt example of the decentering and ironic postmodernism that Linda Hutcheon, among others, has seen as particularly characteristic of "feminist and Canadian fiction alike" (*Canadian Postmodern* 7).

Other patterns of interconnection are also obvious. Journalism as a metaphor for writing as a metaphor for scripting a life is basic to "Hairball," "Uncles," "The Age of Lead," and "Hack Wednesday." Pulp romances, poetry and biography, survival guides, and painting play much the same role in "True Trash," "Isis in Darkness," "Wilderness Tips," and "Death by Landscape," as does "romance" too, whether mostly real ("True Trash"), mostly imagined ("Isis in Darkness"), or mostly turned into narrative ("The Bog Man"). The tales, metafictionally reflecting themselves and one another, illustrate Atwood's characteristic mirror play and employment of duality and doubling. Thus Portia, in "Wilderness Tips," prepares, perhaps, to drown by "slipping into the water as if between the layers of a mirror," and as she does so, she sees herself reflected in the water and in that reflection earlier versions of herself "at fifteen, . . . at twelve, . . . at nine, at six" (221). This countdown to selves safely before the advent of George is also a countdown to herself at zero, dead and safely beyond George. The end of the marriage also reflects its beginning and Portia's partly stripping to dive into the same lake after his dropped sunglasses as a ploy to launch an affair, not a marriage, just as she herself reflects still other Atwoodian characters drowned and not drowned in still other lakes (as in, most obviously, "This Is a Photograph of Me," *Surfacing*, and *Lady Oracle*).

There is also a distinctly personal cast to all this metafictional mirroring. Thus, in the first story, Joanne's anger at Ronette's unplanned pregnancy is prompted and undercut by Joanne's own "bad habit of novelizing" (19), while, in the final story, writing takes "a grimmer turn" (235) as Marcia considers signs of disorder all around her (the homeless in Toronto, Noriega about to be captured in Panama, children suffering throughout the world). The difference between the two narratives is a measure of Atwood's fictional progression from the more individualistic feminist politics of *The Edible*

Woman and *Surfacing* to the larger social focus that informs later novels such as *Bodily Harm* and *The Handmaid's Tale*.

Thematically, too, the obvious interconnections between the stories modify their meanings, individually and collectively. To look briefly, for example, at just the last four, we can notice how the lead poisoning that caused the death of the members of the nineteenth-century Franklin expedition, in "The Age of Lead," is superseded by AIDS in the same story and then, in the next, "Weight," by the narrator's sense that she's "been drinking heavy metals" (179). Or at the conclusion of "Weight," the protagonist, collecting funds for a battered women's shelter by outmaneuvering a wealthy man at a power lunch, sees the setting of that lunch as "like the *Titanic* just before the iceberg: power and influence disporting themselves, not a care in the world. . . . Piss all, and pass the port" (192). The *Titanic* looks back to the two ships of civilization, the ominously named *Terror* and *Erebus* of the Franklin expedition in the previous story, and forward to the next story, in which the betrayed wife, herself nearly submerged in the lake, notes how the whole wilderness tips (another implication of that loaded title) and seems to be "sliding gradually down, submerging" like "a boat—a huge boat, a passenger liner—tilting, descending, with the lights still on, the music still playing, the people talking on and on, still not aware of the disaster that has already overcome them." Yet the final story gives a wry twist to the apocalyptic vision of "the whole mainland" (221), wilderness and civilization, as a sinking *Titanic*. Both wilderness and tips have now adjoined to the city and gone underground, so to speak, to become a maze of malls and tunnels as well as "the 'You Are Here' diagrams placed at intervals to help out those lacking in orientation skills" (231). Apocalypse is also comically muted when the protagonist "smiles . . . and is happy" even as "the world shifts and crumbles and rearranges itself, and time [and life] goes on" (245).

Nevertheless, a wilderness is still present at the end of this story and at the end of the stories taken together as a kind of novel. Marcia imagines how her Christmas will go and how, toward the end of Christmas Day, a little drunk on eggnog, locked in the bathroom and hugging the cat, she will cry for her grown children, for the child she can no longer have, for all the children of the world deprived of childhood. "It's all this talk of babies, at Christmas. It's all this hope. She gets distracted by it, and has trouble paying attention to the real news" (247). As the final words of the last story evoke the title of the first one, we realize that those problematic entities— true trash, real news—have still not been defined, and in that conjoined double failure, the text circumscribes not its own emptiness but its fullness.

CONTRIBUTORS AND SURVEY PARTICIPANTS

The editors are grateful to the contributors and to the teachers who participated in a survey on teaching Atwood's works or proposed topics for essays.

Jane Augustine, *Pratt Institute*
Ann Barnard, *Blackburn College*
Marleen Barr, *Virginia Polytechnic Institute and State University*
Eileen Barrett, *California State University, Hayward*
Shuli Barzilai, *Hebrew University*
Sandra Batson, *McGill University*
Donna Bennett, *University of Toronto, Scarborough Campus*
Carol L. Benton, *Central Missouri State University*
Carol L. Beran, *Saint Mary's College, CA*
Scot Bishop, *Ataguttaaluk High School, Igloolik, NT*
Carolyn Bliss, *University of Utah*
J. Brooks Bouson, *Loyola University, Chicago*
George Bowering, *Simon Fraser University*
Pamela Bromberg, *Simmons College*
Diana Brydon, *University of Guelph*
Cynthia Burack, *George Washington University*
Helen Buss, *University of Calgary*
Virginia Carroll, *Kent State University, Stark Regional Campus*
Jan Garden Castro, *Saint Louis, Missouri*
K. Chellappan, *Bharathidasan University, Tiruchchirappalli, India*
Nathalie Cooke, *McGill University*
Carolyn Creed, *Brandon University*
Arnold E. Davidson, *Duke University*
Dennis Denisoff, *McGill University*
Sandra Donaldson, *University of North Dakota*
Janet M. Ellerby, *University of North Carolina, Wilmington*
Cecilia K. Farr, *College of Saint Catherine*
Joan Gailey, *Kent State University, East Liverpool Regional Campus*
Tom Gerry, *Laurentian University*
Gayle Greene, *Scripps College*
Carole Fitzgerald Hayes, *Woodlands Academy, Lake Forest, IL*
Pamela Hewitt, *University of Northern Colorado*
Earl Ingersoll, *State University of New York, Brockport*
Christine Isler, *Winterthur, Switzerland*
Sally A. Jacobsen, *Northern Kentucky University*
Karl Jirgens, *Toronto, Ontario*
Marlene Kadar, *York University, North York*
Anne Kaler, *Gwynedd-Mercy College*
Mary K. Kirtz, *University of Akron*
Barbara Korte, *Universität zu Köln*

Reinhold Kramer, *Brandon University*
Janet Larson, *Rutgers University, Newark*
Estella Lauter, *University of Wisconsin, Oshkosh*
Valerie Legge, *Memorial University of Newfoundland*
Garry Leonard, *University of Toronto, Scarborough Campus*
Helane Levine-Keating, *Pace University, New York*
Kathleen E. B. Manley, *University of Northern Colorado*
Judith McCombs, *Silver Spring, Maryland*
Patricia Merivale, *University of British Columbia*
Magali Cornier Michael, *Duquesne University*
Patrick D. Murphy, *Indiana University of Pennsylvania*
Alice Palumbo, *University of Toronto, Saint George Campus*
Sally Parry, *Illinois State University*
Nita P. Ramaiya, *SNDT University, Bombay, India*
Carolyn Redl, *Keyano College*
Beth Richards, *Northwest Missouri State University*
Barbara Hill Rigney, *Ohio State University, Columbus*
Jerome Rosenberg, *Miami University, Oxford*
Roberta Rosenberg, *Christopher Newport University*
Roberta Rubenstein, *American University*
George Scheper, *Essex Community College, MD*
Trina Schimmoeller, *Frankfort, Kentucky*
Meryl F. Schwartz, *University of Wisconsin, Madison*
Theodore F. Sheckels, Jr., *Randolph-Macon College*
Karen Smythe, *University of Regina*
Hilda Staels, *Katholieke Universiteit Leuven, Belgium*
Karen F. Stein, *University of Rhode Island*
Paul Matthew St. Pierre, *Simon Fraser University*
Cynthia Sutherland-O'Nan, *University of Pittsburgh, Pittsburgh*
Ruud Teeuwen, *National Sun Yat-sen University, Kaohsiung, Taiwan*
Colette Giles Tennant, *Western Baptist College*
Virgina Tiger, *Rutgers University, Newark*
Kathryn VanSpanckeren, *University of Tampa*
Laurie Vickroy, *Bradley University*
Cheryl Walker, *Scripps College*
John Whalen-Bridge, *University of the Ryukyus, Okinawa, Japan*
Catherine Wiley, *University of Colorado, Denver*
Carol Shiner Wilson, *Muhlenberg College*
Lorraine M. York, *McMaster University*

VOLUME EDITORS

Sharon R. Wilson, *University of Northern Colorado*
Thomas B. Friedman, *University College of the Cariboo*
Shannon Hengen, *Laurentian University*

WORKS CITED

Books and Articles

Aarne, Antti, and Stith Thompson. *The Types of the Folktale: A Classification and Bibliography*. Trans. and enlarged by Stith Thompson. 2nd rev. Folklore Fellows Communications 75, no. 184. Ed. Walter Anderson et al. Helsinki: Academia Scientiarum Fennica, 1961.

Allen, Carolyn. "Margaret Atwood: Power of Transformation, Power of Knowledge." *Essays on Canadian Writing* 6 (1977): 5–17.

Allen, Paula Gunn. *The Sacred Hoop: Recovering the Feminine in American Indian Traditions*. Boston: Beacon, 1986.

Andersen, Hans Christian. *The Complete Hans Christian Andersen Fairy Tales*. Ed. Lily Owens. New York: Avenel, 1981.

Arnason, David, gen. ed. *Themes in Canadian Literature*. 16 vols. Toronto: Macmillan, 1975–77.

Arnow, Harriette. *The Dollmaker*. 1954. New York: Collier-Macmillan, 1961.

Ashcroft, Bill, Gareth Griffiths, and Helen Tiffin. *The Empire Writes Back: Theory and Practice in Post-colonial Literatures*. London: Routledge, 1989.

"Atwood, Margaret (Eleanor) 1939–." *Contemporary Authors*. Ed. Deborah A. Straub. New Revision Series 24. Detroit: Gale, 1988. 17–26.

Atwood, Margaret. "After *Survival*. . . . Excerpts from a Speech Delivered at Princeton University, April 29, 1985." *CEA Critic* 50.1 (1987): 35–50.

———. Afterword. *A Jest of God*. By Margaret Laurence. New Canadian Library. Toronto: McClelland, 1988.

———. Afterword. *The Mare's Egg: A New World Folk Tale Retold by Carole Spray*. By Carole Spray. Illus. Kim La Fave. Camden East, Ont.: Camden, 1981.

———. *The Animals in That Country*. Toronto: Oxford UP, 1968.

———. *Anna's Pet*. With Joyce C. Barkhouse. Kids of Canada. Toronto: Lorimer, 1980.

———. "The Art of Fiction CXXI: Margaret Atwood." Interview with Mary Morris. *Paris Review* 32.117 (1990): 68–88.

———. Audiotape recording for Sharon R. Wilson. August 1985.

———. "Backdrop Addresses Cowboy." *The Animals in That Country* 50–51. Rpt. in *Selected Poems*, Oxford UP, Houghton, 70–71.

———, ed., with Shannon Ravenel. *The Best American Short Stories, 1989*. Introd. Atwood. Boston: Houghton, 1989.

———. *Bluebeard's Egg*. Toronto: McClelland, 1983.

———. *Bluebeard's Egg and Other Stories*. New York: Fawcett, 1987.

———. *Bodily Harm*. Toronto: McClelland, 1981.

————. *Bodily Harm.* New York: Bantam Windstone, 1983.

————. *The CanLit Foodbook: From Pen to Palate—A Collection of Tasty Literary Fare.* Toronto: Totem, 1987.

————. *Cat's Eye.* Toronto: McClelland, 1988.

————. *Cat's Eye.* New York: Bantam, 1989.

————. *The Circle Game.* Illus. Charles Pachter. Bloomfield Hills: Cranbrook Acad. of Art, 1964.

————. *The Circle Game.* Toronto: Contact, 1966.

————. *The Circle Game.* Toronto: Oxford UP, 1966.

————. *The Circle Game.* Toronto: Anansi, 1966.

————. "Concerning Franklin and His Gallant Crew." *Books in Canada* 20.4 (1991): 20–26. Rpt. in *Strange Things.*

————. *Dancing Girls.* Toronto: McClelland, 1977.

————. *Dancing Girls and Other Stories.* New York: Simon, 1982.

————. *Days of the Rebels: 1815–1840.* Canada's Illustrated Heritage 4. Toronto: Natural Science of Canada, 1977.

————. "Defying Distinctions." Interview with Karla Hammond. 1978. Ingersoll *Margaret Atwood* 99–108. Orig. pub. as "A Margaret Atwood Interview with Karla Hammond." *Concerning Poetry* 12.2 (1979): 73–81.

————. "A Disneyland of the Soul." *The Writer and Human Rights.* Ed. Toronto Arts Group for Human Rights. Toronto: Lester, 1983. 129–32.

————. "A Double-Bladed Knife: Subversive Laughter in Two Stories by Thomas King." *Native Writers and Canadian Writing.* Ed. W. H. New. Vancouver: U of British Columbia P, 1990. 243–50.

————. *Double Persephone.* Toronto: Hawkshead, 1961.

————. *The Edible Woman.* Toronto: McClelland, 1969.

————. *The Edible Woman.* Boston: Little, 1969.

————. *The Edible Woman.* London: Deutsch, 1969.

————. *The Edible Woman.* Introd. Alan Dawe. New Canadian Library 93. Toronto: McClelland, 1973.

————. *The Edible Woman.* London: Virago, 1980. Introd. Atwood; rpt. in *Second Words*, Anansi, Beacon.

————. *The Edible Woman.* Toronto: McClelland-Bantam, 1981.

————. *The Edible Woman.* Afterword. Linda Hutcheon. New Canadian Library. Toronto: McClelland, 1989.

————. Foreword. *Cambridge Guide to Literature in English.* Ed. Ian Ousby. Cambridge: Cambridge UP, 1988.

————. Foreword. *Charles Pachter.* By Bogomila Welsh-Ovcharov. Toronto: McClelland, 1992.

————. *For the Birds.* Illus. John Bianchi. Boxes and sidebars by Shelley Tanaka. Earthcare Books. Toronto: Douglas, 1990.

————. *Good Bones.* Toronto: Coach, 1992.

————. *Good Bones.* London: Bloomsbury, 1992.

———. *Good Bones and Simple Murders*. New York: Talese-Doubleday, 1994.

———. "Great Unexpectations: An Autobiographical Foreword." VanSpanckeren and Castro xiii–xvi. Orig. pub. in *Ms*. July–Aug. 1987: 78+.

———. *The Handmaid's Tale*. Toronto: McClelland, 1985.

———. *The Handmaid's Tale*. Toronto: Seal-McClelland-Bantam, 1986.

———. *The Handmaid's Tale*. Boston: Houghton; 1986.

———. *The Handmaid's Tale*. New York: Fawcett, 1986.

———. "If You Can't Say Something Nice, Don't Say Anything at All." Scheier, Sheard, and Wachtel 15–25.

———. *Interlunar*. Toronto: Oxford, 1984.

———. Introduction. *Roughing It in the Bush; or, Forest Life in Canada*. By Susanna Moodie. Virago/Beacon Travelers Series. London: Virago, 1986; Boston: Beacon, 1987. vii–xiv.

———. *The Journals of Susanna Moodie: Poems by Margaret Atwood*. Toronto: Oxford UP, 1970.

———. *Lady Oracle*. Toronto: McClelland, 1976.

———. *Lady Oracle*. New York: Fawcett, 1976.

———. *Lady Oracle*. Toronto: Bantam-Seal, 1981.

———. *Life before Man*. 1979. New York: Warner, 1983.

———. *Morning in the Burned House*. Toronto: McClelland, 1995.

———. *Morning in the Burned House*. London: Virago, 1995.

———. *Morning in the Burned House*. New York: Houghton, 1995.

———. *Murder in the Dark: Short Fictions and Prose Poems*. Toronto: Coach, 1983.

———. "The Only Position They've Ever Adopted towards Us, Country to Country, Has Been the Missionary Position." *If You Love This Country: Facts and Feelings on Free Trade*. Ed. Laurier La Pierre. Toronto: McClelland, 1987. 17–23.

———, ed., with Robert Weaver. *The Oxford Book of Canadian Short Stories in English*. Introd. Atwood. Introd. Weaver. Toronto: Oxford UP, 1986.

———, ed. *The Oxford Book of Canadian Verse in English*. Introd. Atwood. Toronto: Oxford UP, 1982.

———. Papers. Manuscript Collection 200. Thomas Fisher Rare Book Library, University of Toronto.

———. "Playing Around." Interview with J. R. (Tim) Struthers. Ingersoll, *Margaret Atwood* 58–68. Taken from Struthers 18–27.

———. *Power Politics*. Toronto: Anansi, 1971.

———. *Princess Prunella and the Purple Peanut*. Toronto: Key Porter, 1995.

———. *Procedures for Underground*. Toronto: Oxford UP, 1970.

———. "A Reply." *Signs* 2 (1976): 340–41.

———. *The Robber Bride*. Toronto: McClelland, 1993.

———. *The Robber Bride*. New York: Talese-Doubleday, 1993.

———. *Second Words: Selected Critical Prose*. Toronto: Anansi, 1982.

————. *Second Words: Selected Critical Prose*. Boston: Beacon, 1984.

————. *Selected Poems*. Toronto: Oxford UP, 1976.

————. *Selected Poems*. Boston: Houghton, 1976.

————. *Selected Poems, 1965–1975*. Boston: Houghton, 1987. Reissued as *Poems 1965–1975*. London: Virago, 1991.

————. *Selected Poems: 1966–1984*. Toronto: Oxford UP, 1990.

————. *Selected Poems II: Poems Selected and New 1976–1986*. Toronto: Oxford UP, 1986.

————. *Selected Poems II: Poems Selected and New 1976–1986*. Boston: Houghton, 1987.

————. *Strange Things: The Malevolent North in Canadian Literature*. Oxford: Clarendon, 1995.

————. *Surfacing*. London: Virago, 1972.

————. *Surfacing*. Toronto: McClelland, 1972.

————. *Surfacing*. New York: Fawcett 1972, 1987.

————. *Surfacing*. New York: Popular Library, 1976.

————. *Surfacing*. Afterword by Marie-Claire Blais. Toronto: McClelland, 1994.

————. *Survival: A Thematic Guide to Canadian Literature*. Toronto: Anansi, 1972.

————. "Travels Back." *Maclean's* Jan. 1973: 28 + .

————. *True Stories*. Toronto: Oxford UP, 1981.

————. *Two-Headed Poems*. Toronto: Oxford UP, 1978.

————. *Up in the Tree*. Illus. "Charlatan Botchner" [Atwood]. Toronto: McClelland, 1978.

————. *Wilderness Tips*. Toronto: McClelland, 1991.

————. *Wilderness Tips*. Toronto: Seal-Bantam, 1992.

————. *Wilderness Tips*. New York: Bantam, 1993.

————. *You Are Happy*. New York: Harper, 1974.

Auser, Cortland P. "The Mask Is the Face: 'Personae' in Teaching Multi-ethnic American Literature." *MELUS: The Journal of the Society for the Study of the Multi-ethnic Literature of the United States*. Spec. issue on ethnicity and pedagogy. 16.2 (1989–90): 69–76.

Baer, Elizabeth R. "Pilgrimage Inward: Quest and Fairy Tale Motifs in *Surfacing*." VanSpanckeren and Castro 24–34.

Bakhtin, M. M. *The Dialogic Imagination*. Trans. Caryl Emerson and Michael Holquist. Austin: U of Texas P, 1981.

————. *Rabelais and His World*. Trans. Hélène Iswolsky. Bloomington: Indiana UP, 1984.

Bal, Mieke. *Narratology: Introduction to the Theory of Narrative*. Trans. Christine van Boheemen. Toronto: U of Toronto P, 1985.

Baldick, Chris. *The Concise Oxford Dictionary of Literary Terms*. Oxford: Oxford UP, 1990.

Barbeau, Marius, and Michael Hornyansky. *The Golden Phoenix and Other French-Canadian Fairy Tales*. New York: Walck, 1967.

Barr, Marleen S., ed. *Future Females: A Critical Anthology.* Bowling Green: Bowling Green State Popular P, 1981.

Barthes, Roland. Ed. and introd. Susan Sontag. *A Barthes Reader.* New York: Hill, 1982.

Bartkowski, Frances. *Feminist Utopias.* Lincoln: U of Nebraska P, 1989.

Barzilai, Shuli. "A Rhetoric of Ambivalence: Margaret Atwood's *Survival.*" Rhetoric of "Can. Lit." session. MLA Convention. Toronto. 29 Dec. 1993.

Baudelaire, Charles. *Les fleurs du mal. Oeuvres complètes.* Paris: Pleiade, 1961.

———. *The Parisian Prowler: Spleen de Paris/Petits poèmes en prose.* 1869. Trans. Edward K. Kaplan. Athens: U of Georgia P, 1989.

———. *Le spleen de Paris.* Paris: Livre de Poche, 1971.

Bauer, Dale. *Feminist Dialogics: A Theory of Failed Community.* Albany: State U of New York P, 1988.

Beauvoir, Simone de. *The Second Sex.* 1949. Trans. and ed. H. M. Parshley. New York: Bantam, 1961.

Bedrosian, Margaret. "Teaching Multi-ethnic Literature: Some Psychological Considerations." *MELUS: The Journal of the Society for the Study of the Multi-ethnic Literature of the United States.* Spec. issue on ethnicity and pedagogy. 16.2 (1989–90): 5–15.

Belenky, Mary Field, et al. *Women's Ways of Knowing: The Development of Self, Voice, and Mind.* New York: Basic, 1986.

Benedikt, Michael, ed. *The Prose Poem: An International Anthology.* New York: Dell, 1976.

Benton, Carol L. *Raised Eyebrows: The Comic Impulse in the Poetry of Margaret Atwood.* Diss. Southern Illinois U, 1988. Ann Arbor: UMI, 1989.

Beran, Carol. "The Canadian Mosaic: Functional Ethnicity in Margaret Atwood's *Life before Man.*" *Essays on Canadian Writing* 41 (1990): 59–73.

———. "George, Leda, and a Poured Concrete Balcony: A Study of Three Aspects of the Evolution of *Lady Oracle.*" *Canadian Literature* 112 (1987): 18–28.

———. "Images of Women's Power in Contemporary Canadian Fiction by Women." *Studies in Canadian Literature* 15.2 (1990): 55–76.

———. "Intertexts of Margaret Atwood's *Life before Man.*" *American Review of Canadian Studies* 22.2 (1992): 199–214.

———. *Living over the Abyss: Margaret Atwood's* Life before Man. Toronto: ECW, 1994.

Berger, John. *Ways of Seeing: A Book Made by John Berger.* London: BBC, 1972; New York: Penguin, 1972, 1981.

Bergmann, Harriet F. " 'Teaching Them to Read': A Fishing Expedition in *The Handmaid's Tale.*" *College English* 51 (1989): 847–54.

Birney, Earle. "Can. Lit." *Ice, Cod, Bell, or Stone: A Collection of New Poems.* Toronto: McClelland, 1962. Rpt. in *The Collected Poems of Earle Birney.* Vol. 1. Toronto: McClelland, 1975. 138. 2 vols.

Bliss, Michael. "Fragmented Past, Fragmented Future." *University of Toronto Magazine* 19.2 (1991): 6–11.

Bloch, Ernst. *The Principle of Hope*. Trans. Neville Plaice, Stephen Plaice, and Paul Knight. Cambridge: MIT P, 1986. Trans. of *Das Prinzip Hoffnung*. 1954–59.

Bone, Jan, and Ron Johnson. *Understanding the Film*. Lincolnwood: NTC, 1991.

Booth, Wayne. *The Rhetoric of Fiction*. Chicago: U of Chicago P, 1961.

Bordwell, David. *Making Meaning: Inference and Rhetoric in the Interpretation of Cinema*. Cambridge: Harvard UP, 1989.

Bordwell, David, and Kristin Thompson. *Film History: An Introduction*. New York: McGraw, 1994.

Bouson, J. Brooks. *Brutal Choreographies: Oppositional Strategies and Narrative Design in the Novels of Margaret Atwood*. Amherst: U of Massachusetts P, 1993.

Brady, Elizabeth. "Towards a Happier History: Women and Domination." *Domination: Essays*. Ed. Alkis Kontos. Toronto: U of Toronto P, 1975. 17–31.

Brans, Jo. "Using What You're Given: An Interview with Margaret Atwood." *Southwest Review* 68.4 (1983): 301–15.

Brossard, Nicole, ed. *Les Stratégies du réel/The Story So Far*. Montreal: Nouvelle Barre du Jour; Toronto: Coach, 1979.

Brown, Russell. "On Reading for Themes in Canadian Literature." Unpublished paper, 1992.

Brown, Russell, and Donna Bennett, eds. *An Anthology of Canadian Literature in English*. 2 vols. Toronto: Oxford UP, 1982.

Brownmiller, Susan. "Clothes." *Femininity*. New York: Linden-Simon, 1984. 77–102.

Burnett, David. *Colville*. Toronto: Art Gallery of Ontario and McClelland, 1983.

Buss, Helen M. "Maternality and Narrative Strategies in the Novels of Margaret Atwood." *Atlantis* 15.1 (1989): 76–83.

Cameron, Elspeth. *Atwood—The Edible Woman: Notes*. Coles Notes. Toronto: Coles, 1983.

———. "Famininity, or Parody of Autonomy: Anorexia Nervosa and *The Edible Woman*." *Journal of Canadian Studies/Revue d'Etudes Canadiennes* 20.2 (1985): 45–69.

Campbell, Josie P. "The Woman as Hero in Margaret Atwood's *Surfacing*." *Mosaic* 11.3 (1978): 17–28.

Caws, Mary Ann, and Hermine Riffaterre, eds. *The Prose Poem in France*. New York: Columbia UP, 1983.

Chernin, Kim. *The Hungry Self*. New York: Harper, 1986.

Chodorow, Nancy. *The Reproduction of Mothering: Psychoanalysis and the Sociology of Gender*. Berkeley: U of California P, 1978.

Christ, Carol. *Diving Deep and Surfacing: Women Writers on Spiritual Quest*. Boston: Beacon, 1980.

———. "Margaret Atwood: The Surfacing of Women's Spiritual Quest and Vision." *Signs* 2 (1976): 316–30.

Cixous, Hélène. "The Laugh of the Medusa." Trans. Keith Cohen and Paula Cohen. *Signs* 1 (1976): 875–99.

Cluett, Robert. *Canadian Literary Prose: A Preliminary Stylistic Atlas*. Toronto: ECW, 1990.

Cohen, Leonard. *Beautiful Losers*. 1966. Toronto: McClelland, 1991.

Coles Editorial Board. *Atwood—Surfacing: Notes*. Coles Notes. Toronto: Coles, 1982.

Cooper, Sarah. Fax to Jerome Rosenberg. 9 Aug. 1993.

Corn, Wanda M. *The Art of Andrew Wyeth*. With contributions by Brian O'Doherty, Richard Meryman, and E. P. Richardson. Greenwich: New York Graphic Soc., 1973.

Cranny-Francis, Anne. *Feminist Fiction: Feminist Uses of Generic Fiction*. New York: St. Martin's, 1990.

Culler, Jonathan. *Framing the Sign: Criticism and Its Institutions*. Oxford: Blackwell, 1988.

Davey, Frank. "Margaret Atwood." *From There to Here: A Guide to English-Canadian Literature since 1960*. Erin, Ont.: Porcépic, 1974. 30–36.

———. *Margaret Atwood: A Feminist Poetics*. Vancouver: Talonbooks, 1984.

———. *Reading Canadian Reading*. Winnipeg: Turnstone, 1988.

Davidson, Arnold E. "Future Tense: Making History in *The Handmaid's Tale*." VanSpanckeren and Castro 113–21.

———, ed. *Studies on Canadian Literature: Introductory and Critical Essays*. New York: MLA, 1990.

Davidson, Arnold E., and Cathy N. Davidson, eds. *The Art of Margaret Atwood: Essays in Criticism*. Toronto: Anansi, 1981.

Davidson, Cathy N. "A Feminist 1984." *Ms.* Feb. 1986: 24–26.

de Lauretis, Teresa. *Alice Doesn't: Feminism, Semiotics, Cinema*. Bloomington: Indiana UP, 1984.

Dembo, L. S., ed. *Interviews with Contemporary Writers, 1972–1982*. 2nd series. Madison: U of Wisconsin P, 1983.

DeShazer, Mary K. *Inspiring Women: Reimagining the Muse*. New York: Pergamon P, 1986.

Devall, Bill, and George Sessions. *Deep Ecology: Living as If Nature Mattered*. Salt Lake City: Smith, 1985.

Dewart, Edward Hartley, ed. *Selections from Canadian Poets, with Occasional Critical and Biographical Notes, and an Introductory Essay on Canadian Poetry*. 1864. Toronto: U of Toronto P, 1973.

Donaldson, Sandra. "Notes & Queries." *Newsletter of the Margaret Atwood Society* 9 (1992): 16–17.

Dooley, David. "In Margaret Atwood's Zoology Lab." *Moral Vision in the Canadian Novel*. Toronto: Clarke, 1979.

Draine, Betsy. "An Interview with Margaret Atwood." Dembo 366–81.

Dunlop, William. *Tiger Dunlop's Upper Canada; Comprising Recollections of the American War 1812–1814 and Statistical Sketches of Upper Canada for the Use of Emigrants, by a Backwoodsman*. 1832. Toronto: McClelland, 1967.

DuPlessis, Rachel Blau. *Writing beyond the Ending: Narrative Strategies of Twentieth-Century Women Writers.* Bloomington: Indiana UP, 1985.

Dworkin, Andrea. *Pornography: Men Possessing Women.* New York: Putnam, 1981.

——. *Woman Hating.* New York: Dutton, 1974.

Dworkin, Andrea, and Catharine A. MacKinnon. *Pornography and Civil Rights: A New Day for Women's Equality.* Minneapolis: Organizing against Pornography, 1988.

Eco, Umberto. *Postscript to* The Name of the Rose. Trans. William Weaver. San Diego: Harcourt, 1984.

Edwards, Betty. *Drawing on the Right Side of the Brain: A Course in Enhancing Creativity and Artistic Confidence.* Los Angeles: Tarcher, 1979.

Eisler, Riane. *The Chalice and the Blade: Our History, Our Future.* New York: Harper, 1987.

Eliot, T. S. *The Waste Land. Collected Poems 1909–1935.* London: Faber, 1936. 59–84.

Elliott, Robert C. *The Power of Satire: Magic, Ritual, Art.* Princeton: Princeton UP, 1960.

Engel, Marian. *Bear: A Novel.* Toronto: McClelland, 1976.

Fawcett, Brian. "Field Notes: Me and My Gang." *Books in Canada* 20.9 (1990): 8–9.

Fee, Margery. *The Fat Lady Dances: Margaret Atwood's* Lady Oracle. Toronto: ECW, 1993.

Felski, Rita. *Beyond Feminist Aesthetics: Feminist Literature and Social Change.* Cambridge: Harvard UP, 1989.

Fetterley, Judith. *The Resisting Reader: A Feminist Approach to American Fiction.* Bloomington: Indiana UP, 1978.

Fish, Stanley E. *Is There a Text in This Class?* Cambridge: Harvard UP, 1980.

——. *Self-Consuming Artifacts: The Experience of Seventeenth-Century Literature.* Berkeley: U of California P, 1972.

——. *Surprised by Sin: The Reader in* Paradise Lost. Berkeley: U of California P, 1967.

FitzGerald, Gregory, and Kathryn Crabbe. "Evading the Pigeonholers." Ingersoll, *Margaret Atwood: Conversations* 131–39.

Forché, Carolyn. *The Country between Us.* New York: Harper, 1981.

Foucault, Michel. *Technologies of the Self: A Seminar with Michel Foucault.* Ed. Luther H. Martin et al. Amherst: U of Massachusetts P, 1988.

Fox-Genovese, Elizabeth. *Feminism without Illusions: A Critique of Individualism.* Chapel Hill: U of North Carolina P, 1991.

Freibert, Lucy M. "Control and Creativity: The Politics of Risk in Margaret Atwood's *The Handmaid's Tale.*" McCombs, *Critical Essays* 280–91.

Freire, Paulo. *Pedagogy of the Oppressed.* Trans. Myra Bergman Ramos. New York: Seabury, 1970.

Freud, Sigmund. "Creative Writers and Day-Dreaming." Vol. 9 of *Standard Edition* 142–53.

——. "Femininity." *New Introductory Lectures on Psychoanalysis.* Vol. 22 of *Standard Edition* 112–35.

——. *The Standard Edition of the Complete Psychological Works of Sigmund Freud.* Ed. and trans. James Strachey. 24 vols. London: Hogarth, 1953–74.

Friedan, Betty. *The Feminine Mystique.* New York: Norton, 1963.

Frye, Northrop. *Anatomy of Criticism: Four Essays.* 1957. Princeton: Princeton UP, 1973.

——. *The Bush Garden: Essays on the Canadian Imagination.* Toronto: Anansi, 1971.

——. *The Educated Imagination.* Bloomington: Indiana UP, 1964.

——. *Fables of Identity: Studies in Poetic Mythology.* New York: Harbinger-Harcourt, 1963.

——. "National Consciousness in. Canadian Culture." *Divisions on a Ground: Essays on Canadian Culture.* Ed. James Polk. Toronto: Anansi, 1982. 41–55.

——. *The Secular Scripture: A Study of the Structure of Romance.* Cambridge: Harvard UP, 1976.

Fulford, Robert. "The Images of Atwood." Sandler, *Symposium* 95–98.

Gates, Henry Louis, Jr., ed. Editor's Introduction. *"Race," Writing, and Difference.* Chicago: U of Chicago P, 1986.

——. *The Signifying Monkey: Towards a Theory of Literary History.* New York: Oxford UP, 1985.

Gibson, Walker. *Persona: A Style Study for Readers and Writers.* New York: Random, 1969.

Gilbert, Sandra M., and Susan Gubar. *The Madwoman in the Attic: The Woman Writer and the Nineteenth-Century Literary Imagination.* New Haven: Yale UP, 1979.

——, eds. *The Norton Anthology of Literature by Women: The Tradition in English.* New York: Norton, 1985.

Gilligan, Carol. *In a Different Voice: Psychological Theory and Women's Development.* Cambridge: Harvard UP, 1982.

Gilman, Charlotte Perkins. *Herland.* New York: Pantheon, 1979.

——. *The Yellow Wallpaper.* 1899. New York: Feminist, 1973.

Godard, Barbara, ed. *Gynocritics: Feminist Approaches to Canadian and Quebec Women's Writing/Gynocritiques: Démarches féministes à l'ecriture des Canadiennes et Québécoises.* Toronto: ECW, 1987.

——. "Telling It Over Again: Atwood's Art of Parody." *Canadian Poetry* 21 (1987): 1–30.

Grace, Sherrill E. "In Search of Demeter: The Lost, Silent Mother in *Surfacing.*" VanSpanckeren and Castro 35–47.

——. "Stories 'beneath the Page': Atwood's New Fiction." *CRNLE Reviews Journal* 1 (1984): 68–71.

——. *Violent Duality: A Study of Margaret Atwood.* Montreal: Véhicule, 1980.

Grace, Sherrill E., and Lorraine Weir, eds. *Margaret Atwood: Language, Text, and System.* Vancouver: U of British Columbia P, 1983.

Grant, George. *Technology and Empire: Perspectives on North America*. Toronto: Anansi, 1969.

———. *Technology and Justice*. Toronto: Anansi, 1986.

Graubard, Stephen R., ed. *In Search of Canada*. New Brunswick: Transaction, 1989.

Greene, Gayle. Rev. of *Cat's Eye*, by Margaret Atwood. *Women's Studies* 18.4 (1991): 445–55.

———. *Changing the Story: Feminist Fiction and the Tradition*. Bloomington: Indiana UP, 1991.

———. "Choice of Evils." Rev. of *The Handmaid's Tale*, by Margaret Atwood. *Women's Review of Books* 3.10 (1986): 14–15.

Greer, Germaine. *Sex and Destiny: The Politics of Human Fertility*. New York: Harper, 1984.

Grimm. Jacob. *Grimm's Fairy Tales*. London: Scolar, 1979.

Grimm, Jakob, and Wilhelm Grimm. *The Grimms' German Folk Tales*. Trans. Francis P. Magoun, Jr., and Alexander H. Krappe. Carbondale: Southern Illinois UP, 1960.

Guerin, Wilfred L., Earle Labor, et al. *A Handbook of Critical Approaches to Literature*. 3rd ed. New York: Oxford UP, 1992.

Hancock, Geoff. *Canadian Writers at Work: Interviews*. Toronto: Oxford UP, 1987.

Hansen, Elaine Tuttle. "Fiction and (Post)Feminism in Atwood's *Bodily Harm*." *Novel* 19 (1985): 5–21.

Hawthorne, Nathaniel. 1850. *The Scarlet Letter*. New York: Holt, 1963.

Hays, H. R. *The Dangerous Sex: The Myth of Feminine Evil*. New York: Putnam, 1964.

Hengen, Shannon. *Margaret Atwood's Power: Mirrors, Reflections and Images in Select Fiction and Poetry*. Toronto: Second Story, 1993.

Hiebert, Paul. *Sarah Binks*. 1947. New Canadian Library 44. Toronto: McClelland, 1971.

Highet, Gilbert. *The Anatomy of Satire*. Princeton: Princeton UP, 1962.

Hirsch, Marianne. *The Mother/Daughter Plot: Narrative, Psychoanalysis, Feminism*. Bloomington: Indiana UP, 1989.

Hofstede, Geert. *Culture's Consequences: International Differences in Work-Related Values*. Beverly Hills: Sage, 1980.

Horne, Alan J. "Margaret Atwood: An Annotated Bibliography (Prose)." *The Annotated Bibliography of Canada's Major Authors*. Ed. Robert Lecker and Jack David. Vol. 2. Downsview, Ont.: ECW, 1979. 13–46. "Margaret Atwood: An Annotated Bibliography (Poetry)." 1980. 13–53.

Howells, Coral Ann. *Private and Fictional Words: Canadian Women Novelists of the 1970s and 1980s*. London: Methuen, 1987.

———. *York Notes on* The Handmaid's Tale. Harlow, Essex: Longman, 1993.

Hunt, Margaret, and James Stern, trans. *The Complete Grimm's Fairy Tales*. New York: Pantheon, 1972.

Hutcheon, Linda. *The Canadian Postmodern: A Study of Contemporary English-Canadian Fiction*. Toronto: Oxford UP, 1988.

——. " 'Circling the Downspout of Empire.' " *Past the Last Post: Theorizing Post-colonialism and Post-modernism*. Ed. Ian Adam and Helen Tiffin. Calgary: U of Calgary P, 1990. 167–89.

——. *Splitting Images: Contemporary Canadian Ironies*. Don Mills, Ont.: Oxford UP, 1991.

Ingarden, Roman. *The Cognition of the Literary Work of Art*. Trans. Ruth Ann Crowley and Kenneth R. Olson. Evanston: Northwestern UP, 1973.

——. *The Literary Work of Art*. Trans. George G. Grabowicz. Evanston: Northwestern UP, 1973.

——. *Selected Papers in Aesthetics*. Ed. Peter J. McCormick. Washington: Catholic U of America P, 1985.

Ingersoll, Earl, ed. *Margaret Atwood: Conversations*. Willowdale, Ont.: Firefly, 1990; Princeton: Ontario Review, 1990. Introd. Philip Howard. London: Virago, 1992.

——. "Margaret Atwood's *Cat's Eye*: Re-viewing Women in a Postmodern World." *Ariel* 22.4 (1991): 17–27.

Irigaray, Luce. "The Blind Spot of an Old Dream of Symmetry." *Speculum of the Other Woman*. Trans. Gillian C. Gill. New York: Cornell UP, 1985. 11–129.

Irvine, Lorna. *Collecting Clues: Margaret Atwood's Bodily Harm*. Toronto: ECW, 1994.

——. "Murder and Mayhem: Margaret Atwood Deconstructs." *Contemporary Literature* 39.2 (1988): 265–76.

——. *Sub/version*. Toronto: ECW, 1986.

Iser, Wolfgang. *The Act of Reading: A Theory of Aesthetic Response*. Baltimore: Johns Hopkins UP, 1978.

——. *The Implied Reader: Patterns of Communication in Prose Fiction from Bunyan to Beckett*. Baltimore: Johns Hopkins UP, 1974.

Jackson, Rosemary. *Fantasy: The Literature of Subversion*. London: Methuen, 1981.

Jacobsen, Sally. "Daughters of the Dark Goddess: *Tales of Hoffmann*, 'Pop Goes the Weasel,' and the Manuscript of *The Robber Bride*." Margaret Atwood's *The Robber Bride* session. MLA Convention. San Diego. 28 Dec. 1994.

JanMohamed, Abdul R. *Manichean Aesthetics: The Politics of Literature in Colonial Africa*. Amherst: U of Massachusetts P, 1983.

Jensen, Emily. "Margaret Atwood's *Lady Oracle*: A Modern Parable." *Essays on Canadian Writing* 33 (1986): 29–49.

Johnson, Brian D. "Fascism's Handmaid." *Maclean's* 26 Feb. 1990: 42.

——. "Hollywood Meets the New Europe." *Maclean's* 26 Feb. 1990: 38–41.

——. "Returning to a New Berlin." *Maclean's* 26 Feb. 1990: 44–45.

——. "Uphill Battle: Handmaid's Hard Times." *Maclean's* 26 Feb. 1990: 43.

Jones, Douglas G. *Butterfly on Rock: A Study of Themes and Images in Canadian Literature*. Toronto: U of Toronto P, 1970.

Joyce, James. *A Portrait of the Artist as a Young Man*. 1916. New York: Penguin, 1976.

Juhasz, Suzanne. *Naked and Fiery Forms: Modern American Poetry by Women.* New York: Farrar, 1978.

Juneja, Om P., and Chandra Mohan, eds. *Ambivalence: Studies in Canadian Literature.* New Delhi: Allied, 1990.

Jung, Carl Gustav. *Collected Works.* Ed. Herbert Read, Michael Fordham, and Gerhard Adler. New York: Pantheon, 1959.

Kadar, Marlene, ed. *Essays on Life Writing: From Genre to Critical Practice.* Toronto: U of Toronto P, 1992.

Kaler, Anne K. *The Picara: From Hera to Fantasy Heroine.* Bowling Green: Bowling Green State Popular P, 1991.

———. " 'A Sister Dipped in Blood': Satiric Inversion of the Formation Techniques of Women Religious in Margaret Atwood's Novel *The Handmaid's Tale.*" *Christianity and Literature* 38.2 (1989): 43–62.

Kaminsky, Stuart M. *American Film Genres.* Chicago: Nelson Hall, 1988.

Kaplan, Edward K. *Baudelaire's Prose Poems: The Esthetic, the Ethical, and the Religious in* The Parisian Prowler. Athens: U of Georgia P, 1990.

Kauffman, Linda. "Special Delivery: Twenty-First Century Epistolarity in *The Handmaid's Tale.*" *Writing the Female Voice: Essays on Epistolary Literature.* Ed. Elizabeth C. Goldsmith. Boston: Northeastern UP, 1989. 221–44.

Keith, W. J. *Canadian Literature in English.* New York: Longman, 1985.

———. *Introducing Margaret Atwood's* The Edible Woman: *A Reader's Guide.* Canadian Fiction Studies 3. Toronto: ECW, 1989.

Kennedy, X. J., ed. *Literature: An Introduction to Fiction, Poetry, and Drama.* 5th ed. New York: Harper, 1991.

Kernan, Alvin B. *The Plot of Satire.* New Haven: Yale UP, 1965.

Ketterer, David. "Margaret Atwood's *The Handmaid's Tale*: A Contextual Dystopia." *Science-Fiction Studies* 16 (1989): 209–17.

King, Thomas, ed. *All My Relations: An Anthology of Contemporary Canadian Native Fiction.* Toronto: McClelland, 1989.

Klinck, Carl F. *Literary History of Canada: Canadian Literature in English.* 2nd ed. Toronto: U of Toronto P, 1990.

Kolodny, Annette. "Some Notes on Defining a Feminist Literary Criticism." *Critical Inquiry* 2.1 (1975): 75–92.

Korte, Barbara. "Margaret Atwoods Roman *The Handmaid's Tale*: Interpretationshinweise für eine Verwendung im Englishchunterricht der Sekundarstufe II." *Neueren Sprachen* 89.3 (1990): 224–42.

Kristeva, Julia. "Stabat Mater." Trans. Annette Kuhn. *Contemporary Literary Criticism: Literary and Cultural Studies.* Ed. Robert Con Davis and Ronald Schliefer. 2nd ed. New York: Longman, 1989. 186–203.

Kroetsch, Robert. "Beyond Nationalism: A Prologue." *The Canadian Literary Scene in Global Perspective.* Ed. Evelyn Hinz. Spec. issue of *Mosaic* 14.2 (1981): v–xi. Rpt. in Kroetsch, *Lovely Treachery* 64–72.

———. *The Lovely Treachery of Words: Essays Selected and New.* Toronto: Oxford UP, 1989.

———. "Unhiding the Hidden: Recent Canadian Fiction." *Journal of Canadian Fiction* 3.3 (1974): 43–45. Rpt. as "Unhiding the Hidden," in Kroetsch, *Lovely Treachery* 58–63.

Lacan, Jacques. "The Signification of the Phallus." *Ecrits: A Selection*. Trans. Alan Sheridan. New York: Norton, 1977. 281–91.

Lacombe, Michele. "The Writing on the Wall: Amputated Speech in Margaret Atwood's *The Handmaid's Tale.*" *Wascana Review* 21.2 (1986): 3–20.

Langton, Anne. *A Gentlewoman in Upper Canada*. Ed. H. H. Langton. Toronto: Clarke, Irwin, 1950.

Laurence, Margaret. *The Diviners*. Toronto: McClelland, 1974. New York: Bantam, 1975.

———. *Heart of a Stranger*. Toronto: McClelland, 1976.

Lauter, Estella. "Remedios Varo: The Creative Woman and the Female Quest." Lauter, *Women as Mythmakers* 79–97.

———. *Women as Mythmakers: Poetry and Visual Art by Twentieth-Century Women*. Bloomington: U of Indiana P, 1984.

Lawson, Alan. " 'A Maze of Circular Arguments': Literature and Life in Canadian Criticism of the 1970s." Rhetoric of "Can. Lit." session. MLA Convention. Toronto. 29 Dec. 1993.

Lecker, Robert, ed. *Canadian Canons: Essays in Literary Value*. Toronto: U of Toronto P, 1991.

Lee, Dennis. "Cadence, Country, Silence: Writing in a Colonial Space." *Open Letter* 2.6 (1973): 34–53. Rpt. in *Boundary 2* 3.1 (1974): 151–68.

———. "Seventh Elegy." *Civil Elegies*. Toronto: Anansi, 1968. N. pag.

Lessing, Doris. *The Golden Notebook*. 1962. New York: Bantam, 1973.

Levine-Keating, Helane. "Myth and Archetype from a Female Perspective: An Exploration of Twentieth-Century North and South American Women Poets." Diss. New York U, 1980.

Lewis, Mary Ellen B. "The Study of Folklore in Literature: An Expanded View." *Southern Folklore Quarterly* 40 (1976): 343–51.

Lindsay, Joan. *Picnic at Hanging Rock*. Harmondsworth: Penguin, 1970.

Lustig, Myron W. "Value Differences in Intercultural Communication." *Intercultural Communication: A Reader*. Samovar and Porter 55–61.

Lüthi, Max. *Once upon a Time: On the Nature of Fairy Tales*. Bloomington: Indiana UP, 1970.

Lyons, Bonnie. "An Interview with Margaret Atwood." *Shenandoah* 37.2 (1987): 69–89.

MacEwen, Gwendolyn. "Dark Pines under Water." *The Shadow-Maker*. Toronto: Macmillan, 1969. 50.

Maclean, Marie. *Narrative as Performance: The Baudelairean Experiment*. New York: Routledge, 1988.

MacLulich, T. D. "Atwood's Adult Fairy Tale: Lévi-Strauss, Bettelheim, and *The Edible Woman.*" *Essays on Canadian Writing* 11 (1977): 111–29.

Malak, Amin. "Margaret Atwood's *The Handmaid's Tale* and the Dystopian Tradition." *Canadian Literature* 112 (1987): 9–16.

Mallinson, Jean. *Margaret Atwood and Her Works.* Toronto: ECW, 1984.

Mandel, Eli. "Atwood Gothic." Sandler, *Symposium* 165–74.

———. "The City in Canadian Poetry." *Another Time.* Erin, Ont.: Porcépic, 1977. 114–23.

———, ed. *Contexts of Canadian Criticism.* Chicago: U of Chicago P, 1971.

Mandel, Eli, and David Taras, eds. *A Passion for Identity: Introduction to Canadian Studies.* Toronto: Methuen, 1987.

Martyn, Katherine, comp. *Guide to the Margaret Atwood Papers.* Thomas Fisher Rare Book Library. University of Toronto. 1983. Rev. 1986 and 1990.

McCarthy, Mary. "Breeders, Wives and Unwomen." Rev. of *The Handmaid's Tale,* by Margaret Atwood. *New York Times Book Review* 9 Feb. 1986: 1+.

McCombs, Judith. "Atwood's Fictive Portraits of the Artist: From Victim to Surfacer, from Oracle to Birth." *Women's Studies* 12.1 (1986): 69–88.

———. "Contrary Re-memberings: The Creating Self and Feminism in *Cat's Eye.*" *Canadian Literature* 129 (1991): 9–23.

———. "Country, Politics, and Gender in Canadian Studies: A Report from Twenty Years of Atwood Criticism." *Literatures in Canada/Littératures au Canada.* Ed. Deborah C. Poff. Vol. 10 of *Canadian Issues/Thèmes canadiens* Ottawa: Assn. for Canadian Studies and Intl. Council for Canadian Studies, 1988. 27–47.

———, ed. *Critical Essays on Margaret Atwood.* Boston: Hall, 1988.

———. *First Surfacings: The Creative Metamorphoses in Margaret Atwood's Manuscripts.* Forthcoming.

———. "Politics, Structure, and Poetic Development in Atwood's Canadian-American Sequences: From an Apprentice Pair to *The Circle Game* to *Two-Headed Poems.*" VanSpanckeren and Castro 142–62.

———. "*Power Politics*: The Book and Its Cover." *Moving Out* 3.2 (1973): 54–69.

———. "*The Robber Bride*: Atwood's Pre-modern Feminist Bildungsroman." Margaret Atwood's *The Robber Bride* session. MLA Convention. San Diego. 28 Dec. 1994.

McCombs, Judith, and Carole L. Palmer. *Margaret Atwood: A Reference Guide.* Boston: Hall, 1991.

McDougal, Stuart Y. *Made into Movies: From Literature to Film.* New York: Holt, Rinehart, 1985.

McKibben, Bill. *The End of Nature.* New York: Random, 1989.

McLaren, Peter. "Multiculturalism and the Postmodern Critique: Towards a Pedagogy of Resistance and Transformation." *Cultural Studies* 7.1 (1993): 118–46.

McNaught, Kenneth. *The Pelican History of Canada.* Harmondsworth: Penguin, 1982.

Mendez-Egle, Beatrice, ed. *Margaret Atwood: Reflection and Reality.* Edinburg: Pan American UP, 1987.

Miller, Jean Baker. *Toward a New Feminist Psychology of Women*. 2nd ed. Boston: Beacon, 1986.

Miller, Nancy K., ed. *The Poetics of Gender*. New York: Columbia UP, 1986.

Miller, Perry. *Errand into the Wilderness*. Cambridge: Belknap–Harvard UP, 1956.

Milstead, John W., et al. *Sociology through Science Fiction*. New York: St. Martin's, 1974.

Miner, Valerie. "Atwood in Metamorphosis: An Authentic Canadian Fairy Tale." *Her Own Woman: Profiles of Ten Canadian Women*. Ed. Myrna Kostash et al. Toronto: Macmillan, 1975. 173–94.

Mohanty, Chandra Talpade. "On Race and Voice: Challenges for Liberal Education in the 1990s." *Cultural Critique* (1989–90): 179–208.

Moi, Toril. *Sexual/Textual Politics: Feminist Literary Theory*. London: Methuen, 1985.

Montefiore, Jan. *Feminism and Poetry: Language, Experience, Identity in Women's Writing*. New York: Pandora, 1987.

Moodie, Susanna. *Life in the Clearings*. 1853. Toronto: Macmillan, 1959.

———. *Roughing It in the Bush*. 1852. Toronto: McClelland, 1962.

———. *Roughing It in the Bush; or, Forest Life in Canada*. 1852. Virago/Beacon Travelers Series. Introd. Margaret Atwood. London: Virago, 1986; Boston: Beacon, 1987.

More, Thomas. *Utopia*. Ed. George M. Logan and Robert M. Adams. New York: Cambridge UP, 1989.

Morson, Gary Saul. *The Boundaries of Genre: Dostoevsky's Diary of a Writer and the Traditions of Literary Utopia*. Slavic Series 4. Austin: U of Texas P, 1981.

Moss, John. *Patterns of Isolation in English Canadian Fiction*. Toronto: McClelland, 1974.

Mulvey, Laura. *Visual and Other Pleasures*. Bloomington: Indiana UP, 1988.

Munro, Alice. *Lives of Girls and Women*. 1971. New York: Signet-NAL, 1974.

Murphy, Patrick D. "Reducing the Dystopian Distance: Pseudo-Documentary Framing in Near-Future Fiction." *Science-Fiction Studies* 17 (1990): 25–41.

Mycak, Sonia. *In Search of the Split Subject: Psychoanalysis, Phenomenology, and the Novels of Margaret Atwood*. Toronto: ECW, 1996.

Neuman, Shirley. "Life Writing." New, *Literary History* 333–70.

Neuman, Shirley, and Smaro Kamboureli, eds. *A Mazing Space: Writing Canadian Women Writing*. Edmonton: Longspoon, 1986.

Neumann, Erich. *The Great Mother: An Analysis of the Archetype*. Trans. Ralph Manheim. 2nd ed. 1955. Princeton: Bollingen Foundation–Princeton UP, 1974.

New, William H. *Dreams of Speech and Violence: The Art of the Short Story in Canada and New Zealand*. Toronto: U of Toronto P, 1987.

———, gen. ed. *Literary History of Canada: Canadian Literature in English*. Vol. 4. 2nd ed. Toronto: U of Toronto P, 1990.

Newlove, John. "Samuel Hearne in Wintertime." *Black Night Window*. Toronto: McClelland, 1968. 84–85.

Ngũgĩ wa Thiong'o. *Decolonising the Mind: The Politics of Language in African Literature.* London: Currey, 1986.

Nicholson, Colin, ed. *Margaret Atwood: Writing and Subjectivity.* Houndmills, Eng.: Macmillan, 1994; New York: St. Martin's, 1994.

Nodelman, Perry. "Trusting the Untrustworthy." *Journal of Canadian Fiction* 21 (1977–78): 73–82.

Northey, Margot. *The Haunted Wilderness: The Gothic and Grotesque in Canadian Fiction.* Toronto: U of Toronto P, 1976.

O'Donnell, Patrick, and Robert Con Davis. Introduction. *Intertextuality and Contemporary American Fiction.* Ed. O'Donnell and Davis. Baltimore: Johns Hopkins UP, 1989. ix–xxii.

O'Keeffe, Georgia. *Georgia O'Keeffe.* New York: Studio-Viking, 1976.

Ondaatje, Michael. *Coming through Slaughter.* New York: Norton, 1976.

Ortner, Sherry B. *Sexual Meanings: The Cultural Construction of Gender and Sexuality.* Cambridge: Cambridge UP, 1981.

Orwell, George. *1984.* 1949. New York: NAL, 1977.

Ostriker, Alicia. "The Thieves of Language: Women Poets and Revisionist Mythmaking." *Signs* 8 (1982): 68–90. Rpt. in Showalter, *New Feminist Criticism* 314–38.

Oxford Companion to Canadian Literature. Toronto: Oxford UP, 1983.

Page, P. K. *The Sun and the Moon and Other Fictions.* Toronto: Anansi, 1973.

Page, Sheila. "Supermarket Survival: A Critical Analysis of Margaret Atwood's *The Edible Woman.*" *Sphinx* 1 (1974): 9–19.

Patton, Marilyn. "Tourists and Terrorists: The Creation of *Bodily Harm.*" *Papers on Language and Literature* 28.2 (1992): 150–73.

Petrone, Penny, ed. *First People, First Voices.* Toronto: U of Toronto P, 1988.

Plaskow, Judith. "On Carol Christ on Margaret Atwood: Some Theological Reflections." *Signs* 2 (1976): 331–39.

Plato. *The Republic.* New York: Norton, 1985.

Pollard, Arthur. *Satire.* Critical Idiom. Ed. John D. Jump. London: Methuen, 1970.

Poulet, Georges. "Phenomenology of Reading." *New Literary History* 1.1 (1969): 53–68.

Pratt, Annis. "Margaret Atwood and the Elixir of Maternity." *Archetypal Patterns in Women's Fiction.* Bloomington: Indiana UP, 1981. 157–61.

Rabkin, Eric, Martin Greenberg, and Joseph Olander, eds. *No Place Else: Explorations in Utopian and Dystopian Fiction.* Carbondale: Southern Illinois UP, 1983.

Rao, Eleonora. *Strategies for Identity: The Fiction of Margaret Atwood.* New York: Lang, 1993.

Relke, Diana M. A. "Double Voice, Single Vision: A Feminist Reading of Margaret Atwood's *The Journals of Susanna Moodie.*" *Atlantis* 9 (1983): 35–48.

Rich, Adrienne. *Adrienne Rich's Poetry and Prose: Poems, Prose, Reviews, and Criticism.* Ed. Barbara Charlesworth Gelpi and Charles Gelpi. New York: Norton, 1993.

————. *Of Woman Born: Motherhood as Experience and Institution.* New York: Norton, 1976.

Richler, Mordecai. *Solomon Gursky Was Here.* Markham, Ont.: Penguin, 1988.

Rigney, Barbara Hill. *Madness and Sexual Politics in the Feminist Novel: Studies in Brontë, Woolf, Lessing, and Atwood.* Madison: U of Wisconsin P, 1978.

————. *Margaret Atwood.* Houndmills, Eng.: Macmillan, 1987. Totowa: Barnes, 1987.

Rosenberg, Jerome. " 'For of Such Is the Kingdom . . . ': Margaret Atwood's *Two-Headed Poems.*" *Essays on Canadian Writing* 16 (1979): 130–39.

————. *Margaret Atwood.* Boston: Twayne, 1984.

————. Unpublished conversation with Margaret Atwood, 16 Aug. 1978.

Ross, Sinclair. *As for Me and My House.* 1941. New Canadian Library 4. Toronto: McClelland, 1982.

Rubenstein, Roberta. *Boundaries of the Self: Gender, Culture, Fiction.* Urbana: U of Illinois P, 1987.

————. "*Surfacing*: Margaret Atwood's Journey to the Interior." *Modern Fiction Studies* 22 (1976): 387–99.

Samovar, Larry A., and Richard E. Porter. "Approaching Intercultural Communication." *Intercultural Communication: A Reader.* Ed. Samovar and Porter. 5th ed. Belmont: Wadsworth, 1988. 15–30.

Sanders, Thomas E., and Walter W. Peek. *Literature of the American Indian.* New York: Glencoe, 1973.

Sandler, Linda. "Interview with Margaret Atwood." Sandler, *Symposium* 7–27.

————, ed. *Margaret Atwood: A Symposium.* Spec. issue of *Malahat Review* 41 (1977): 1–228.

Scheier, Libby, Sarah Sheard, and Eleanor Wachtel, eds. *Language in Her Eye: Views on Writing and Gender by Canadian Women Writing in English.* Toronto: Coach, 1990.

Scholes, Robert. *Semiotics and Interpretation.* New Haven: Yale UP, 1982.

Schor, Naomi. "Feminist and Gender Studies." *Introduction to Scholarship in Modern Languages and Literatures.* Ed. Joseph Gibaldi. New York: MLA, 1992. 262–87.

Schreiber, Le Anne. "Female Trouble." *Vogue* Jan. 1986: 208–09.

Scott, Peter Dale. "The Difference Perspective Makes: Literary Studies in Canada and the United States." *Essays on Canadian Writing* 44 (1991): 1–60.

Shadbolt, Doris. *The Art of Emily Carr.* 1979. Vancouver: Douglas, 1987.

Shklovsky, Victor. "Art as Technique." Shklovsky, *Russian Formalist Criticism* 3–24.

————. *Russian Formalist Criticism: Four Essays.* Trans. Lee T. Lemon and Marion J. Reis. Lincoln: U of Nebraska P, 1965.

————. "Sterne's *Tristram Shandy*: Stylistic Commentary." Shklovsky, *Russian Formalist Criticism* 25–60.

Showalter, Elaine. "Feminist Criticism in the Wilderness." *Critical Inquiry* 8 (1981): 179–205.

————, ed. *The New Feminist Criticism*. New York: Pantheon, 1985.

————. "Towards a Feminist Poetics." Showalter, *New Feminist Criticism* 125–43.

Sinclair, David, ed. *Nineteenth-Century Narrative Poems*. New Canadian Library 8. Toronto: McClelland, 1972.

Smith, Paul. *Discerning the Subject*. Theory and History of Literature 55. Minneapolis: U of Minnesota P, 1988.

Snitow, Ann. "Back to the Future." *Mother Jones* April–May 1986: 59–60.

Sollors, Werner, ed. *The Return of Thematic Criticism*. Harvard English Studies 18. Cambridge: Harvard UP, 1993.

Spivak, Gayatri Chakravorty. "Can the Subaltern Speak? Speculations on Widow-Sacrifice." *Wedge* 7–8 (1985): 120–30.

————. *In Other Worlds: Essays in Cultural Politics*. New York: Routledge, 1988.

————. *The Post-colonial Critic: Interviews, Strategies, Dialogues*. Ed. Sarah Harasym. New York: Routledge, 1990.

————. "Poststructuralism, Marginality, Post-coloniality and Value." *Literary Theory Today*. Ed. Peter Collier and Helga Geyer-Ryan. Ithaca: Cornell UP, 1990. 219–44.

Spriet, Pierre. "Margaret Atwood's Postmodernism in *Murder in the Dark*." *Commonwealth Essays and Studies* 11.2 (1989): 24–30.

Staels, Hilde. *Margaret Atwood's Novels: A Study of Narrative Discourse*. Transatlantic Perspectives. Tübingen: Francke, 1995.

St. Andrews, Bonnie. *Forbidden Fruit: On the Relationship between Women and Knowledge in Doris Lessing, Selma Lagerlöf, Kate Chopin, Margaret Atwood*. Troy: Whitston, 1986.

Steele, James. "The Literary Criticism of Margaret Atwood." *In Our Own House: Social Perspectives on Canadian Literature*. Ed. Paul Cappon. Toronto: McClelland, 1978. 73–81.

Stewart, Grace. *A New Mythos: The Novel of the Artist as Heroine, 1877–1977*. Montreal: Eden, 1979.

Stimpson, Catharine. "Atwood Woman." *Nation* 31 May 1986: 764–67.

Struthers, J. R. (Tim). "An Interview with Margaret Atwood." *Essays on Canadian Writing* 6 (1977): 18–27.

Stuewe, Paul. *Clearing the Ground: English-Canadian Literature after* Survival. Toronto: Proper Tales, 1984.

Swift, Jonathan. *Gulliver's Travels*. Ed. Paul Turner. New York: Oxford UP, 1986.

————. "A Modest Proposal." *The Norton Anthology of English Literature: The Major Authors*. Ed. M. H. Abrams. 5th ed. New York: Norton, 1987. 1078–85.

Tennyson, Alfred. "Sense and Conscience." *The Devil and the Lady and Unpublished Early Poems*. Ed. Charles Tennyson. Bloomington: Indiana UP, 1964. 42–46.

Test, George A. *Satire: Spirit and Art*. Tampa: U of South Florida P, 1991.

Thomas, Clara. "Feminist or Heroine?" Rev. of *Lady Oracle*, by Margaret Atwood. *Essays on Canadian Writing* 6 (1977): 28–31.

Thompson, Lars. *A Teacher's Guide for* The Handmaid's Tale *by Margaret Atwood*.

Companions to Literature. Becci Hayes, contributing ed. Mississauga, Ont.: S.B.F., 1990.

Thompson, Lee Briscoe. "Minutes and Madness: Margaret Atwood's *Dancing Girls*." Davidson and Davidson 107–22.

Thompson, Samuel. *Reminiscences of a Canadian Pioneer for the Last Fifty Years, 1833–1883*. 1884. Toronto: McClelland, 1968.

Thompson, Stith. *Motif-Index of Folk-Literature: A Classification of Narrative Elements in Folktales, Ballads, Myths, Fables, Mediaeval Romances, Exempla, Fabliaux, Jest-Books, and Local Legends*. Rev. and enlarged ed. 6 vols. Bloomington: Indiana UP, 1955.

Thüsen, Joachim von der. "De idylle: De antropologie van een literair genre." *De Gids* 152 (1989): 273–83.

Traill, Catherine Parr. *The Backwoods of Canada, Being Letters from the Wife of an Emigrant Officer, Illustrative of the Domestic Economy of British America*. 1836. Selections. Toronto: McClelland, 1966.

Trinh, T. Minh-ha. *Woman, Native, Other: Writing Postcoloniality and Feminism*. Bloomington: Indiana UP, 1989.

Turner, Victor. *The Ritual Process: Structure and Anti-structure*. Chicago: Aldine, 1969.

TuSmith, Bonnie. "The Cultural Translator: Toward an Ethnic Womanist Pedagogy." *MELUS: The Journal of the Society for the Study of the Multi-ethnic Literature of the United States* 16.2 (1989–90): 18–29.

Van Gelder, Lindsy. "Margaret Atwood." *Ms.* Jan. 1987: 49+.

VanSpanckeren, Kathryn. "Magic in the Novels of Margaret Atwood." Mendez-Egle 1–13.

———. "Shamanism in the Works of Margaret Atwood." VanSpanckeren and Castro 183–204.

VanSpanckeren, Kathryn, and Jan Garden Castro, eds. *Margaret Atwood: Vision and Forms*. Carbondale: Southern Illinois UP, 1988.

Verduyn, Christl. "*Murder in the Dark*: Fiction/Theory by Margaret Atwood." *Canadian Fiction Magazine* 57 (1986): 124–31.

Vinaver, Eugéne. *Form and Meaning in Medieval Romance*. Cambridge, Eng.: Modern Humanities Research, 1966.

———. *The Rise of Romance*. Cambridge, Eng.: Brewer; Totowa: Barnes, 1984.

Waddington, Miriam. *Driving Home: Poems New and Selected*. Toronto: Oxford UP, 1972.

Wagner, Linda. "The Making of *Selected Poems*, the Process of *Surfacing*." Davidson and Davidson 81–94.

Walker, Barbara G. *The Woman's Encyclopedia of Myths and Secrets*. San Francisco: Harper, 1983.

Waugh, Patricia. *Feminine Fictions: Revisiting the Postmodern*. New York: Routledge, 1989.

Wiebe, Rudy. *A Discovery of Strangers*. Toronto: Knopf, 1994.

———. *The Mad Trapper*. Toronto: McClelland, 1980.

————. *The Scorched Wood People.* Toronto: McClelland 1973.

————. *The Temptations of Big Bear.* Toronto: McClelland, 1973.

Wieland, Joyce. *Joyce Wieland: Art Gallery of Ontario.* Toronto: Key Porter, 1987.

Wilson, Ethel. *Swamp Angel.* 1954. Toronto: McClelland, 1990.

Wilson, Sharon R. "Deconstructing Text and Self: Mirroring in Atwood's *Surfacing* and Beckett's *Molloy.*" *Journal of Popular Literature* 3 (1987): 53–69.

————. *Margaret Atwood's Fairy-Tale Sexual Politics.* Jackson: U of Mississippi P, 1993.

————. "Sexual Politics in Margaret Atwood's Visual Art." VanSpanckeren and Castro 205–14.

————. "Turning Life into Popular Art: *Bodily Harm*'s Life-Tourist." *Studies in Canadian Literature* 10.1–2 (1985): 136–45.

Winnicott, D. W. "Transitional Objects and Transitional Phenomena." *Playing and Reality.* Harmondsworth: Pelican, 1974. 1–30.

Woodcock, George. "Bashful but Bold: Notes on Margaret Atwood as Critic." Davidson and Davidson 223–41.

————. *Introducing Margaret Atwood's* Surfacing: *A Reader's Guide.* Toronto: ECW, 1990.

————. "Margaret Atwood." *The Literary Half-Yearly* 13.2 (1972): 233–42.

————. "Margaret Atwood: Poet as Novelist." *The Canadian Novel in the Twentieth Century: Essays from Canadian Literature.* Toronto: McClelland, 1975. 312–27.

Woolf, Virginia. *A Room of One's Own.* 1929. New York: Harbinger-Harcourt, 1957.

————. *To the Lighthouse.* 1927. New York: Harvest-Harcourt, 1955.

Worth, Fabienne. "Postmodern Pedagogy in the Multicultural Classroom: For Inappropriate Teachers and Imperfect Spectators." *Cultural Critique* (1993): 5–32.

Writers' Development Trust. *Resource Guides for the Teaching of Canadian Literature.* 11 vols. Toronto: Teachers and Writers Educ. Project, 1977.

Wyatt, Jean. *Reconstructing Desire: The Role of the Unconscious in Women's Reading and Writing.* Chapel Hill: U of North Carolina P, 1990.

Yalom, Marilyn. "Margaret Atwood: *Surfacing.*" *Maternity, Mortality, and the Literature of Madness.* Ed. Yalom. University Park: Pennsylvania State UP, 1985. 71–88, 119–20.

York, Lorraine M. "The Habits of Language: Uniform(ity), Transgression and Margaret Atwood." *Canadian Literature* 126 (1990): 6–19.

————, ed. *Various Atwoods: Essays on the Later Poems, Short Fiction, and Novels.* Toronto: Anansi, 1995.

Young, Robert. *White Mythologies: Writing History and the West.* London: Routledge, 1990.

Zinn, Howard. *People's History of the United States.* New York: Harper, 1990.

Zipes, Jack, trans. and ed. *Beauties, Beasts, and Enchantment: Classic French Fairy Tales.* New York: NAL, 1989.

————. *Fairy Tales and the Art of Subversion: The Classical Genre for Children and the Process of Civilization.* New York: Methuen, 1988.

————. *The Trials and Tribulations of Little Red Riding Hood.* South Hadley: Bergin, 1983.

Audiovisual Aids

Bluebeard's Egg and Other Stories. Read by Patricia Vandenberg Blom. 3 audiocassettes. Brilliance, 1987. 4 hours.

Cat's Eye. Read by Kate Nelligan. 2 audiocassettes. Bantam, 1989. 3 hours.

The Handmaid's Tale. Dir. Volker Schlondorff. Screenplay by Harold Pinter. Cinecom, 1989. Released on videocassette by HBO, 1990. 109 mins.

The Handmaid's Tale. Read by Julie Christie. Abridged by Betty Stephenson. 2 audiocassettes. Durkin Hayes–Listen for Pleasure, 1987. US version released by Durkin Hayes, 1992.

Interview with Jan Castro. Conducted in St. Louis, 1983. Audiocassette. Amer. Audio Prose, n.d. 56 mins.

Interview with Hermione Lee. *Writers in Conversation–Writers Talk. Ideas of Our Time.* 2 videocassettes. Inst. of Contemporary Arts, n.d. 92 mins. Reissued as *Writers on Writing* 2. Videocassette. Roland, n.d. 52 mins.

The Journals of Susanna Moodie. Read by Mia Anderson. Recording. *Canadian Poets* 2. CBC, 1969.

The Journals of Susanna Moodie. Screenplay by Margaret Atwood and Marie Waisberg. Black-and-white film. Tranby, 1972. 15 mins.

Margaret Atwood: Once in August. Dir. Michael Rubbo. Natl. Film Board of Canada, 1984. 57 mins. Available in videocassette (Wombat, 1987). Released in film by NFB as *Atwood and Family.* 1985. 30 mins.

Margaret Atwood Reading from Her Own Work, Including Selections from The Circle Game, The Animals in That Country, *and* Power Politics. Recording. High Barnet, 1973.

Margaret Atwood Reads from A [sic] Handmaid's Tale *and Talks about This Futuristic Fable of Misogyny as Compared to Orwell's* 1984. Movable Feast 17. Audiocassette. Amer. Audio Prose, [1986]. 30 mins.

Margaret Atwood Reads from Bodily Harm. Movable Feast 1. Audiocassette. Amer. Audio Prose, n.d. 30 mins.

Margaret Atwood Reads "Unearthing Suite." Recording. Amer. Audio Prose, 1983. 30 mins.

Murder in the Dark. Read by Clare Coulter. Audiocassette. Coach–Music Gallery, 1989.

Not a Love Story: A Film about Pornography. Natl. Film Board of Canada, 1981. 68 mins.

The Poetry and Voice of Margaret Atwood. Selections from *The Animals in That Country* and *Power Politics*, read by the author at the 92nd Street YM-YWHA,

New York. Audiocassette and 12-in. record. Caedmon, 1977. 36 mins. Issued in slightly shorter version, 1992.

Reflections: Progressive Insanities of a Pioneer. Dir. Paul Quigley. Cinematics Canada, 1972. Universal, 1974. 6 mins.

The Robber Bride. Read by Blythe Danner. 4 audiocassettes. Bantam, 1993. 290 mins.

Stories from Wilderness Tips. Read by Helen Shaver. 2 audiocassettes. Bantam, 1991. 3 hours.

Surfacing. Dir. Claude Jutra. Adapt. Bernard Gordon. Pan-Canadian, 1979. 88 mins.

The Twist of Feeling. Discussion and reading of *Power Politics.* Broadcast on *Ideas,* Nov. 1971. LP. CBC Learning Systems, [1980]. 30 mins.

INDEX

Modern Language Association of America
Approaches to Teaching World Literature
Joseph Gibaldi, series editor

Metaphysical Poets. Ed. Sidney Gottlieb. 1990.

Miller's Death of a Salesman. Ed. Matthew C. Roudané. 1995.

Milton's Paradise Lost. Ed. Galbraith M. Crump. 1986.

Molière's Tartuffe *and Other Plays.* Ed. James F. Gaines and
  Michael S. Koppisch. 1995.

Momaday's The Way to Rainy Mountain. Ed. Kenneth M. Roemer. 1988.

Montaigne's Essays. Ed. Patrick Henry. 1994.

Murasaki Shikibu's The Tale of Genji. Ed. Edward Kamens. 1993.

Pope's Poetry. Ed. Wallace Jackson and R. Paul Yoder. 1993.

Shakespeare's King Lear. Ed. Robert H. Ray. 1986.

Shakespeare's The Tempest *and Other Late Romances.* Ed. Maurice Hunt. 1992.

Shelley's Frankenstein. Ed. Stephen C. Behrendt. 1990.

Shelley's Poetry. Ed. Spencer Hall. 1990.

Sir Gawain and the Green Knight. Ed. Miriam Youngerman Miller and
  Jane Chance. 1986.

Spenser's Faerie Queene. Ed. David Lee Miller and Alexander Dunlop. 1994.

Sterne's Tristram Shandy. Ed. Melvyn New. 1989.

Swift's Gulliver's Travels. Ed. Edward J. Rielly. 1988.

Thoreau's Walden *and Other Works.* Ed. Richard J. Schneider. 1996.

Voltaire's Candide. Ed. Renée Waldinger. 1987.

Whitman's Leaves of Grass. Ed. Donald D. Kummings. 1990.

Wordsworth's Poetry. Ed. Spencer Hall, with Jonathan Ramsey. 1986.